WILD
TO THE LAST

WILD
TO THE LAST

ENVIRONMENTAL CONFLICT
IN THE CLEARWATER COUNTRY

CHARLES PEZESHKI

WSU
PRESS

Washington State University Press
Pullman, Washington

Washington State University Press, PO Box 645910,
Pullman, WA 99164-5910
Phone 800-354-7360; FAX 509-335-8568

Front cover photo of the Mallard-Larkins Pioneer Area from Fire Lakes Butte courtesy Gerry Snyder. Back cover photo of the author courtesy of the author.

Library of Congress Cataloging-in-Publication Data
Pezeshki, Charles, 1962-
    Wild to the last : environmental conflict in the clearwater country /
Charles Pezeshki.
        p.   cm.
    Includes bibliographical references and index.
    ISBN 0-87422-159-5 (pbk.)
    1. Clearwater County (Idaho)—Environmental conditions.   2. Environmentalism—Idaho.   3. Environmentalists—Idaho—Interviews.   4.   Pezeshki,   Charles,   1962-   .   5. Environmentalists—United States—Biography.   I. Title.
GE 155.I2P49   1998
363.7'009796'88—dc21   97-49101
                                                          CIP

Breaking with tradition, this book is dedicated to landscape—the Floodwood State Forest, located next to nowhere, in the former wild heart of the Clearwater Country. Her giant white pines are cut, her streams clogged with silt and landslides, her record-breaking steelhead dead, murdered by Dworshak Dam and monumental human stupidity. This book is written in memory of all the wild animals that perished when the State of Idaho destroyed the Floodwoods, a state endowment forest, in the name of the schoolchildren of Idaho.

To a life of shame and failure,
Of sorrow, and despair.
To a life undiversified by hope or joy.
All desire gone,
All hopes ground into dust.
To a malevolent God,
To jail,
To fate.
And to the Wild Rockies,
Wild now, wild still, wild to the last.

—Wild Rockies Earth First! drinking toast

Contents

Acknowledgments

J IM HEPWORTH TOLD ME once that writing a book is a community effort, and this one is no exception. I would like to thank all the people in my community who humored me during the course of writing.

Dr. Bart Stryhas supplied the information regarding the geology of the area. Roy Keene of the Public Forestry Foundation taught me the basics of silviculture. LeRoy Lee drug me around the woods showing me the good, bad, and ugly. Gerry Snyder started the original Forest Watch group that I joined, looking for an outlet for my latent do-goodism. A lot of what I know about fish, watersheds, and internal Forest Service politics started under Al Espinosa's careful tutelage. Larry McLaud has served during the past three years as my main partner in forest activism. Bob Greene relentlessly kept me on task at the end. Thanks also go to Sioux Westervelt and Kelly Mitchell for their endless moral support. My larger Northern Rockies activist community has served as inspiration and teacher to me over the past eight years. Kayaking buddies Beck Malloy, Ron Doebler, Craig Thomas, and others provided diversion for my mental condition.

Many people read this manuscript and encouraged me early on in the process. Diane Prorak, Steve Brown, Mel Siebe, Keith Russell, Phil Druker, and Michael Frome all showed great patience with my prose when I was in the process of learning that I didn't know how to write. Mike Beiser allowed me to hold an entire student backcountry ski group captive in Bow Hut and read the manuscript aloud over the course of a Thanksgiving week. Dr. Morgan Wright and Dr. Michael Murphy and Cathy Murphy provided generous financial support. Peggy Pace, Jim Hepworth, and Keith Petersen provided entrance into the literary community that helped get this book published. Greg McNamee took the first professional swing at turning the manuscript into a book.

My wife, Kelley, my dogs—Mary and Tommy—and my family all provided endless encouragement, there is no question. But there is one person who shall go unnamed. Without his help, this book would never have been written. It was he who edited my first prose, when I had the temerity to believe that I could write a book, yet had absolutely none of the requisite skill or ability. I cannot name him because the process of doing so would compromise him. May the world change to the point where those who stand up for the last of America's wild country are honored, not cursed, in their own land.

Preface

IT WAS MY FATHER who gave me the Clearwater River when I was fourteen. It was an accidental gift, delivered at a roadside diner in Syringa on a hot July day, next to a logging truck, surrounded by forested hills—clearcut now—like a found nickel given to a small child, or in hindsight, more like Huntington's disease, an irresistible affliction of the later years of my life. I can remember the van ride along the river on Highway 12—we were on our way to the put-in for a river trip down the Salmon River, outside of North Fork, Idaho, and we stopped along the Lochsa River, next to Lochsa Falls. "A bunch of goddamn trees and rocks," he said. If there was higher intention behind the gift, my father hid it.

My father was an obstetrician in a small rural county in southern Ohio, in the foothills of the Appalachians. Born in Iran, he had come to America to escape the ignorance and deprivation of living in the Third World, the abuse of women, and the selling of children. He was partially raised by a woman whom the family had bought when she was very young. Maybe he even wished to escape the notion of charity behind the selling of children; my father often told me that his nanny would have been sold into prostitution had his parents not bought her. He came over to this country, which ostensibly had law and order, truth, justice, and the American Way. He ended up in Appalachia, delivering his share of twelve-year-olds having babies. He told me that he originally went into the field of obstetrics because he thought that it would be the happiest of all the medical fields. I don't know that he has ever recovered from being a constant bystander in cases of underage pregnancy and incest. I can remember him talking with one of his poorer patients on the phone once. She was a smoker, but was tired of being pregnant and wanted my father to induce labor. My father was trying to reason with her, telling her that smokers had smaller babies, and that she needed to let the pregnancy run as long as possible, for the baby. Finally, in a fit of anger and desperation, my father yelled into the phone: "Don't you care if this baby dies?" And she responded, "It's all right—I can always have another."

My father and I had difficulties. He had a drinking problem during much of the time I was growing up, and I had all the usual adolescent problems, which, upon reflection, probably helped to exacerbate my father's drinking problem. In retrospect, my father was (and is) too much like me, or rather the reverse—I am too much like him, and the combination of high strung, sensitive personalities in a small space, in a world that I think neither of us understood—he was an immigrant from Iran, and I was, well, an adolescent—combined to make an explosive situation on more than one instance.

But that is all past us now. We get along, truly, in our separate realms. I am happy to go home to southern Ohio, and he is happy to see me when I arrive. I know that I am lucky. Many children never resolve conflicts with their fathers, and that unfortunate circumstance haunts them all of their lives. I go home because I want to. And I think, now that the years have passed, that I understand him a little better, too. And maybe that matters in the long run, because he is too old to change.

But my father and my mother have taught me much that I know, as far as matters of consequence, and I have not forgotten that debt. My father is small now, only 5'5", shrinking—skinny legs, grey hair, little pot-belly and black glasses, old Bermuda shorts and a white tank top. He is interested in the leftovers in the refrigerator as well as in recycling, because, in reality, my father is the ultimate environmentalist.

I never knew my father young, although I can remember his stories of riding with the Kurds in the Alburz Mountains, wild people, feeling the power of the Himalaya beneath small, thundering horse hooves. He was a political organizer, and he waged his battles with the forces of darkness of his time—the Shah and his father. He tells only funny stories now, but protesting the dominant order in Iran meant torture or death, even for a young doctor, and to see my father is to see a history of hardness. He raised one family, his brothers and sister, in the worst of times before he came to the United States on the SS *France*. And I think he is still fearless, though changed. Maybe softer now, slower to react, calmer. He can still get mad. But he pauses more before he speaks, and conflict is no longer foremost in his mind. As his hand shakes with Parkinson's disease, I think that my father thinks now only of reconciliation with his children.

My father, the ultimate environmentalist, doesn't belong to any national groups. He does not campaign for wetlands. He does not save the whales. What he does do is dumpster dive. He finds things in the trash throughout Cleveland, where he lives most of the time, rescues them, puts some of his treasures in his small apartment (he has twenty clocks), and gives lots of stuff to the thrift store. One day he greeted me at the door of his place with a hat and shirt from a fast-food restaurant. He told me he had to do something to occupy his off-hours. He was lying, of course. He had found them in the dumpster. One time, when I visited, he had a queen-sized mattress leaned up against one wall. He already had a mattress to sleep on, so I asked him what this one was for. He replied "I just like it there." He told me he had found the mattress four blocks away, in the dumpster. When I offered to help take the mattress to Goodwill, he refused. He wanted it to stay. I stopped, looked at the mattress, then at him, small man, recovering from a coronary bypass operation. Then I understood.

When many men start feeling the ebb of life, they suffer a masculinity crisis. I am sure that I will not be exempt. What they then do is fly to some place like Cabo San Lucas, charter a boat, and go marlin fishing. Marlins are huge fish, and the effort of catching a champion can take all day. After the old man has fought with the fish and landed it, it is hauled up on a boom, a small flag is flown to commemorate the "victory," and the marlin is hauled back to port to be stuffed and hung on the conqueror's wall. But my father is an environmentalist. I am sure that he had his old man's crisis in the dumpster. He fought with that mattress all day long, finally managing to heave it over the edge and onto the ground. After that, he hauled it back to his apartment. There he hung it on the wall. There was no need to have it stuffed, since the mattress already was, so he dispensed with that formality.

My father gave me a present that day, though I do not think that he knew it. He gave me the present of a beautiful fish—blue, five hundred pounds, with a long, straight bill, swimming out in the ocean on a tropical, sunny day, chasing amberjack against an oceanic horizon. I will never see my father's gift, never interact with it, touch it, call it by name. But it will live forever in my dreams, and I can feel it, cool water and hot sun, and I will die with my dream. I will always think of the eye of my fish—alien, unknowing of me—and I will race with my fish, swim fast, feel the freedom of the water. And maybe for a moment, the fish will share with me its wild heart.

To fix the woes of the world, we need the generations to stand behind each other. Father, I remember the you that existed before me, with the Kurds, and wild mountain snowstorms, and the fish that will exist after I am gone. Stand behind me.

Part I

Landscape

THE CLEARWATER COUNTRY STRETCHES ACROSS north-central Idaho, the part of the state that you'd grab if you tried to choke up your grip on the Panhandle. Low and green, full of life and forests—big old ones—the Clearwater Country is the transition, the place where the coast changes into the Rocky Mountains. And it's not in Montana, either. It's in Idaho, the millions of acres, the land of cougars, bears, lynxes, and pine martens. And wolverines if you're ever lucky enough to see one. It's a land of geographic transition, undergoing a social and ecological transition, one of the last big wild places left in the Lower 48. Those transitions are what this book is about.

This is the country where the Nez Perce fished for salmon for thousands of years, the country they crossed on the Lolo Trail on their way to the buffalo lands of Montana, the country that Lewis and Clark walked through, before getting into boats. Lewis and Clark came through here because the pass—Lolo Pass—was low and they could actually get through. They met the Nez Perce in Weippe, not too far from where I paddle my kayak down Lolo Creek in the springtime.

Some of this land is preserved for posterity, protected by the federal Wilderness Act of 1964, as well as the Wild and Scenic Rivers Act. The Selway, one of the main tributaries of the Middle Fork of the Clearwater, drains the Selway/Bitterroot Wilderness Area, and the South Fork of the Clearwater takes care of the Gospel Hump Wilderness Area. The Lochsa, Selway, and Middle Fork of the Clearwater are all federally protected Wild and Scenic rivers. But most of the Clearwater—Kelly Creek, Cayuse Creek, the Great Burn, the Mallard Larkins, White Sand, Meadow Creek—is unprotected, bare, under the gun from the old and new sins of the West that simply refuse to fade or make peace with the sustainable capability of the landscape—logging, mining, grazing, as well as overuse, off-road vehicles, and exploitation.

Compared to the rest of the Lower 48, this is still an unknown place. I want you to know it. Start by reading this book. Then visit. Don't believe a word I say. Do the walking—verify it for yourself. But do it quickly, because it's going fast. Real fast.

One of the region's roadless treasures, Weitas Creek is at the forefront of the debate on whether to log or protect the remaining wild areas of the Clearwater Country. *Gerry Snyder photo.*

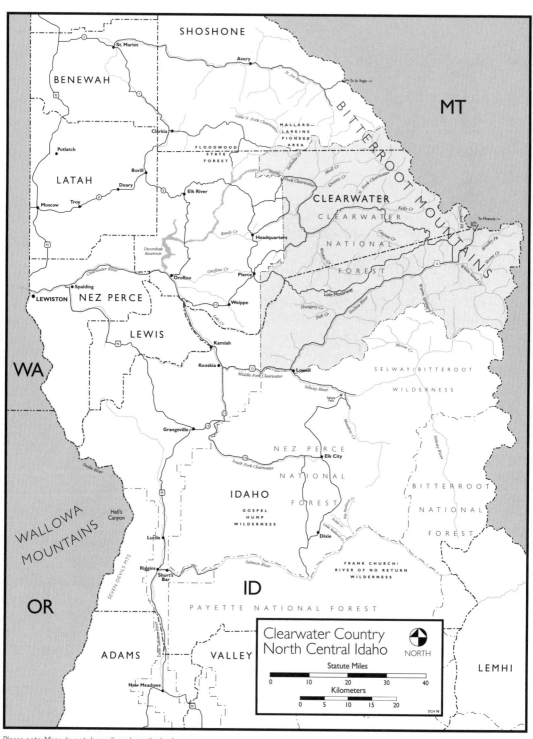

Please note: Maps do not show all roads on the landscape.
Outside of designated wilderness and roadless areas, the majority of landscapes
are spiderwebbed with roads, with densities approaching urban levels.

A Sense of Place

IT IS NOT A BIG CHUNK OF LAND, not a large place to save. Three days for a wandering grizzly bear to cross, six days for a salmon to swim to her high mountain home, maybe five days for a lone wolf to bisect from top to bottom. The Bitterroot Crest—the low country, the tangled lodgepole forests, and deep cedar groves in pockets of seacoast weather stolen from the western shores far away. The Northern Rockies—Douglas fir in the middle, subalpine fir and mountain hemlock up top, and old ponderosa pine on the southern river breaklands, refugees in a temporal space, established at the end of the Little Ice Age three hundred years ago.

Rivers define the land, from top to bottom, north to south: the St. Joe, flowing west-northwest, toward Lake Coeur d'Alene; the North Fork of the Clearwater, winding a big southward bend before heading west, ending ignominiously in the slackwaters of Dworshak Reservoir; the Lochsa and Selway rivers, forming a vee at Lowell, the Selway being the only big river in the continental United States to drain a pristine forested and almost completely protected watershed, from the headwaters to Selway Falls; the South Fork of the Clearwater, salmon river, errant sister, stolen from the Salmon a very long age ago; and the Salmon, with its famous Middle Fork and hidden South Fork bounding off the country in the south, running north almost to the Idaho/Montana border then heading west, dissecting the state before the confluence with the Snake below Pittsburg Landing. All of the rivers cut across the panhandle before heading for the Snake, the Columbia, and the sea.

So much of this land is clean, granite. The animals are itinerants, wandering, using the resources of this last place only in parsimonious amounts. The ungulates, elk and moose, live in the high country in the summer, frequenting green pastures and meadows on top of fire-cleared knobs. Black bears look for ladybug caches on ridgetops in tall, standing snags. River otters avoid the iced over rivers. The salmon cleverly use the protection of the barren upper headwaters of creek beds to avoid predators for their smolts, then harness the force of warm spring rain melting snow to send their young hurtling toward the rich, warm ocean four hundred miles away in the springtime. The bull trout, feeding on the salmon smolts in the hatch, move one hundred miles farther down to the big rivers to seek cool, deep pools in the intensity of midsummer's heat.

Humans have names for this place: the St. Joe and Clearwater Country, the Selway/Bitterroot Wilderness, the North and South Lochsa Face, the Great Burn, the Bighorn/Weitas Country, the Kelley/Cayuse Creek Complex, the northern section of the Frank Church/River of No Return Wilderness. The government administers the Clearwater and the adjacent landscape—most of it is publicly owned, if not managed for the public interest, in national forests: the Panhandle, the Clearwater, the Nez Perce, and the Payette. The boundaries set for these man-made constructs are arbitrary, based on human need, roads, rivers sometimes. The animals do not understand the word "Idaho."

If one wanted to, one could drive around this place. Interstate 90 passes just to the north of the country, from Spokane through low hills toward Missoula. From there, US 93 runs down to Salmon and Challis. A westward turn on state roads goes to Stanley, Banner Summit, Lowman, then Banks. From Banks, one can travel the western edge on Idaho 55, turning into US 95, through Riggins, Grangeville, Lewiston, then back to Spokane on US 195, up through the wheat-desert of the Palouse. The land on the western side is greater than the road, though, and it spills over, cannot be contained by a thin, black strip of asphalt. There is the Snake River, Hell's Canyon, and then up into the Wallowa Country, some of the most beautiful country in the world, the old home of Chief Joseph's people, the Nez Perce. Hell, it is all beautiful, amazing, complete, whole, going, going, gone.

The driving on winding, backwoods country roads would take at the most two days—the last complete, wild, forest in the Lower 48 of the United States. Two days. Less if you drove fast. I've done it. Fast.

Of the roads that go through, there are few places where humans can cross, especially in the winter when the cold winds from the north blow down the Bitterroot spine, making great snowstorms and blocking the mountains with white. US 12 cuts up from west of Lewiston, through Orofino, Kamiah, Kooskia, Syringa, Lowell, then nothing human, except Powell and the ranger station. From there, it's another forty-five miles to Lolo, Montana, and US 93. That is, there is nothing here in the human sense—just the great forest, the last low-elevation pieces of forested wilderness left in the Lower 48, moose hanging out at the snowplow barn by a pile of gravel. The other crossings are graveled roads, but never open in the winter: the Lolo Motorway, following the old Indian trail that Lewis and Clark followed; maybe up by Red Ives and the St. Joe, if one has a lot of time; or the Magruder Corridor Road, the human construct dividing the Selway/Bitterroot and Frank Church wildernesses.

This version of the West is not the huge, uplifted inland sea, sage-brush, mountains lined up in narrow ridges, separating dry valleys, basin and range, horst and graben. It is not canyonlands cut by slow erosive action over millions of years. It is foothills leading to tall peaks hundreds of miles away, hiding behind the battlements of the Montana mountains. It sits on top of the Upper Belt Complex, made 350 million years ago, folded and bent during the Antler orogeny, the birth of mountains when trilo-bites had only just started to swim in the warm inland sea. The land itself, most of it, is called by geologists the Idaho Batholith, a huge, multilobed bubble of igneous rock that drifted toward the surface some seventy-odd million years ago.

I call it the Heart of the World, and when I sit in the hot springs scattered across the face of the land, I can still feel the passion and the magic of creation drifting up beneath me. The Heart of the World is not cool.

Later geology wielded a different paintbrush across the landscapes. The Columbia River basalts flowed up the canyon of the Clearwater and Lolo Creek only three million years ago, changing the course of the rivers more than once, from the Middle Fork of the Clearwater to Big Cedar Creek, then back again. The South Fork of the Clearwater flowed into the Salmon. Glaciers shaped the mountains: the Grave Peak, Canteen Lake, and Legend Lake glaciations washed the arêtes and dished the canyons where I walk today. All these scientific reasons pacify my monkey mind, but I do not need to know how, why the land was formed to feel the connectivity running through it.

I came to this land through rivers. As a young boy growing up in southern Ohio on the edge of the Billion Dollar Coalfield, my rivers were flat, slow, warm, polluted. I can remember floating down the Scioto on a log raft, with a found Labrador retriever and my friends as company, soggy sandwiches drifting in plastic bags in a cooler. The Scioto wandered through farmlands and gravel pits. All of the outside turns were lined with old cars, refrigerators, and washing machines. Slope stabilization, so I was told, ug-liness for the benefit of mankind. I would always look up, above the high water line, to the surrounding hills, and the big oaks: chinquapin, red, black, swamp, blackjack, and post. My eyes would run to the hills and skies, the next vista, the next bend in the river. Later, when my parents bought me a canoe and lifejacket, my friend Tony and I would float the length of our stretch of the river entirely out of the boat, worried about Old Man Catfish grabbing our foot if we stepped on the bottom. We had heard that they had blown up one weighing one hundred and fifty pounds once while dynamiting down on one of the Ohio dams. At home I dreamed of rivers, of the next turn in the bend, anything to take me away from home, my alcoholic father, our constant unhappiness and fighting. Take me away, to Idaho. I had seen the pictures of the mountains.

In 1976, my father brought me out to Lewiston, to run the main Salmon River, the River of No Return, starting outside of North Fork, at Corn Creek, and floating across the state to Riggins. If you wanted, you could drink out of the Salmon then, the years before *giardia lamblia*. There were few ranches on the river. It was a true wilderness float. I could not believe such a land, such a clean land. No refrigerators, old cars, or washing machines on the banks. Just big rock, high sky, and twilight ripples on the edges of slim aquamarine and red rowboats. Each bore the name of a lost place painted on its bow, tragic history unknown to me. The names read *Lake Tahoe*, or *Glen Canyon*; I had never heard of these places before. I was only fourteen and reading fantasy novels at the time. These were to be the new places of my dreams, these vanished paradises lost to development or concrete dams. I ran up and down the mountains, a young grizzly cub myself, and paddled an inflatable kayak in the hot July sun. When one of the guides took sick, I rowed his boat for miles, relentlessly. I remembered so few flat stretches from that trip—in my memory, almost all of it was white. When I paddled the same stretch with my kayak eighteen years later it seemed all flat. I can remember rattlesnakes, no houses, and maybe two ranches. That has all changed. On my last trip, I walked through the grounds of the Polly B, a huge condominium/resort complex, across from one of the original pioneer river ranches, the Shepp Ranch. The primacy and divine right of money had been established even in this last wild space. Buckskin Bill, the last of the wild old mountain men who lived on the Salmon, fired his cannon for me, and showed a young fourteen-year-old boy pickled cougar fetuses. He is dead now. His descendants, such as they are, sell candy bars in his old fort.

I did not return to Idaho for twelve years. In the meantime, I attended university, then graduate school. I ran the Grand Canyon, discovered kayaking, and proceeded to march up and down the Appalachian chain running every small creek in North Carolina, Georgia, and West Virginia in my plastic boat. I was comfortable there. I was and still consider myself a hillbilly. I was raised with the long conversations, slow nasal drawls, and grinding tragedies of the mountain people and their communities. Sitting on a porch discussing someone's chickens is still second nature to me, and I can pass the hours doing nothing, though I know I have changed, too. I married. I dreamed of the West, but my West now was Colorado and her cold, mountain rivers. Idaho was too far. On a river your sight is limited. I know this now.

I graduated from Duke in 1987, looked for a job, and one year later, after a divorce, came here. The Lochsa is the reason I give for moving, leaving my kin, and maybe in the end that is the truth. I have let rivers define me, and of all of the justifications that I have for the paths taken in my life, I think that it is at least the most consistent.

The Clearwater Country is defined by rivers, and I started coming to terms with the environmental issues involving this place as a result of accidental exposure on my many kayaking trips. When I paddled Orofino Creek, outside the town of the same name, between clearcut banks stripped of their cedars, I was only slightly unsettled that I sank up to my hips in silt getting out of my boat at the takeout. But only three weeks later, on a trip down the Middle Fork of the Salmon, flagship river of the federal Wild and Scenic River system, on my night to do dishes, I could dig no dirt out between hard-packed cobbles to help me with my chore. No silt to wash my pots. No silt. Clean.

But rivers could only teach me so much. In the end, I had to confront my ignorance of my own backyard, the country in-between the canyons. I was forced to walk. And so these stories in this book go—starting with kayaking and rivers, then moving toward walking on high ridges, the crests of mountains, and forests. And there are people involved, too—new voices to show the way, leading inevitably to crisis, as the fate of the Lower 48's last standing unknown forest, a place that few know, is decided.

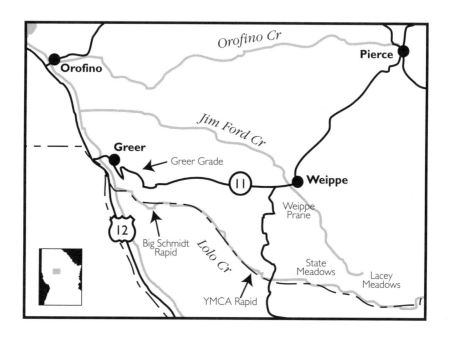

Lolo Creek

THE SOUL OF THE EARTH IS STRONG HERE, in these exposed rocks. I am standing next to Lolo Creek under wavering shade from big cedars, and the sun is shining.

Lolo Creek is a small place, hidden on the maps underneath the county line dividing Clearwater and Idaho counties, draining into the main stem of the Clearwater River above the town of Greer, Idaho. Flowing through a pocket wilderness tracing down the center of the Weippe Prairie in the north-central part of the state, the canyon and stream create a haven for elk, deer, and bear in the middle of the cultivated wheatlands that stand like high islands around the deep canyon incisions of the lower Clearwater and its tributary streams. Originating up in the Musselshell country on the boundary of the North Fork Clearwater drainage, Lolo Creek follows a gentle path past basalt pillows, upland timber country, and clearcuts in the top of the watershed. After meandering through a large open valley, State Meadows, it confronts a large chunk of rock on the edge of the Idaho Batholith. There, it slashes an eighteen-mile canyon through the bones of the prairie, with walls of schist rising fifteen hundred feet above its rocky bed. Between the put-in and the main stem of the Clearwater lies some of the best runable Class IV-V whitewater (on a scale from I to VI) in Idaho.

Driving across the plateau this morning, I think of the old forest that used to grace these open fields, filled with giant white pines now lost to me. But I have been raised with rural sensibilities and agrarian intent, and if the forest is gone, at the least it has been replaced with well-ordered farms, small woodlots dotting the draws, and rushes and hedgerows where small quail and grouse quake in the late spring breeze.

I am here with my buddy Beck to paddle this river. This is no first descent, no exploratory run. This is Beck's and my backyard, literally. Beck's girlfriend's father John lives a half mile up from the take-out, and today he is driving us to the put-in in his white van.

Beck is a small-time logger, making his living selling firewood that is much like Beck himself—big and stout. Beck's load of wood for me last year consisted of forty rounds from a 150-year-old Doug fir stricken by root-rot; *Armillaria* fungus fans spread beneath the bark. I met Beck soon after arriving in Idaho, in a karate class. I dropped out, but he continued, and he can kick my ass. But Beck is a good kayaking friend. If I were in jeopardy, pinned on a rock in the current, he would risk his life to save mine. Such contracts are not taken lightly—the price of such friendship.

At the put-in, our dogs romp in the water, then are shepherded back into John's van. We put our kayaks in the small flow. The current moves slowly into the breach. The final canyon of Lolo Creek was carved by a basalt-dammed North Fork of the Clearwater, two million years ago, before the river changed its mind again and took another course, the path followed by its main stem today. Around the corner, a transformation in the river takes place, as it accelerates into the bend. Signaled by a sharp vertical rock fin, the river turns white, picking up speed.

I have no ignorance to comfort me about the state of this canyon bottom. Lolo Creek and its headwaters—Eldorado Creek, Yakus Creek, Upper Lolo Creek—have been classified as distressed watersheds by the Clearwater National Forest. When the National Marine Fisheries Service swept through Idaho to designate "critical habitat" for the endangered salmon, it passed over Lolo Creek and the entire upper Clearwater, though I have seen a chinook jumping up the falls at Big Schmidt rapid. Potlatch Corporation owns a large part of the upper watershed, and has razed the forest for miles off the basalt bluffs. The Forest Service has itself done its share of damage, too. There are tributary streams in the upper drainage where logging operations have run their bulldozers back and forth across the streambed in the process of yarding the big timber, taking away the precious shade that cools the water for coldwater fish species, as well as dumping silt into the creek bed, filling up the slackwater pools in between rapids where cutthroat trout wait out the cold Idaho winters.

Beck and I are not paying attention today. It catches up with us in a long Class V rapid that we call the YMCA, the start of the big drops on this section. The YMCA consists of several four-foot drops placed in a twisting sequence between a high wall on the left and rocky bank on the right. There is a small, deceptive deep crack on the left at the bottom of the rapids, a locker room, where water pools up against a large, rounded boulder splitting the main channel. The current wants to take my boat toward the crack. I have made this move before, but am not wary enough today.

Coming out of an eddy above the boulder, I overshoot the main channel. My boat broaches sideways on the boulder, the nose bridging the small chute, caught on a flake of schist on the left wall. In an instant, I am leaning upstream on my paddle, braced off the bottom. After popping my sprayskirt, I will have five seconds to get out of my kayak before the current folds the plastic deck on my legs and shoves the hull under, down to the bottom of the crack, where, trapped, I will drown. I release my paddle.

The force of the river pivots the boat violently. As I pull my skirt, the boat starts to fold. I am almost out, my body swaying in the mainstream, my foot caught by the cockpit rim, arms stretched out over my head, waving underwater like an awkward clown. I jerk once, feel my hip distend, then suddenly my foot is released, and I am swimming, free, twisting my body, floating toward shore, where Beck pulls me, gasping and shocked, up on a flat rock. We watch my red boat, obscured by the water, submerge lethally in the crack, before it pops free five minutes later. Beck retrieves my craft. We pause, breathe, eat his supply of glucose tablets. The small, purple drysack containing my lunch is lost.

I recover. We kick the dents out of the boat and finish the run. Beck shares his lunch with me underneath my favorite big red cedar, at the end of the first canyon. A large sandhill crane, a transient in this place, floats in front of us in the lower canyon. It is an auspicious sign. I have never seen one here before. We pass through the final long rapid in sharp, late-afternoon sunlight, then on down to the confluence with the Clearwater and my truck.

A year has passed. They are logging this final canyon of Lolo Creek this gray spring morning, up at the top, below the bridge. Earlier, I had looked at my ownership map of the area and had thought that this whole section was public land, BLM ground, managed by my friend LuVerne Grussing. He had told me that they weren't going to log here. Later, I check my map again: BLM ownership starts a mile down the canyon. This first mile is all private ground.

As we float down, my face wrenched with dismay, we survey the damage. Many of the big cedars along the first mile have been cut. One big tree has been felled across the creek as a bridge. A tailhold for the skyline logging system has been established across the creek. Trees are cut down to water's edge. I think of reporting this job to the state Department of Lands.

No good there—if there were any violations of the Idaho Forest Practices Act, the landowner would receive only a ticket, but no fine. After that, he would probably cut off access to this run, as a penalty for his trouble. Local press? Without a violation, there is no story. What would be the result anyway? In Idaho, commenting on your neighbor's land practice makes for fighting words, and in the end, still no results.

The upper river is choked with logging debris. We carry once. The YMCA is not runable—the entrance slot is walled off with more slash. There is a new log in one of the slots. We carry again. As we stop for lunch, the sound of the helicopter interrupts our sandwich. They are logging the upper rim, the land not in BLM ownership. I see the helicopter dropping down off a bluff to what appears to be a new road, lower in the canyon. Big ponderosa pines dangle, midair, from a yarding cable.

It's private land, I tell myself. There is nothing I can do. I stand alone under my favorite cedar, cold, witnessing the beginning of dismemberment of my favorite place.

Later, I check with LuVerne. He goes down to the canyon, walks the timber sale, making sure that BLM ground has not been damaged or logged. He says, bad job or not, they followed the toothless, industry-written Idaho Forest Practices Act. I protest, naming the big cedars next to the creek. They left a few, he replied. They followed the law. He'll be watching.

All I can do is grieve.

Author in the high water of Big Schmidt Rapids on Lolo Creek.

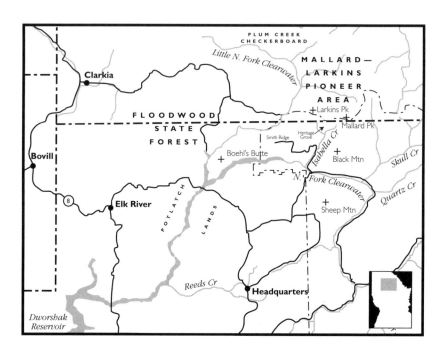

PLUM CREEK
CHECKERBOARD

Little N. Fork Clearwater

MALLARD—
LARKINS
PIONEER
AREA

Clarkia

+ Larkins Pk

FLOODWOOD
STATE
FOREST

Mallard Pk

Smith Ridge

Heritage
Grove

Isabella Cr

+ Black Mtn

Skull Cr

Boehl's Butte

Bovill

N. Fork Clearwater

Quartz Cr

8

Elk River

P O T L A T C H

L A N D S

+ Sheep Mtn

Reeds Cr

Headquarters

Dworshak
Reservoir

Mallard-Larkins

Watershed and wildlife habitat conditions have been pushed to the limit by past [logging] activities....The "front country" is exhausted...and...private land activities are limiting national forest opportunities because...watersheds are approaching or have already exceeded State water quality thresholds.

—Fred Trevey, forest supervisor, Clearwater National Forest, 1990

THIS WAY TO THE MALLARD-LARKINS SUCKS, driving through Elk River. On the advice of a friend, I am on the back route, driving through miles and miles of clearcuts owned by Potlatch, the local timber giant with the huge air-polluting pulp mill in Lewiston. The State of Idaho owns a good chunk of the property back here too—the Floodwood State Forest, a Third World part of a Third World state, hacked bad for the ostensible benefit of the schoolchildren of Idaho. The Floodwoods are part of "trust" lands, given to the state over a hundred years ago by the federal government, and supposedly managed by the Idaho Department of Lands to produce revenue for the public school system in the state.

My friend had told me that he thought the trip was beautiful. He himself did it ten years ago, and all he remembered was green forest. The drive earlier today, to Elk River through second-growth lodgepole, hadn't looked too bad. But past Elk River, the industrial forest commenced in earnest, heavily logged and roaded. As I drive along in my small pick-up, the ground lies bare and ragged.

Down the winding road from Elk River, Dworshak Reservoir hides behind low hills, only partially filled, sporting its bathtub ring under Grandad Bridge. My wife, Kelley, is with me today, and we travel up out of the basin, over Bingo Saddle, and down toward the flowing section of the North Fork of the Clearwater River, through the roaded front of the Clearwater National Forest. The road twists. Kelley and the dogs get sick, and we have to stop. Finally, the North Fork stretches before us at the bridge at the Aquarius campground. After crossing the river, we make our way up the last eleven miles to Smith Ridge, past clearcuts on steep angles, 45 degrees and more, steeper than I would ski with my telemark gear. Who would climb down there with a chainsaw? I'd be afraid of falling down with the damn thing running.

The weather is gray up on top of Smith Ridge, with marbled clouds hanging closely on the ridgelines, spitting rain, framing the forty-acre squares of clearcut, the industrial forest stretching to the horizon to the south. The trail starts at 4,400 feet, on the west side of the Mallard-Larkins Pioneer Area. Looking out over the surrounding countryside, I remember a conversation with Art Bourassa, district ranger for the North Fork District of the Clearwater National Forest. He is the man in charge of this area for the Forest Service, the agency dedicated to managing these lands for "multiple use." The Forest Service is supposed to provide for a number of uses of the forest—some timber harvest, some hunting, fishing, motorized recreation, hiking, and so on. On paper, the idea looks great. But in reality, here on the North Fork District, on the roaded front—the part of the forest laced with roads and thus easily accessible by humans—Bourassa has told me that the program for harvesting timber is twenty years ahead of the schedule.

From my vantage point on Smith Ridge, it sure looks like he's right. So much for multiple use. All they're doing across the valley is chopping down trees like no tomorrow. And Art can't seem to stop, either. Every quarter, new timber sales come up on the block, prepared by his district. If he knows that they are twenty years ahead of a sustainable program, and he has been ranger here for as long as I have lived in the area, why can't he kick the habit?

Stopping along Smith Ridge in our truck, it becomes evident that the Mallard-Larkins is a castle, a fortress surrounded by a sea of bad policy. The part called the Pioneer Area has been set aside under a holdover Forest Service designation from the past, reserved for places that the Forest Service has recommended for national wilderness designation under the Wilderness Act but that have not been formally acted upon by Congress.

But the Pioneer Area is only a part of the greater Mallard-Larkins Roadless Area that covers the northwestern corner of the Clearwater and the southwestern corner of the St. Joe National Forest. Protection only encompasses the high country, a C-shaped chunk of land running the ridges, surrounding Larkin Peak, Crag Peak, Heart Peak, Mallard Peak, and Black Mountain to the south, connected by Goat Ridge. The entire complex of mountaintop glacial cirques and subalpine lakes, though scenic and offering humans a high-altitude playground, is a gerrymandered hunk of rocks and ice. The country, the ecosystem, stretches further down the mountain. Isabella and Elmer creeks, draining the high ridges, are in the center of the C-shaped map boundaries. Avalanche Creek and Collins Creek protect the eastern edge—thick, low-elevation timber country. The Little North Fork of the Clearwater runs to the north and west, between the roadless area and the overharvested, square-mile checkerboard lands of the Plum Creek Timber Corporation. The majority of the forest has been carefully drawn out of the Pioneer Area.

The lower section of Isabella Creek is scheduled for logging and roading, what the Forest Service calls "development," though this will mean annihilation of the lower streambed because of inevitable road slumps into the creek. The soil types underlying the forest are unstable for roadbuilding—another time, driving up the Isabella Creek Road, I have seen the unraveling taking place, road blowouts and tree roots hanging over the edge of the road cut banks. Isabella Creek also houses one of the remaining patches of coastal disjunct forests remaining in Idaho—a displaced patch of the Cascade forests, hundreds of miles away from the seacoast. Logging will mean the end of dozens of sensitive plant species that grow only in this rare habitat—the Pacific dogwood and bank monkeyflower that inhabit this area are almost extinct.

The temperature is in the upper forties, cold out here, even for early July. We walk along the upper slopes of Larkin Peak, covered with old-growth subalpine fir, Douglas fir, and alder thicket. Kelley and I look for wildlife. Many elk and deer spend their summers browsing on clean grasses, the purple aster and Indian paintbrush. Black bear take advantage of the huckleberries coating the south slopes. But there are no grizzlies, no wolves. They have all been killed.

The wind blows over Smith Ridge out of the north. From our perch, we can see three thousand feet below us into the canyon of the Little North Fork. Our dogs are slowed by their packs, a relief since we are in unknown terrain, and they stay close. On the feeder trail down to Larkin Lake, we encounter a mountain goat holding ground on the path. The dogs stare uncertainly, face to face with a tenacious adversary. I am confused; mountain goats are supposed to run from people. The land around here is mineral-poor, and the goat is probably looking for salt. But the habituation of the big animal is still unsettling. As the goat finally moves off, we trip on down the trail toward camp and a rendezvous with two friends.

Evening comes. Three elk and two deer venture into camp, looking for handouts of Twinkies and salt, their lack of fear indicating that they have been hand-fed before. A group of horse campers, already set up and standing around a large fire, informs us about the elk. With folk wisdom elevated to the power of myth, they tell us "This is their land." They then tell us about the popular habit of feeding the native fauna salt out of a pan.

But it is not their land, as can be witnessed around our campfire. The deer, elk, and mountain goats have lost their wildness in this heavily-traveled and popular area. They have been deprived of their natural instincts alternately by campers offering them Pavlovian rewards of junk food and sodium, and hunters blasting them with 30-06s and hardened steel arrows. They live on their island, isolated by geography and clearcuts, prisoners on a small reservation. They have lost their fear of man. And there are consequences that the Mallard-Larkins has been turned into a huge petting zoo for the gamut of Idaho ungulates.

Keith Haley, a Moscow, Idaho, resident, hiker, and hunter, was camping with his wife and two sons at Larkin Lake in early August of 1993. After setting up, he went fishing with his son, Daniel. When he returned from this small expedition, he noticed a cow elk and calf and a number of mule deer circling his camp. Watching the sun set, he also spotted a mountain goat coming around the lake toward him. As he sat quietly with Daniel on a boulder outside of his camp, the mountain goat came trotting up the path. The family dog started barking at the goat. But instead of turning and fleeing, the goat charged the dog. A melee ensued between goat and dog, which ended only after Keith yelled at the dog to back off. As soon as the dog retreated, the goat turned on Keith, charging up the rock. Fortunately, Keith was seated and met the charge with his boots. Panicked, he ordered his son to jump off the rock and get help from his mother. The boy refused. Keith wrestled with the goat for more than fifteen minutes— once, the goat's horn got caught in his pant leg, and he thought the goat would pull him off the rock.

Finally, his wife Pattie heard the commotion and began a frantic attempt to find the small gun, a 22 mag, that they had brought to the lake. She finally found the gun and bullets, and managed to approach the rock where Keith and his son were perched. She handed the gun carefully to their son, trembling, saying "Daniel, it's loaded and pointed at me. Don't touch the trigger. Please hand it to Daddy carefully." Daniel put the gun in his father's right hand. Keith slowly lowered the gun and attempted to shoot the goat in its left eye. When the gun went off, the goat charged one more time, knocking Keith off the back of the rock into an alder thicket. Recovering, Keith fired two more shots at the now-retreating goat. One hour later, Keith walked back up the trail. The goat, with a red spot below its eye, was standing on a boulder overlooking camp, glowering at him. But the excitement for the night did not end there.

After the attack had passed, the family gathered around the campfire and tried to calm down. At that time, the cow elk and calf that had been loitering around the camp started pulling clothing off their clothesline and pawing cooking pots by the fire. Keith started yelling and throwing rocks. This did not seem to affect them. Next, he started firing shots in the air, also with no apparent effect. Finally, caveman style, Keith charged the elk with burning sticks from the fire. The elk, uninterested, found their food pack, hung high in a tree, and pulled it down, propping her front legs up against the trunk. After ripping it down, she stood there, holding it, as Keith said, "like a black lab holding a Frisbee." Keith hit her with another rock, and she finally dropped it.

Unnerved by now, Keith hung the pack even higher in another tree. Unable to sleep, he laid in his sleeping bag, watching the elk. At about 3 a.m., the elk found the pack again, tore it to tatters and ate all of the food. In the morning, Keith and his family packed up quickly and hiked out, hungry. The cow elk, calf, and mule deer still stood around the camp, watching them hike up to the edge of the lake bowl.

A replay of Keith's elk experience starts unfolding at our campsite. The two deer and three elk start nosing toward our packs, seeking unknown goodies. I chase them from our circle, snapping pictures of their brown coats in the yellow evening sun. Finally, we go to sleep, tired from our hike. Mary, my border collie, is left outside to dig her sleep-hole. The deer and elk invade the camp again and raid our friends' stash of oranges and coffee, destroying a dog pack in the process. We wake in the morning to survey the damage. I catch two cutthroats to compensate our friends for their lost breakfast, and after eating them, they depart. The horsepackers pack up as well, leaving Kelley and me alone. It is the Fourth of July.

I saw many small, smiling frogs around the lake today. The frogs bode well for the country. Because amphibians drink their daily water through their skin, they are perennial canaries-in-the-coal mine for all aquatic environments. It appears that acid rain has not yet arrived in these glacial cirque lakes. Within the boundaries of this sky island, the only intrusion is from myself, Idaho Fish and Game, and the local Backcountry Horsemen, who have seen fit to stock these lakes, most naturally barren of fish, with imported trout.

Whether this program is good or bad remains to be seen. No study was done on the effects of fish stocking of these lakes. Miscegenation has occurred up here—an unnatural hybridization of cutthroat and rainbows, an anathema to particular fishermen and fish biologists. Hybridization causes losses of pure strains of fish, an extinction of a species, as well as often producing fish that are sterile and cannot breed. In the case of the Mallard-Larkins, there were probably never fish in these lakes to begin with, and introducing a new, exotic predator into the food chain can do no good. How my friends the frogs will fare is also unknown. Still, today, I can enjoy their brief company as they hop into the water at the sound of my footsteps.

All over wild America, the appropriateness of stocking high-elevation lakes with exotic fish species has recently been resurrected as an issue by interested environmental groups and ecologists. Fish stocked in high alpine lakes, while increasing tourism and benefitting recreational fisheries, have wreaked havoc on the functioning of native ecosystems. Because of their voracious, predaceous nature, fish have eliminated not only amphibian populations, but also mayflies, caddisflies, and water beetles, according to Roland Knapp, a research biologist with the University of California's Sierra Nevada Aquatic Research Laboratory. Since most of these benthic invertebrates have a stage of development that occurs on land, elimination may jeopardize unique bird species that live high in the mountains and eat these insects. In California, since stocking with California golden trout and its subsequent predation on the local fauna, the zooplankton communities, the building blocks of the aquatic ecosystem in fishless lakes, have changed types, altering the ecosystem. The Yellow-Legged Frog, which used to be the most common amphibian in Sierra Nevada lakes above 8,000 feet, has virtually been eliminated, and many herpetologists view the listing of the frog under the Endangered Species Act as inevitable. According to Joseph Grinnell, who surveyed the Yosemite region and its wild animals between 1914 and 1916, the frog was found virtually everywhere. But since 70 percent of the high-elevation lakes have been stocked in the past century, their range has been drastically reduced. Additionally, because stocking occurred in a scattershot fashion, many of the frog populations in the remaining lakes have been fragmented. The physical distances separating groups of frogs may now be too great for population interbreeding, causing genetic deterioration over a longer period of time.

Reversing such stocking policies is intensely controversial. Fishing groups, horsemen, and other recreational users often visit these areas for the sole purpose of fishing. The Forest Service and the state fish agencies have no desire to touch such an issue, seeing only more controversy surrounding wilderness and alienation of the general public for what many feel is an esoteric issue. Even moderate environmentalists, fearful of isolating themselves from a broader constituency and projecting too "extreme" a worldview, often denounce biodiversity advocates who want to stop fish stocking. The debate touches the heart of the purpose of our wild areas—whether they are to preserve a vestige of primitive, untouched America, supporting all native species, or whether recreational interests should supersede the requirements of healthy ecosystems.

The Pioneer Area is a hotbed for fishing. The lakes off the edge of Smith Ridge, Larkin Lake, Crag Lake, Heart Lake, Northbound Lake, and Skyland Lake, have been stocked with a variety of species of game fish—cutthroat, brook trout, German brown, and rainbow—creating a recreational smorgasbord.

There is nothing I can do to help restore the ecosystem balance up here—except catch the stocked trout in the lake. I can enjoy the act of catching my own meal, as well as enjoy frying them up stuffed with garlic, lemon, and jalapeno pepper, and coated with margarine carried by my dogs up the rocky trail.

My Fourth of July ends with a silence of wind swirling beneath the cliffs. As the sun sets, Kelley spies a mountain goat halfway up the cliffs behind the lake. It is small, unobtrusive, and distant—not begging handouts of cantaloupe and green pepper from our encampment.

Tonight, I can sit and think about our founding fathers, great men who formed our country. Men who spoke against power, but used it themselves. Men who lived in constant contradiction, like Thomas Jefferson, who opposed slavery while keeping slaves of his own. Men who begat the only true American tradition: that of embracing myth against the harsh light of an introspective reality.

Tonight, I maintain my myth. I look at the mountain goat on the cliff, embrace my sweetheart, and smile. Ah, wilderness!

The weather turns cloudy again as we trudge out of our camp at Larkin Lake, facing north. We hike along Goat Ridge, past Crag Lake, Heart Lake, Northbound and Skyland lakes. The temperature is noticeably colder, maybe 40 degrees. The trail is lined with mountain hemlocks, with a history of harsh winds, cold snows, and rains in early autumn written in their shape and their bark.

We wind downhill, tired and cold, to Mallard Lake, to 5,800 feet. We will backtrack tomorrow, and cannot help but think that every foot of elevation lost is one that must be made the following day. The prospect of relief from the cold by losing altitude does not seem to be present. It looks cold all the way down to the big tree-tops, 1,000 feet below. The weather in northern Idaho is usually governed by the ocean, but this storm has come from the northeast, off the cold inland plateau of eastern Alberta.

Upon arrival at Mallard Lake, we seek shelter in the surrounding forest. The trees, mostly subalpine fir, are sparse and gnarled. Most of those growing along the edge of an opening have an unusual L-shaped crook close to the ground before straightening out before heading skyward. I comment to Kelley that the bends in the trees are probably from the snow. The loads on the young subalpine and Douglas firs are intense at the edge of an opening, what with the two hundred inches of wet snow blanketing these northerly slopes every winter. The dogs are frosty, digging, preparing to curl up in their small sleep-holes. They eat quickly, evaporatively. They know they will sleep outside tonight.

Tonight, we camp in the paradigm of rock and ice wilderness—sparse, twisted trees, snow pockets in July, chiseled boulders, and big ocean-breaker fog rolling down the glacial cirque, dissipating above the tops of the old-growth forest far beneath us. Stark and memorable, these upper mountain reaches support little diversity of life year-round. There are only two species of trees up here, and the ground is covered only with heather, moss, and springtime wildflowers. I try catching some fish to help with dinner, but the small cutthroat in the lake are stunted, only six inch fish, with big heads and fragile, china mouths. The prospect of this being the only habitat available for all the animals in the roadless area is frightening. In the winter, the animals have no place to live. Ninety percent of all protected wilderness is just like where we are camping right now. Why can't we protect a real forest?

We leave Mallard Lake today, climb up over Smith Ridge heading south toward Black Mountain and drop down into the Fall Creek/ Isabella Creek drainage, along Avalanche Ridge. Goat Ridge shelters Avalanche Ridge from the northerly winds, creating a small rain forest microclimate filled with four-foot diameter hemlocks, Douglas fir, subalpine fir, and the occasional whitebark pine sprouting along the ridge tops. Whitebark pine nuts are prime grizzly chow, but there are no grizzlies here.

The trail drops down into the trees, the vegetation thick and the trail deeply rutted, improperly contoured up the mountain. Fog hangs over the path to the valley, limiting visibility to one hundred feet on either side. For a moment, we are lost—the trail to Black Mountain is less well traveled than the other trails in the area, and we see no horseshoe prints. However, as we climb out of the swamp trough up toward Black Lake, new elk and bear tracks scratch their way up an erosion gully in the fresh, black mud. Our arrival at Black Lake out of the old-growth is subdued. The day progresses—the trail is hard. We are tired from the six hundred foot climb up to the saddle sheltering Black Lake. Looking down, the water is forest-green blue, surrounded by trees and round cliffs.

After setting up camp, I go fishing and catch two different varieties of cutthroat trout for dinner. One—the Colorado cutthroat—is huge, eighteen inches long, and over a pound. As I reel it in from the depths, it turns silently broadside, then starts its wild thrashing as air hits its gills. I am hungry and excited. I grab it, beat its head with a rock, lay it out, clean it, relax again, and cast my Roostertail back out into the lake. The fog, moving, blows cold, surrounding me as it lifts and sinks from the lungs of Black Mountain. Firs and hemlock fade in and out of white.

The trail to the lookout on top of Black Mountain is steep, with switchbacks running up the southwest face. The day is cool as we walk up the trail through wet skunk cabbage, bear grass, and alpine wildflowers. Kelley spots and names yellow avalanche lily, white trillium, and blue lupine along the trail this morning. Behind my head, a four point buck in velvet bounds through the ground cover, flanking my dogs, who swing their heads without a bark at the brown blur of sinew and tissue striding by them. I am heartened to see the deer flee our presence so quickly, still the master of himself.

We reach the lookout at 10 a.m. To the north and the east are the mountains that make up the Mallard-Larkins area: Larkin Peak, Crag Peak, Heart Peak, and Mallard Peak. To the far east is the Nub, a small outcrop of rock perched atop Lost Ridge. The forest is thick and green, falling down to Avalanche Creek. To the south and west across the river is another story. We stare at the industrial forest, the "managed" landscape, sawn into blocks, stretching south to the horizon.

As I wander around the lookout, I notice a salt block, anchored beneath a boulder. Later, I find out the block is here to capture goats for relocation and has been left behind by errant biologists two weeks earlier, too busy stuffing mountain goats in helicopters for transportation down south. I pick it up and throw it off the cliff—no habituation of my mountain goats in my National Forest. When I return home, I shall write a letter to the district ranger. It will read like this:

Dear Art,

I was hiking in your district the other week, and as a concerned citizen/ owner of our National Forests, I noticed several things that were amiss. Of course, I realize that there is probably no money in the budget to clean up the trash left to the north of Mallard Lake by the outfitters who work that area. Likewise I suppose that there is no funding available to establish proper camping areas around the more popular lakes, even though the proliferation of fire circles does much to harm the native vegetation. I also realize that trail repair to fix the erosion problems caused by improper trail construction is probably out of the question as well. Fiduciarily speaking, these are hard times.

There is one small matter, however, that I believe you might be able to attend to. I visited the Black Mountain Fire Lookout this past week. Sparing you the argument that fire is a natural and necessary process in the forest ecosystems of the Northern Rockies, and in deference to old Smokey himself, I did notice two salt blocks anchored at the north and south ends of the lookout. Considering how many rangers have told me not to feed the animals all my young life (I was a Boy Scout in my younger days), I realized that someone must have sneaked up there and placed those salt blocks against your better wishes. As an owner of our National Forests, I quickly went to work and managed to remove one of the offending blocks. You will be pleased to know that I rendered it in a more natural state (I threw it off the cliff and pulverized it). However, I was unable to remove the other—it was locked down with rebar. I am sure that you realize the danger of habituating wild animals such as mountain goats to human presence; a Moscow resident felt so imperiled by one last year that he felt the need to shoot a large billy with his small 22 Derringer.

I have enclosed a bill for trail services—$1.25, more than enough to cover the cost of a beer and tip at a local Orofino pub. If I am in error, and have committed an unacceptable act of vandalism, please bill me for the amount of a salt block, and accept in advance an expression of my most sincere apologies. I do hope that the lookout removes the other salt block quickly. I would hate to hear of another tragic incident such as the one between the individual and the mountain goat. As usual in those types of incidents, the animals lose.

Most sincerely.....

I rest, satisfied at a good day's work on the trail crew!

Today, we hike out of Black Lake, along Avalanche Ridge and down Isabella Creek. We drop off the ridge at 6,200 feet to 3,200 feet. At the juncture of the downward trail, we encounter a mother bear with two cubs. Spooked by our dogs, the cubs tree instantly. I call the dogs back quickly, and beat a hasty retreat. We pause a hundred yards away, drink water, and ponder Tam's luck at avoiding a sow's paw raised in protection of her young.

The branch of the trail off Avalanche Ridge that follows Isabella Creek drops down fast, past subalpine and Douglas fir. As we descend lower, the trees change to hemlock, Douglas and grand fir. Suddenly, the scent on the path is different. Ancient white pine, so rare, their long, loosely seeded cones scattered over the trail, fill the air with sweet sap. Most white pine in north Idaho have been cut, the tree of choice of Idaho's early timber industry, or killed by blister rust disease, an airborne, exotic fungus exacerbated by roading. There are no roads here.

Wildflowers in profusion dominate the banks on either side of us: reddish-purple monkeyflower, snow lily, avalanche lily, and Queen Anne's lace. But there are many others that I cannot identify—small white bell-shaped flowers and red cigar flowers. The air is sweet with the scent of wild roses. Clear water jumps off the mountain, filling Fall Creek and Crimper Creek.

We arrive at the heart of the Heritage Grove at the confluence of Isabella and Elmer creeks. A bridge and small signs labeling Jug Creek and Isabella Creek frame a small campsite up the path. For the first time in the trip, we are surrounded by the great forest. There are no low branches to throw our hanging-rope over to make a bear-proof cache. The nearest one is fifty feet up.

Filled with giant western red cedars, the Heritage Grove is a remnant of coastal disjunct old-growth forest, one of the most unique biotic communities in northern Idaho. Populated with species found west of the Cascades, this is the homeland of the Mallard-Larkins country. It has received special designation because it is one of the few examples of this forest type left in the area. The lowland forest through here used to all be like this—old-growth patches separated by younger groves. Now it is such an oddity that the Forest Service has to give it a special name. I worry aloud to Kelley over people forgetting what places like this actually look like, and adjusting their standards for beauty downward as more wild country is destroyed. I think of the bare hills of Scotland, replete with tourists waxing poetically over denuded hillsides covered with heather, the site of the old Caledonian forest. I think of the great oak forest that built the navies of England, and wonder if this will be the fate of my place.

The morning comes, brought in by a small thunderstorm. It lasts long enough to soak our tent and gear. After we shake the water off our stuff, we begin the long hike back up to Smith Ridge, 3,000 feet above our heads. At the start, the unmaintained trail up Elmer Creek winds through the big trees, open and clear. But it is not long until the path is virtually impassable, blocked by six-foot-diameter red cedar windthrow. The dogs with their packs scramble around the deadfall. They slam their chests into the wooden obstacles repeatedly, undeterred from leading us up the trail. We finally remove their packs, and as we straddle and pull ourselves over the bolts of wood thrown randomly about, the dogs squirm like moles underneath the huge branches and out the other side. We sweat, soaked by dew. We drink water by the bucket.

The trail up the mountain ends in ignominy, with Kelley and me scattering to find remnants that will take us up to the ridgetop. I take a bearing with my compass and topo map. We bushwhack to a hunting camp, then up to Goat Ridge and back down to the trail to my red pickup. I give my dogs, my hearts of gold, the last of my water. They are grateful, and so am I. Back in the car, driving down the Smith Ridge road, we see two elk cows leap through a clearcut and back into an opening gap between two trees. As I turn toward Kelley, they are gone.

Snow at Black Lake in the Mallard-Larkins Pioneer Area. *Author photo.*

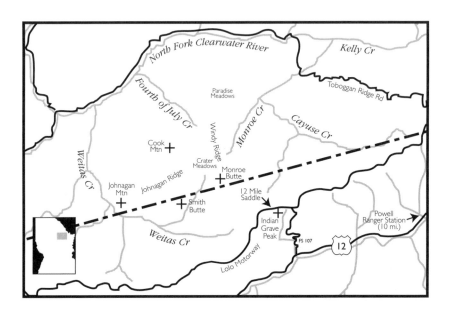

Cayuse Country

IT IS A BROAD SWEEP OF LAND, the undiscovered country, the place in the middle, between I-90 with the expanding Coeur d'Alene/Kellogg/Clark Fork/Missoula road strip and the known wilderness, the Selway/Bitterroot. If the unprotected roadless Clearwater Country can be said to have a center, it is the Kelly Creek/Cayuse Creek complex, together with the upper North Fork forming the headwaters of the big river, the real North Fork of the Clearwater.

I have come here for a week with Steve Paulson of the Gray Wolf Committee. We are tracking wolves, hiking on the ridge between Monroe Creek and Fourth of July Creek, two of the most remote drainages in the Clearwater Country, off the Lolo Motorway from Twelve Mile Saddle. We are traveling to Cook Mountain, to Windy Ridge, to Windy Bill Summit, maybe even to Paradise Meadows. It is hot, and time is limited.

Soft-spoken and sweet, Steve runs through his personal history on the trail—growing up in Idaho, bowhunting cougar, the Marines, and his ten years as a smokejumper. Steve speaks fondly of spending time in the woods as well as his start in activism and his interest in Forest Service timber sales. We discuss his contribution to the fight over the bank monkeyflower, a sensitive species made famous by Idaho's ex-senator Steve Symms's commitment to mow down any in the way of logging road construction.

We hike in eight miles to a hunter's camp, pitch my tent, rest, and wait. We will hike this evening, look for wolf scat, howl for the gray wolf. Steve has seen wolf sign here before. I take a brief stroll out from camp to Crater Meadows, to an overlook across the southern end of the Great Burn country, the name given to the crescent of land encompassing Weitas Creek, Kelly Creek, Cayuse Creek, and up across the border into Montana.

Fires burned hot across the Clearwater Country in the years between 1910 and 1919, creating the Great Burn, whose extent was increased by a dry climatic period in the Clearwater that extended up into the 1930s.

Started by lightning and logging slash disposal, and driven by summer rainfalls of low single digits, whole landscapes, from Cook Mountain north to Kelly Creek and even the Coeur d'Alene mountains, were scorched. Smoke hung so thick over the small towns surrounding the Clearwater Country that, according to Ralph Space, who grew up outside Weippe, chickens went to roost in early afternoon. In 1910 the mining town of Wallace burned. And in 1914 the town of Bovill almost burned up as well, a victim of a crown fire started by Potlatch Lumber Company incinerating piles of woody debris in August.

But such fires are typical in Clearwater history. Most of the country where we hike today is lodgepole, running on the hundred-year fire cycle of the species, save for dark, mixed groves of firs trimmed by larch down by the creeks. Lewis and Clark, during their travel through the Great Burn, talked about crossing burned breaklands, as well as Native Americans who set trees to flame. In his book *The Clearwater Story*, Space talks about the history and extent of the great fires, and the determined efforts made by the Forest Service to fight the burns. Driven by what many considered holy cause, individuals made gallant attempts to stop the fires, especially when they burned close to ranger stations and people's homes. But reading between the lines, it seems that the best that most could do, armed with minimal equipment, was to keep the fires from burning man-made structures. When it came to the forest, the fire did what it wanted. Looking across the expanse of the shrub fields in upper Weitas Creek, from backcountry horizon to horizon, it is obvious that the fires spread where the laws of physics dictated.

Hiking up the Cook Mountain trail at sunset, we come across a ridge to the roof of the western Cayuse Creek country. It is there: rounded mountains lining the edge, dimming sunshine falling down through burnt lodgepole pine snags and young subalpine fir. There is a moose cow and calf at the edge of the world—mother dark, fading into the gray dusk, baby sorrel, pressed tightly against his mother's side. There are also mosquitoes at the edge—the world was not made solely for the comfort of humanity.

Up on the edge, Steve and I talk red wolf reintroduction in the Southeast. We are at the beginnings of gray wolf recovery in the Northern Rockies, and important to the environmental community at large are the lessons of reintroduction of large predators in other parts of the country. The red wolf was one of the first animals protected under the Endangered Species Act, and certainly the story of its tentative salvation is important. But equally important is the chain of events that happen to an animal just before being eliminated from the planet. What is the face of extinction?

Curtis Carley, with the U.S. Fish and Wildlife Service in Albuquerque, New Mexico, tells this story in his report on red wolf recovery, one of the original recovery documents from the 1970s, when he lived in Beaumont, Texas:

> The animals [red wolves] we encounter are often in unbelievably poor condition due to the harshness of the coastal environment and parasites. The most serious external parasite is the mange mite. This parasite denudes the animal and causes skin lesions which often become infected....Our first attempt to cure an advanced mange condition came when a litter of three wild canine pups was given to the field program by a cooperating rancher in July of 1974. The pups, one female and two males, were about three months old and were heavily parasitized by mange mites and hookworms. They had been so weakened by their condition that they were easily captured by hand in an open pasture....All adult canines examined by the field program have been infested with heartworms, the most serious of the internal parasites....The hearts of these animals are often enlarged and deformed by the parasite mass contained in their chambers.

A grainy photograph accompanies the report. The wolf pups are crouched pathetically against a woven wire fence, ears drooped and legs splayed. Curtis Carley does a good job of attempting to tell it like it is within the limits of his profession. Regarding the situation of the red wolf, he describes bodies covered with mange, half hairless, huddled together in final desperation. Social animals deprived of their last contact—it is human denial to think that those intelligent animals were not also losing their minds. He stops short of emotional impact, hoping to be heard as a voice of reason. But when I read the above passage, when I for a moment attempt to walk one mile in another species' paws, my only reaction is rage.

As part of the mandated recovery effort for the red wolf, the U.S. Fish and Wildlife Service brought all the existing red wolves in from the wild— a heroic feat. After a successful captive breeding program, wolves were released in spots in coastal North Carolina as an experiment, then finally reestablished in the Great Smoky Mountains National Park. In order to allay fears of livestock predation, the population released into the wild was designated a "nonessential experimental population," a provision under the Endangered Species Act introduced under the Reagan administration that would allow killing any problem wolves. This clause could only be used if there were no populations of the species present in the reintroduction area. Since all the red wolves had been brought in from the wild, the possibility of accidentally killing remnant wild populations did not exist. Accompanying the release was an extensive landowner education program regarding the wolves and the Service's intentions.

Steve and I talk gray wolves now—more specifically their impending reintroduction into the Northern Rockies. The gray wolf was once abundant in Idaho, as well as throughout North America. However, with the extermination of the great bison herds and annihilation of other ungulates that were the wolves' prey, as well as wholesale slaughter of wolves, grizzlies, and other predators through predator control efforts, the wolf was eliminated as a viable species throughout the West by the 1920s. By the 1930s, the wolf was considered extinct in Idaho. The last documented wild wolf in the greater Yellowstone ecosystem was killed in 1944. Though lone wolves have been spotted throughout Idaho and Montana since that time, the only supportable wolf populations have been in northwestern Montana, consisting of five packs ranging from outside Missoula to Glacier National Park.

In the Environmental Impact Statement (EIS) for the gray wolf recovery in the Northern Rockies, the U.S. Fish and Wildlife Service, in charge of the reintroduction, is not nearly as direct in their prose as was Curtis Carley. The Fish and Wildlife Service would like to use "nonessential experimental populations," and would put two separate populations of wolves into Wyoming and Idaho.

"Nonessential experimental populations"—since when is any member of an endangered species "nonessential"? And what are the ethics of doing "experiments" on rare animals? As pabulum to be passed to the public, "nonessential" is an attempt to lead the citizenry into thinking that reintroduction is irrelevant. And "experimental" glosses a lacquer-thin coat of scientific validity to an otherwise specious outcome—shooting wolves if they don't happen to bend to local whim.

So often when dealing with issues of extinction, scientists and bureaucrats employ this kind of language—the vocabulary of sterility. Animals don't die, according to this lexicon—populations "wink out." Even terms like "extinction" or "habitat degradation" are emotionless words, and convey no descriptive images of death and destruction. This is intentional, of course—the choice of words defines the way that the public will consider the issue.

In reality, though, limiting vocabulary confines the debate. Ordinary people with spiritual perspectives are eliminated. In order to even participate in the debate regarding the fate of much of our ancient forests, or the wild itself, it is almost a prerequisite to be a scientist, bureaucrat, or someone with a monetary interest. Speaking out in favor of truth and beauty won't get you a seat at the table.

Regarding the face of extinction, animals don't just "wink out." Species on the edge of extinction, like the red wolf, are usually there because they have been starved out, their homes have been wrecked, they're dying of their version of the plague, they're freezing to death, or they've been executed by bullets, cyanide, or poison pellets. The reality of extinction, especially for an intelligent social creature like the red wolf, is the worst nightmare any individual in a species can possibly experience, a group loss of community, future, and love—an unspeakable loneliness and darkness. And extinction does not just affect the amorphous concept of species. Real individuals feel the pain directly.

The Service wants to use Section 10(j) of the ESA—those experimental populations of wolves—as a political move to ease the concept of reintroduction of the large predator in both central Idaho and the greater Yellowstone area. One group would be "soft released" in Yellowstone after acclimatization. The other population, about fifteen wolves, would be "hard released," dumped into the center of either the Frank Church/River of No Return or the Selway/Bitterroot Wilderness. One thing is certain with hard release—wherever the wolves are placed, the probability is high that they won't be in the same place the following day.

Nonessential populations can be removed if there are difficulties, or eliminated if there is a problem with livestock loss. The Service's attitude is that this worked in North Carolina and the Great Smokies and it can work here. But many members of the environmental movement in the Northern Rockies are not behind the Service. Steve supports another alternative: natural recovery. He is convinced that wolves are out here, denning, reproducing. "Maybe down in Monroe Creek, here, or Fourth of July Creek. These are two of the most remote places on the Clearwater Forest." They're just damn hard to find, he says. From our experience so far, I would have to agree.

The environmentalists have no beef with the greater Yellowstone release, only problems with the central Idaho plan. The reason is because they know that wolves are already there. Wolf sightings have been on the rise in central Idaho throughout the '80s and '90s. And the environmental community is not too excited to see the protections of the ESA withdrawn from the resident wolf population, as well as wolves that will naturally migrate into Idaho. Besides, the language of the ESA states that the Service cannot use experimental populations when those are geographically connected with naturally occurring wolves. The gray wolves in Montana can reach Idaho in a day.

It is hard to judge whether the people in the Service actually think that natural recovery has a chance. There is evidence offered in favor of such a plan in a letter from Charles Lobdell, head of the Service in Boise, Idaho, to the Wolf EIS Director, Ed Bangs. In the letter are strong words that wolves are coming from Montana, and that in the near future the Service "envision(s) that eventually, there will be no stark disjunction of wolf packs between any of the three recovery areas [Montana, greater Yellowstone, central Idaho]." In fact, in this letter, it appears that the Idaho office of the U.S. Fish and Wildlife Service crew thinks that natural reintroduction is going to work. Then who upstairs in the Service is pulling the strings for "experimental" reintroduction? And for what reason? The politicos at the top are obsessed with control of the natural environment and must want to shoot wolves if there are any inconveniences at all. But the majority of people in Idaho, Montana, and Wyoming, the three states affected by wolf reintroduction, support the idea of wolves in their backyard. And across the United States, by a two to one margin, citizens support bringing back the wolf.

The agricultural industry, conversely, advocates removal of the wolf in Montana, Wyoming, and Idaho from the list of endangered species. Fearing livestock depredation and land-use restrictions, groups such as the American Farm Bureau state in the draft EIS for the recovery plan that "there is virtually no chance of acceptance of an introduction program without a program to compensate farmers, ranchers and others for losses caused by introduced wolves. Losses for which compensation must be provided should not only include livestock losses. Compensation should also be provided for property damages, personal injury, and 'taking' of private property under the Fifth Amendment." The Idaho Cattle Association's comments are more strident concerning livestock loss: "You fail to address the potentially catastrophic losses that may be suffered by these few ranchers. Hint: That is why we killed all the wolves in Idaho in the first place!"

An exhaustive study by Steve Fritts, Wolf Recovery Coordinator for the Northwestern United States of the U.S. Fish and Wildlife Service, documented that cattle losses in the greater Yellowstone area averaged only nineteen cattle and thirty sheep killed or injured each year. This out of over 146,000 cattle and calves and 265,000 sheep and lambs grazing on the six national forests in the greater Yellowstone ecosystem every summer! In central Idaho, because cattle and sheep are generally taken up into the wilderness to graze after the calving and lambing season, losses are only expected to be ten cattle and fifty seven sheep on average, from a completely recovered wolf population of one hundred wolves—the cost in dollars only $11,083. But facts don't really matter to those who tolerate no losses—according to the Service, out of four wolves to come to Idaho in the recent past, two have been shot.

The real issue is, of course, not forty-some cattle or one hundred sheep. The real issue is control of the myth of the West. The Old West, structured with marginal economies that have never been nature-friendly, is familiar with the idea of dressing up non-issues with hysterics, such as "catastrophic livestock losses," or "collapse of the entire timber industry." Doughty pioneers struggling against a relentless natural world plays well during funding time at the federal trough. But reintroducing wolves into the West flies in the face of the "common sense" pabulum peddled by Western senators. Maybe being a cowboy is never having to say you're wrong, or you're sorry. Wolf reintroduction, by stating that killing off the wolf was a tragedy so fundamental to the essence of the land that it must be repaired at any cost, might open up other questions. What other things have these pioneers been doing out here on the frontier?

The only place I can hear wolf feet now is in my dreams, following ridgelines through brush and new snow. It is still summer. But as Steve and I stand on the edge of the world, the wind changes, cold out of the north, drying sweat. The seasons change quickly in the Cayuse Country, I think. Except for winter.

Steve and I howl for the wolves. On my first howl, we hear a response southwest from the ridge. I howl again; a pure wolf note howls back.

I am jumping off the edge of the world now, under the sunset, into another green world below. As I am falling, I am dreaming. I see a black wolf with blue eyes, howling, singing deep songs for me. Centuries pass. I watch. He fades into the brush, shifting from black to red-speckled gray, and now back again, into Wolf, tail standing flat from his back, hump over shoulders. Changing and shifting, he sings to his world and me, pleading for me to keep his world separate from mine.

I wake up this morning at five. Last night, Steve and I had decided that our chances of wolf contact would be better in early morning or late evening, when their primary prey, the Rocky Mountain elk, are also more active. Steve is slow, groggy, snoring. I run out of the tent, up the mountain behind the camp. I've got better things to do than watch Steve's wrinkled face eat cereal. I want to run with the wolves.

On a small knoll just out of Crater Meadows, I let out a howl to the west through the brown-green needles of the lodgepole forest. I wait. Wolves have a simple howling protocol that must be followed in order to prevent being discovered as an impostor; one twenty second howl, followed by a two minute wait, followed by another twenty second howl. After this sequence, one must wait at least thirty minutes before howling again. This waiting period can be difficult for the impatient, like myself. When one does achieve success, one wants to howl again immediately. To the wolves, though, such immediate response is improper and unmannerly. They will not dignify your boorish behavior with a response.

Earlier, Steve had taught me the appropriate howling protocol. He shuddered his shoulders, took three deep breaths, and, well, howled. It sounded very much like the long note on a fire engine siren.

Mary obviously thought that Steve's demonstration howl was a good one. She returned from her leadership position one hundred yards up the trail to check out the fuss. She circled Steve, craned her head and neck toward his mouth, and yipped a peremptory check to his noise, indignant at the abuse of dog-speech and culture.

By the light of a rising day, I let out two more howls across Smith Butte. The echoes bounce back from Windy Creek. A wolf howls back, out of the west. One deep, sonorous note. He holds it on the breeze, like a wilderness Enrico Caruso, for his twenty seconds. Then several coyotes start yipping, back-up singers in the canine choir.

I run down the ridge, jumping and tripping over downed lodgepole, running with Mary. I am going to attain Smith Butte, howl out over Weitas Creek. And then I run into the ceanothus brush field.

Ceanothus is a woody, waxy-leafed shrub common in the Northern Rockies. It is generally found on catastrophic fire sites, where the fire has burned so hot that all the organic layer of humus has been removed, leaving only mineral soil. Industrial silviculturalists hate ceanothus. It is persistent, virtually impossible to get rid of easily, and blocks reforestation/ tree planting efforts by screening light from the seral species of trees most prized for their commercial value.

Yet ceanothus has a higher purpose than industrial man can see. It provides elk with summer cover. Where I stand, the smell of elk urine hangs on the top of the ground like a wet diaper. A preferred food, elk flock to ceanothus like kids to ice cream. And most importantly for the forest, it is a nitrogen fixing plant, restoring nutrients to the soil after a fire. Ceanothus has a ninety-year life span on fire sites and must have a burn site to germinate. During the time ceanothus is present, it redeposits the humus layer lost in the fire. It repairs the soil with this organic matter, so that when finally all conditions achieve critical mass, a young forest will burst up through the waxy leaves, strong and disease-resistant. Young white pines are already beginning this process on these southern facing slopes. Once they regain their preeminence, ceanothus will go to sleep in the seed bank, waiting for another catastrophic event to call forward its role in the forest ecosystem.

Ceanothus brush fields are thick, though, with twisted roots and curved branches formed by the changing condition of yearly snowpack. It brings back memories of hiking in mountain laurel growing in the Blue Ridge, back in my college days, gnarled and choked, frustrating my passage. There would be no more running today, only picking my way down the mountain on paths cleared by downed logs and meandering elk. Mary scoots off after a small chipmunk, flying low under the claustrophobic branches.

There are always consolations, though, for giving up romantic images for a more practical reality. Interspersed in the ceanothus are bushes of ripening huckleberries, turning from dull red to deep purple in the morning sun. I eat huckleberries instead of running with the wolves. After picking and munching several handfuls, I sit on a rock outcrop and howl at a cow elk five hundred yards below me at a small salt lick. She seems most impressed with my imitation, until she spots Mary and me. She snorts and bugles her desultations at us, finally trotting off around the far side of Smith Butte, leaving me with smeared purple on hands and mouth in the presence of Weitas and Liz Butte, on the morning of a bright, sunny day.

The following morning, Steve and I break camp and head north and east for the Kelly Creek country. It is hot and buggy on the trail today, with black flies buzzing in my ears, stinging the back of my knees where they can smell my blood. I am aggravated and irritated, walking through this baking lodgepole forest, whose trees give no shade. I drink water, cursing the southern exposure slope. I beg to walk in a breeze.

All of it does no good. I smear mosquito repellent on my legs and dunk my cap in a cold stream. The flies circle, waiting for the chemical evaporative moment, waiting for lunch to be served.

Steve is dawdling on the trail again, moving slowly, looking for wolf sign. I have always been impatient. When I was thirteen, I would pour toluene glue over plastic airplane models like hot maple syrup on a stack of pancakes, then press the agglomeration together to form an idea of a B-17. I cannot do this for a wolf study.

Steve is looking for tracks, hard to find, especially in this powdery trail dust. He is also looking for wolf scat. The techniques used for examining scat are not for the squeamish. The primary activity is poking and prodding a given sample to determine its state of decay. Once located, a canine-shaped piece of poop must be measured. Girth must be at least three centimeters in order to qualify. Additionally, wolves have a lever-action jaw when compared to other canines. This evolutionary adaptation enables wolves to crack the bones of their prey to get at the marrow inside. This in turn puts bone chips in their stool, an easily identifiable feature when ground under the heel of a hiking boot. Dogs and coyotes can only gnaw on bones. Their feces may contain hair and rodent bones, but no chips of deer femur or pieces of calf elk hoof will be found.

Steve bags his samples carefully, recording in a small notebook the location of a sample, its size, and other environmental features. If greater than three centimeters, Steve carefully places the sample in a bread bag and labels the plastic with hospital tape, using twigs like chopsticks to lift the stool to avoid a certain infective fungus contained within. On this trip to Cook Mountain and along Windy Ridge, we have identified nine possible specimens, and collected three positives.

We push on, ending our day by reaching Paradise Meadows, a large clearing on top of Windy Ridge running out to the Kelly Creek Canyon. We camp for the night and cook. Elk gather in a herd above our camp beneath young spruce and fir. Steve manages to call a young cow down into camp with his rubberband calf call. The cow had probably just lost a calf, and the sound of a distressed baby offered the promise of relief from the pain of lactation. She barks, whines, and groans for ten minutes while I sit in the bushes with Mary and my camera. These elk are wary, different from their Mallard-Larkin's cousins. Less traffic and more hunters.

At dusk, we hear a coyote yipping down in the salt lick in Paradise Meadows. We crawl on our bellies through the tall grass, mosquitoes biting our lips and cheeks. The coyote yips at his image of us, at a bull elk up the meadow, and at his mate hunkered down in the salt lick. Mary trembles. Steve puts Mary, our decoy, out on a short lead in front. The coyote in the salt lick is surprised to see a black and white image of itself floating between the beargrass hummocks. Steve dreams of finding a coyote kill. I wonder if there will be a spot on me without a bug bite.

Steve crawls across the marshy streambed, using the act of Mary's deception as a cover. Behind a young spruce, he blows his calf call. Coyote is confused now. The yipping increases. The trickster is being tricked. Mary barks on cue.

Finally, the scene, the gag, is over. Steve stands up, laughs. I rise, and Coyote laughs as he trots off into the woods on the far side of the pasture. We walk down into the salt lick, Mary bounding over hummocks, as the sun sets and a great blue heron floats down out of heaven, into an old hemlock lining the edge of a summer twilight sky.

Three years have passed since Steve and I stood on top of Cook Mountain and howled for wolves, and much has happened. After the U.S. Fish and Wildlife Service completed the EIS, wolf reintroduction was handed over to the Nez Perce tribe. In January 1995, fifteen wolves were released into the central Idaho wilderness, followed by a release of twenty wolves in 1996. The original plan had been to release fifteen wolves per year for five years. But in the end, the political enemies of wolf reintroduction won out. Headed by Senator Conrad Burns of Montana, the opposition cut funding levels by $200,000 for the effort, and the second release was made possible only by contributions from private donors.

Grassroots activists' fears concerning ranchers shooting wolves were realized with the famous Gene Hussey incident, where a rancher from Salmon, Idaho, found a wolf shot next to one of his dead calves. U.S. Fish and Wildlife agents arrived to investigate the shooting, possessing a legitimate search warrant. Hussey claimed they used excessive force, and congressional hearings championed by Representative Helen Chenoweth and Senator Larry Craig from Idaho were held regarding the agents' conduct. However, a tape of the incident showed that Hussey cursed and threw rocks at the two agents, who were trying to investigate the scene of the shooting and were acting professionally. An autopsy of the calf showed that it had been stillborn, and the unlucky wolf had happened upon an easy meal.

Three more of the central Idaho wolves perished during initial reintroduction: one was winter-killed; another was killed by a cougar; and a third, preying on livestock, drowned in a stream after a leghold trap intended for the wolf set by the Animal Damage Control Service got caught in brush. And as this book went to press, a report of a young male wolf being shot outside of Elk River, a tourist and timber town on the western edge of the Clearwater Country, appeared in local papers. Malice seems to be the only explanation for the killing. No livestock was present and Elk River has no significant livestock industry anyway. The wolf, a transient from the Nine Mile pack in Montana, had been observed hunting mice in a roadside pasture. U.S. Fish and Wildlife officials are investigating.

But grassroots activists underestimated the wolves' natural fecundity. The reintroduced wolves have formed six breeding pairs, which have produced a total of thirty pups. Incidents have quieted down, according to Curt Mack, the coordinator of the management effort with the Nez Perce tribe. The tribe is concentrating on outreach and has set up a livestock cooperative—a loose network of key contacts, whereby the tribe monitors the wolves and their locations and informs ranchers in order to avoid wolf/stock incidents before they happen. "On a statewide basis, losses to livestock are insignificant," Curt says. "But to the individual rancher, that doesn't matter."

Emotions on all sides seem to have settled down, and while the ranching and timber industries still aren't ecstatic about wolf reintroduction, they seldom criticize the work of the tribe. Any more active reintroduction is probably a moot point anyway. "Trends are positive biologically," Curt says. "It's more of a social issue. We've got to learn to live with wolves now."

Aerial view of the confluence of Kelly and Cayuse creeks. *Author photo.*

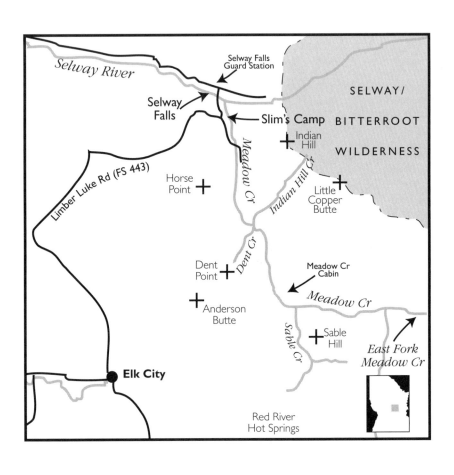

Selway River

Selway Falls
Guard Station

Selway
Falls

Slim's Camp

Indian
Hill

Meadow Cr

Horse
Point

Indian Hill Cr

SELWAY/

BITTERROOT

WILDERNESS

Little
Copper
Butte

Limber Luke Rd (FS 443)

Dent
Point

Dent Cr

Meadow Cr
Cabin

Meadow Cr

Anderson
Butte

Sable Cr

Sable
Hill

East Fork
Meadow Cr

Elk City

Red River
Hot Springs

Meadow Creek

MEADOW CREEK IS A PLACE to walk in a forest. Not some sparse, hot, lodgepole forest, or a windblown, scraggly subalpine fir and whitebark pine forest, but the real thing—old-growth Doug fir and cedar crowding the miles between jumpoff and ending points. One of the largest tributaries of the Selway River, on the western boundary of the Selway/Bitterroot Wilderness on the Nez Perce National Forest, Meadow Creek was excluded from protection in the 1964 Wilderness Act and the 1980 Central Idaho Wilderness Act because of the vastness of its timber resource. The timber industry wants into Meadow Creek. But it is still intact, remaining the last, unlogged, unroaded major drainage on the Nez Perce unprotected by wilderness designation.

Unlike most remaining roadless river courses anywhere in the Lower 48, Meadow Creek does not tumble down off the mountain from a glacial cirque. Its headwaters are in heavy forest, flowing down into an open valley with old-growth western red cedar and grand fir on the western shore, and big open stands of ponderosa pine hundreds of years old on the eastern canyon wall. Meadow Creek Canyon is open until its final miles, where it plunges into a quartzite-schist gorge, dropping an average of one hundred and fifty feet per mile on its way to the Selway River. Butted up against the breaks of the Salmon River, Meadow Creek is the Clearwater Country's southern arm, having the same plants and similar geology and weather. The only human settlements are Red River Hot Springs or Elk City, two small Idaho towns literally in the middle of nowhere. No one goes there much, save hunters during fall elk season. And unlike the Mallard-Larkins, there's not a bunch of cut-over timberland plastered across the landscape. Once over the edge in Meadow Creek canyon, there are no clearcuts.

The way politics are going, Meadow Creek in its unmarred form probably won't be around much longer. But there's also no question that the drainage won't be logged without a vicious fight, and one with historic precedence. The debate over logging or preserving this place has been at the center of controversy ever since passage of the Wilderness Act in 1964.

In closing the deals for the Selway/Bitterroot Wilderness in 1964, as well as the Central Idaho Wilderness Act in 1980, Meadow Creek became a heavily timbered pawn in a game that gave away two critical pieces of habitat to the timber industry in order to avoid gridlock and nonpassage of the various wilderness set-aside bills. Then Secretary of the Interior and former and future governor of Idaho, Cecil Andrus, made an unwritten sweetheart deal to the timber industry, promising them the Cove/Mallard area to the south of Elk City, and the Meadow Creek watershed, to the north, in return for no opposition to the Central Idaho Wilderness Act of 1980. After the bill passed, the Elk City mill, which was most conveniently located to process the trees from the Cove/Mallard area, changed hands from Gwen Shearer to Bennett Lumber Company. Shearer had seen the handwriting on the wall, and had probably decided that no significant timber would come out of that area of the Nez Perce National Forest.

Once the Central Idaho Wilderness Act passed, the Forest Service proceeded with the ugly business of destroying the remaining unprotected roadless areas. This involved building another couple hundred miles of road and selling the timber for clearcutting. Because of the inaccessibility of the area and the increased cost in hauling the logs from this area any-where—the Elk City/Dixie/Red River communities are as far from any-where as a place in the Lower 48 can be; over sixty twisting miles from either Grangeville, Kooskia, or Kamiah, home of competing mills—the Bennetts could count on always underbidding the sales in the official auc-tions that the Forest Service conducts for selling the timber from these areas. The constantly expanding checkerboard of forty-acre clearcut patches ubiquitous in the rest of the Nez Perce Forest would spread through these two timbered watersheds. More riches would be had for the Bennett fam-ily coffers. A compliant workforce would not question such issues as sustainability. Would there be jobs ten years from now? Who cares? In an industry rife with boom, deforest, and bust cycles, most loggers know that as long as the truck payment is met this month, that is all that matters. In the past, there has always been timber over the next hill.

The plans of the administrators of the Nez Perce Forest called for destroying the Cove/Mallard area, south of Dixie, followed by the Wing/Twentymile areas, the forested northern flank of the Gospel Hump Wil-derness. Wing/Twentymile was roaded and partially logged. But the Forest Service received unexpected opposition over the Cove/Mallard area from Earth First!.

But even the Forest Service has appeared strangely reluctant over entering Meadow Creek for timber harvest. Aside from a weak attempt in the early '80s to log the headwaters from the Magruder Road, entry into Meadow Creek in recent history has always been at the forest supervisor's discretion, and the supervisor has always chosen not to cut. Part of the reasoning is logistical. Hauling logs out of Meadow Creek, even by helicopter, would require building a road down over three thousand vertical feet into the four-thousand-foot-deep canyon. Such a road would probably collapse off the mountainside into the stream because of the fragile geology that underlies the area. Additionally, if logs were hauled out over the Selway and down to Lowell, a huge new bridge would have to be built above Selway Falls, and the road along the Lower Selway, a federal Wild and Scenic River, would have to be straightened. Geography and topography alone guard Meadow Creek from a chainsaw fate.

On the surface, the argument over Meadow Creek's ultimate fate is entwined in the "nature versus jobs" debate. Elk City as a timber community may collapse if the Meadow Creek, Cove/Mallard, and Wing/Twentymile areas are not logged. And it is certainly arguable whether a community like Elk City could make it economically on tourism alone. Additionally, its inaccessibility, poor infrastructure, and elevated transportation cost makes attracting soft industry extremely difficult.

In fact, the relative fullness of the log deck at the Bennett mill seems to have little to do with the prosperity of the area. Many times I have driven by the mill on the edge of town and seen logs stacked over twenty feet in the air, then pulled into Elk City to see the same run down trailer shacks lining the few roads in the area. Elk City is never going to be a Chamber of Commerce postcard shot, even when the logs come to town.

But it is worth asking what is being saved versus what is being destroyed when pondering such a decision. Logging these last areas will preserve a poverty-stricken community, complete with all the emblems of the downtrodden—pickups up on concrete blocks parked outside of trailers, and shotgun shacks, as well as the elevated teen pregnancy and domestic abuse rates—for another ten years at most. The problems faced by communities like Elk City will not vanish by destroying the last, few, roadless areas. The only community-based effect will be to let the Forest Service keep their slumlord status over an area that was always only marginally economically viable.

Kelley drives me from Moscow to the bottom of Meadow Creek, up along the Selway River to just above Selway Falls. We sleep overnight next to the small picnic tables at Slim's Camp, just up from the confluence. In the morning, we load up the dogs into a single pickup and drive the winding FS443 road to Elk City, where I plan on hiking into the upper reaches of Meadow Creek by myself, then traversing the country, finally relieving myself of my pack at the confluence.

On the western edge of the watershed, Kelley drops me off. I am almost alone—Mary, my border collie, has come to be my companion. Tall, green cedars and Douglas firs filter sun against a blue Idaho sky. The trailhead sign on the East Fork of the American River says "Anderson Butte - 6, Meadow Creek - 14." It is going to be a long day with a full pack. I am starting at 8:30 on a midsummer day. Kelley says good-bye as I shoulder my pack. Mary is having happy fits, running up and down the trail. As we hike, Mary engages in her favorite hobby: chasing pine squirrels.

The trail up to Anderson Butte is steep, but well-maintained. It is zoned for snowmobiles, trail bikes, and horses, as well as walkers, too good to be just a hiker's trail into the backcountry. Knowing that the Forest Service is always careful to maintain trails used by dirt-bikers and outfitters, I start looking for the predictable outfitter's camp. Most of these are elaborate affairs, permanent structures and corrals hacked out of the surrounding forest on public land. Cresting the top of the Meadow Creek Divide, it is there to my left, complete with woodburning stoves for cooking steak and lobster for rich tourists during the fall elk hunt, and platforms for wall tents. Though this is not designated wilderness, such structures could be considered dubiously legal. They are the result of a Forest Service-issued special-use permit for the area. Such permits are valuable, as the Forest Service issues only a small number for certain areas. Although they are given away free by the government and theoretically cannot be bought and sold by individuals, in reality there is a healthy commerce in the permits among the various outfitters, packaged with old, overpriced gear to legitimize the sale. Huge, industrial hunting camps such as this also abound in designated wilderness areas, places where, as stated in the Wilderness Act, "man is a visitor and does not remain."

I scurry up the hill to the Anderson Butte Lookout. It is an old-fashioned tower, built of steel and rough-hewn boards, guyed to the earth with thick cables. Afraid of heights, I carefully climb the steep stairs as far up as possible, stopping underneath the locked watchhouse on top of the tower. Looking to the west, I see an endless sea of clearcuts, some bad, some worse. But to the east, my goal lies beneath me—Meadow Creek Canyon. Untouched, pristine, intact, it is a rare sight in the Lower 48, where the chainsaw has been king for the past fifty years. I check my topo map one last time, locate my trail, note the vertical elevation loss to the creek— 4,000 feet!—and drop off the edge.

Lost. I am lost in the woods, confined in a small ravine, surrounded by downed western red cedars splintered like smashed bone, thrown about by spring winds.

I had wanted to hike alone for this trip. It was my choice to leave companionship and the security of partners behind. I had intended to confront the issues of solitude, loneliness, extinction. Now, if I slip on the fern-covered 45 degree slopes, misplace my footing in between this rotting, downed windthrow, I will become extinct myself. It is the first day of a five-day hike. Kelley has explicit instructions to wait twenty-four hours after my scheduled arrival before she calls the search-and-rescue squad. By then, I will have been lying on the ground for five days. The circumstances are not good: the closeness of the downed logs, the fact that I am carrying fifty pounds, and that I am off-trail. When I do fall, gravity carrying 275 pounds of combined mass against three square inches of tibia will most certainly cause a compound fracture. My white bone, a sight I have never seen, will extrude above the tongue of my hiking boot. In all probability, if this happens, I will die. It will be slow, painful, and hysterical, full of shock and gangrene.

The trail had been good to Anderson Butte. Off the backside was decidedly less well maintained, yet there were signs to Dent Point, a landmark on the climb down, and Meadow Creek. The trail was also clearly labeled on the topo map. I had not bothered to pick up a Nez Perce National Forest map. I had figured, incorrectly, that all available trails would be located on the topos. To a certain extent, one must count on the existence of trails and trail signs in heavily forested lower elevation terrain. Because of the heavy cover, it was impossible to even see landmarks, let alone triangulate off them to secure my position. This trail was weedy, yet there were signs at every one mile interval, clearly saying "TRAIL."

And then the signs stopped. The trail continued on into an abandoned outfitter's camp. Then there was no more trail. I sat next to a rusting stove damper, unfolded my topo map, and contemplated my next move.

In hindsight, I had placed my position to the south of where I was actually located. I knew that I had to go down, and charted a route with my compass that should have me intersect the trail, if the trail existed at all. And so down I went, through an open, old-growth stand of western red cedar. Descending, I saw a bounding whitetail buck, breaking to the south. I considered it a good sign. Deer do not like dense, spiderweb groves of second-growth trees. Since they cannot run, they feel vulnerable. I followed the path of the deer.

Across the headwaters of a creek I came, tromping through the mud. I followed the contour of the hill and down, slipping on ferns resting in the mud, skating on dry duff beneath tall cedars. After traversing the slope for half a mile, I came to the realization that I was not going to find the trail and that, judging from the forest type where I was, I still had 2,000 feet more to go down until I rested my pack on the canyon floor. Now I knew that I was lost.

Without choices, I head straight down the canyon wall, my feet slipping and ankles pleading, stretching the sides of my hiking boots. I finally stop my descent in a small feeder creek (Dent Creek, as hindsight would educate me), and commit myself to the path of the ravine. In the end, this has to run into Meadow Creek. Large logs block the streamcourse, obstructing my progress. I step slowly, carefully, down the steep banks, using the downed logs as bridges, wading in the streambed, pushing against the fleshy stems of the deadly poison water hemlock that choke every cleared space. Carefully I step, until finally I am reduced to crawling in those small pools, in the creek bed. I can see elusive light far ahead of me. Meadow Creek Canyon? Every step pushes the mirage one step further. There is no place to stop to camp. The gloom of an early evening settles in the ravine.

Mary is with me, though. Tired as well, she gamely scrambles up, in between, and down over the three feet in diameter windthrow. No fire has touched here for over two hundred years. There is no relief, yet she moves quickly through the holes, in the creek, out of the creek, burying her muzzle in the cool water, panting and painting her dog-smile across her jowls. She is my leader, my follower, my friend and good-luck charm. And then finally, at the end of hope and the evening hours, there is light, yellow rays on a canyon floor. I burst onto Meadow Creek, past a dilapidated log cabin, slipping on slimy river rocks covered with algae. I wade into the stream. Mary yowls on the left bank, then plunges into the water. She despises swimming, but hates even more the prospect of abandonment. I had intended to drop my pack on the far shore, then retrieve her, but she could not wait. Me yelling, her whining and barking, we arrive—tired, depressed, elated, a trail, a clearing under monster Doug fir and a sweet bed of cropped grass. I can see Indian Hill Creek just down the trail. I undress and sit in Meadow Creek, my muscles twitching and shivering from shock and low blood sugar. My breath comes in short gasps. After a handful of fruit, I feed Mary, hang the pack, and sleep—precious sleep under a bright belt of white stars.

I am resting today, down on Meadow Creek. It is a good place, with salmon berries and mountain bluebell, next to running water. A small, brown winter wren screams at me as I wash my dishes in a small pool. Like all wild animals, she is indifferent or hateful of my presence. I sleep the afternoon away. Mary does, too, in a small hollow she has dug in the ground. The day passes into night. My strength returns slowly. The opportunity to explore a new place calls dimly. I wake to cook a big dinner, followed by a long night's sleep, filled with deep, unrecoverable dreams.

I did not want to hike this morning when I awoke at 5:30. Mary greeted me underneath an overcast, cloudy sky. I packed anyway, ate breakfast, then set out on the trail. I started walking quickly, hurried for no other reason than the goal of reaching another destination.

Wildflowers slowed me down: mountain bluebell again, cinquefoil, heal-all, water parsnip, flax, cow parsnip, and showy daisy. Then I stopped. I took off my boots, stuffed my socks deep into the toe, and tied them to the back of my pack. I reshouldered my heavy load, and continued walking.

By the laws of Western Civilization, I, as a white man, am not able to make a religion of the respect of nature. I was raised Catholic. Society will accept if I worship Jesus, the Virgin Mary, Vishnu, Mohammed, Buddha, the angel Moroni, or the Reverend Sun Yung Moon—he has enough money. But declaring allegiance to the land—that is another matter. I throw myself open to all sorts of derogatory appellations: tree hugger, New Ager, or, at best, an anachronism.

I am thinking of the San Carlos Apache this morning, fighting for their holy Mt. Graham, the sky island in southern Arizona. The University of Arizona and the Vatican want to build multiple observatories on the top of Mt. Graham, the latest perversely called the Columbus Telescope. But the San Carlos Apache have declared this their sacred ground, to the consternation of University, Church, and Forest Service, which manages the forest on the mountain. The University of Arizona needs another high-profile observatory for its international reputation. The Vatican, besides atoning for sins against Galileo, has officially said that it is considering baptizing extraterrestials, if they can be found. The San Carlos Apache do not have much hope. But they do have the force of law, the 1987 Indian Religious Freedom Act, which gives them the right to hold such places as Mt. Graham as holy.

The tribe at least has the chance to prove sites are sacred. I, in contrast, am a spiritual naked orphan. Many places in central Idaho are sacred to me. I have spent nights on a spot I call the Edge of the World singing and praying my own prayers. But because I am white, I cannot claim this spot of burnt lodgepole forest and goshawk. If I am to argue for protection of the wilderness, my sacred robe must be the tweed jacket and the tie. I must act the professor of engineering, argue the economics of road construction, debate the demerit of gene-pool destruction, advocate things such as riffle armor stability indices of streams, or discuss geomorphic threshold. I cannot argue for the salvation of my soul, the perishing of my spirit, the loss of my existence if these places are destroyed.

And indeed, I cannot claim native beliefs. Though I have sat in the sweatlodge, waited as a guest at the Root Feast of the Nez Perce in Kamiah, and looked with respect at the medicine men I have met, I shall always be famished, unable to eat other's spiritual food. If I am to establish a spiritual tradition, I must find my own way. I have few elders to teach me. I can remember the time I met Bill Means, Lakota Sioux, of the American Indian Movement, at a talk at my university. I told him of the problems with my elders and the problems of rallying older people to save more wilderness. After the talk, I approached him, smiling in the WASP business ethic that I have been inculcated with since youth. I grabbed his hand, shook it. It was limp, flabby in my palm. He thanked me for my question, and turned away. He would not be my elder. To find medicine—well, I was on my own.

I have a start, though. It is not an original thought that Western man has broken the law of peace with the world. Here down on Meadow Creek is example enough. A wilderness bill offered by former Idaho Representative Larry LaRocco is an example of the feeble foolishness offered up as spiritual, Solomonic wisdom to the masses. The legislation, offered as a preservation bill, would have given the thickly covered, red cedar forest on the western side of the river to the timber industry, in the supposed interest of jobs, livelihoods, and contemporary lifestyles. The eastern side, sparsely covered dry slopes of ponderosa pine, would have gone into the present wilderness system. The area is already wilderness. It does not need human labeling to exist intact. If it is not protected, the devastation visible from Anderson Butte will move here, inexorably. The deep, rocky pools will fill up with silt. The functioning intactness will be lost, replaced by the sound of the biting chainsaw and the roar of the idiot motorcycle. In our society, cutting the child in half is called reasonable compromise.

I shall have to discover my own spirit power, my own medicine. I remember the words of an old counselor; he would be my elder: walk barefoot, the barefoot medicine. I walk.

I walk on sharp rocks, cleaved schist across talus slopes, avalanche chutes. The soles of my feet crack, my insteps ache from the load of my pack. The tops of my feet are scratched from thorny vines crossing the trail. Small drops of blood seep. Contact with ground purifies me. Thorns and sticks, now rocks, soft sand, then mud, step by step, I make my barefoot medicine, starting my renewal of contract with the land. It is not enough to ask for forgiveness, for blessing. I must atone.

After three miles, I see a gravel bar, a deep pool. I borrow my only Nez Perce song from the sweat lodge, praying that the old grandfathers are listening—this was their land first. Flecks of mica bounce, my feet thump on the sand, footprints in the mud. I drop my pack, strip my clothes, and run naked into the water, crying, aching, alive.

Oh Creator, if they destroy this place, if they build their roads, chop down these sacred trees, kill the bull trout in the water, drive the elk and bear to the high country, burn the fisher and pine marten out of their groves, leave my precious wildflowers in the ruts of their trucks and bulldozers, please, oh please do not forgive them.

Damn them. Damn them all to hell.

I went fishing today. Not being an elite fisherman, I own no specialized vest nor fancy glasses. I do not fly fish, nor view it as an art. It matters not to me that Jesus was a fisherman. Even when I was young, I was a lousy Catholic. I catch fish to eat, not to release, unless they are all head and tail and make no sense covered with Mrs. Dash and butter in a frying pan. I am the lowest of the low. Given the opportunity, a live cricket, cheeseball, or a piece of corn will work equally well. I am a bait fisherman.

Though I view catch-and-release fishing as a viable contemporary management strategy, I'm not a practitioner of the sport. I have always considered eating sacred. But sport is not sacred, especially when it involves dragging another living creature around in the water, hook buried in a fragile jaw, for the purpose of entertainment; just another manifestation of Western man's separation from nature. There are the rationalizations of enjoyment and fish population protection, and there is absolutely no question that catch-and-release fishing retains real populations of wild, easily caught fish. But if we are to change our definition of our juxtaposition with nature, this is the place to start.

I tried catching dinner out of my fishing hole on Meadow Creek. Fish after fish hit my lure—mostly steelhead and salmon smolts—as soon as my black and white Roostertail hit the water. All were under eight inches, not big enough to eat. I stopped, disassembled my rod, packed it away. I stripped, jumped in the water, and went swimming in my fishing hole. I swam across Meadow Creek to a pile of river-smoothed Belt rocks, hunks of schist from the basement of the world. I sat overlooking the eddy where I had been casting my lure and looked down.

There in formation were all my previous friends, bodies streamlined, undulating in the fast current created as the water rushed between my rock and the bank. Holding their position like a squadron of fighter planes, they would occasionally veer off to the surface to strike a fly. They paid no heed to my presence. Sometimes one would swim under a shelf created by my seat-rock to take a temporary break from the forces of inexorable current.

I started to sweat in the July sun. It wasn't long until biting flies had located my position, beautiful biting flies. Some had iridescent eyes with yellow lace wings, others, black and white striped wings with zebra abdomens. Once they had locked in on my warm scent, they had no choice. They had to land. They were not particularly fast. I would wait for them to align their small razor with a follicle on my skin. Then my hand would land on their back, twisting and breaking their neck and wings. I would gingerly remove their carcass off my sunburned hide, and drop it in the water at the top of the eddy.

When I go fishing, the most exciting moment is not the strike, the setting of the hook in the fish's mouth. Rather, it is when I reel in the fish, when I can see the glint of the bright silver underside as it turns its head and body in an attempt to throw the lure. I crave the chance to admire the sleek, hydrodynamic shape, the subtle curves of this creature as it is slowly reeled to the surface. And in my heart, this is the moment that I think catch-and-release fisher-folk also crave: the chance to be connected with something so exquisite and wild.

The fish below my rock would rise instantly to my dead fly bait. Because the fly would float on the surface right in front of me, I could get my glimpse of small, wild nature, of flashes of silver bellies as a fish would rise to hit my cast-off fly. It wasn't long until the formation had moved directly underneath me, fluid turbulence and sharp glance dictating which member of the squadron would receive the manna from heaven.

I did not eat fish that night. It was by choice. I could have caught two eight-inchers and fried them up with the canola oil buried in my pack. Instead, I exercised a gentleman's forbearance, having received from the fish what I had probably craved in the first place. I could brag about how large the one was that got away, because they all got away. Catch-a-glimpse and release says nothing about memory.

I am going on a hunt today, my weapon an Olympus OM-4 loaded with high-powered ammo—Kodachrome 64. I am hunting wildflowers in general, and one in particular: Indian pipe. I had been told of a sighting up on Sable Creek, south of the Meadow Creek workcenter and cabin. The source had been reliable: a married couple, friends of mine, who had spent four days hiking out of the cabin on the trails in surrounding countryside. I set foot on the trail determined.

Indian pipe has a long stem curved in a U at the top, terminated by a bell-shaped flower and ringed with delicate, white leaves. A saprophytic plant, it has no chlorophyll, leaving it unable to make its own food. It lives its life intertwined with a certain fungus that breaks down the dead organic matter that holds its root network. Some might find Indian pipe morbid, living off the dead. I think of it as a coconut shaving, a translucent time portal, carrying the beauty of living things past into a manifestation in the present of mother-of-pearl cups ringed downward with cocoa.

No pack on today. Mary is energetic, running quickly, scaring off all animate creatures. It is a good thing I am interested only in plants. I see fireweed, monk's hood, more cinquefoil, but no Indian pipe. Finally, high on a ridge above Sable Creek, there grows my consolation prize: clarkia, a small, four-petaled fuschia flower, with each petal shaped like a miniature oak leaf. It is perched right where my Petersen's guide had predicted—a disturbance site, a rough, partially soil-covered slope, with a due south aspect. I turn around, walk back to camp, and pack up to backtrack downriver where I had previously camped.

It is three miles down the trail from my camp when I finally see the white stems bounce out of the corner of my eye, a short distance from where I had removed my boots and had started my barefoot medicine. It is there by the trail, under a tall Doug fir in a clump of moss. I dutifully photograph it, document its place on my map. And then I sit in the trail and watch it. Me of the constant schedule, the full-time job and full-time activist avocation, not-a-weekend-free for two months. I wallow in the luxury of the unscheduled appointment. My eyes are fixed on the many white stems and the downturned, brown-rimmed pearl flower cups. My mind wanders, following the smoke drifting out of the bowls of the cluster, up and up, wrapping itself around the wings of a pair of golden eagles scraping the bottom of the clouds with their backs.

I finish the day the same way I had the previous: naked, on a rock in a small grotto by Meadow Creek, catch-a-glimpse and release fishing. A different squadron of rainbow, cutthroat, and bull trout are here, hovering off the separation point of my rock. The fishing is not so good, though. The sky is overcast, and there are fewer flies to kill with my hand. I see a river mussel, though, and an entire colony of crayfish dressed in hunter's orange, tucked up under the edge of the cliff. Most are safe in their select crevice. However, one is exposed on a flat rock. I approach him with my big toe. He casts off, feeling for an instant the freedom of the water before he dives, tail tucked between legs underneath a small rock across the pool from me.

I walk out of Meadow Creek today. The trail follows the river briefly, and in short order, turns upward, into the giant ponderosa pine forest, broken only by silent hollows and ravines of red cedar. More clarkia rests on a sunny slope at my rest stop, and I carefully glass the river with my small field binoculars to examine the cataracts in the final miles of Meadow Creek. I make a promise to return next June, on the backside of a falling hydrograph, with my kayak, to see Meadow Creek's last canyon from the bottom. I walk, kicking along the last few miles to Slim's Camp, through an open red cedar old-growth forest, trees with diameters of eight feet, scooting pebbles off the trail like a bored, small child. The sun is shining, the pack light. A jump in the Selway River and a Wilderness Burger at the Wilderness Inn in Lowell is only hours away. In future days, this place will be a salve for my soul.

And finally, at the end of the trail, an RV is parked in the road, with an all-terrain vehicle proudly displayed beside it. I wonder if America will let her remaining wildlands be destroyed because of indifference and compassion fatigue. I stand, an incompetent warrior, a rabbit in the grass, waiting and listening.

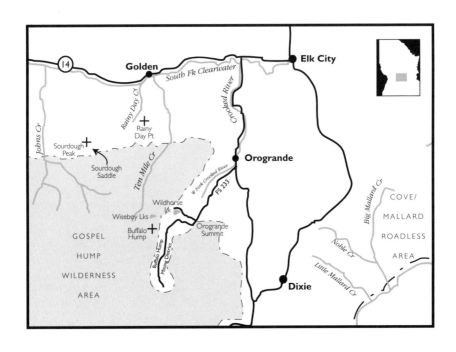

Buffalo Hump

THE ROAD UP HERE IS STEEP, Lord knows. We started at twelve hundred feet down by the Clearwater, and now we're at four thousand feet around Elk City, way to hell and gone. We've got a ways to go, too—three thousand more vertical feet to Orogrande Saddle, over the top to the Buffalo Hump mining district and the Gospel Hump Wilderness Area, our final destination. In an interstate world, seven hours seems like a long time to travel less than two hundred miles.

Kelley and I had stopped at the Nez Perce National Forest supervisor's office in Grangeville, hoping for information to help us plan our hike. The receptionist, friendly but unhelpful, dialed frantically around the building and other ranger districts in response to our requests for information. They seemed surprised to find out that people actually wanted to know about hiking. After five minutes, a deep, masculine voice was located at the Red River Ranger District. He was brief, declared our desired point of entry "good," and the trail, "rocky but locatable." I knew that there had been a lot of mining in the area, and asked him about how much mining had altered the landscape. He pronounced the mining disturbance "noticeable." I asked whether open pits were visible. He said "yes." I ended up with no idea of what to expect. It's supposed to be a wilderness area up there.

We take our first break, stop the truck, and stare at the now-empty cataracts of Golden Canyon on the South Fork Clearwater. It is late summer, and the river is a trickle, the waning run-off of groundwater in a drought year. Back in the truck, Kelley and the dogs are carsick by the Elk City halfway mark.

We turn up the dark, low canyon of Crooked River and stop at a point of interest: "Crooked River Historic Dredging." The trees, short black firs, only forty feet tall, lean ominously over the creek, blocking the dull light filtering through low clouds. Except for a few small spots, the Crooked River has been rototilled by both placer and dredge operations, the entire river bottom turned and sifted for gold. Piles of tailings sit, like a rock quarry, lined up for miles, with pathetic, small conifers growing up out of the mounds of creek gravel and stagnant ponds separated by gravel bars. It is indeed historic. It will be a geological age before the river is restored as a natural stream.

Driving along, I stare at the river and the tailings piles, thinking about the many books claiming to be history that talk in glowing terms about the mining industry, the gold rush days, the boom and bust, and the halcyon times of dance hall girls and saloons. Growing up in a mining area myself, I find it all impossible to believe. I cannot countenance the absence of women and their civilizing touch. I can imagine men feverishly drawn together only for the reason of personal profit, forgoing any sort of balance in their lives, to rip apart the earth in one of the few acts of man that will not pass from the planet on any human time scale. I can imagine men lined up for the few prostitutes living in the gold camps, the monotony of living in a desecrated world, and the inspired business of moving on to another pristine area to ruin. I think of the isolation of those early days, and try to place it in the realm of my own perspective. I have spent nights where the loneliness was thick, like cold fog on river bottom land. The frontier spirit eludes me. The legacy of mining in Idaho still haunts the state—one of its most beautiful lakes, Coeur d'Alene, is possibly the most polluted body of water in the United States, its bottom covered with lead and heavy metals from the upstream mines outside of Kellogg, washed down the South Fork of the Coeur d'Alene River by fast floods off denuded, clearcut hillsides.

But it is typical. Our history is usually glorified: doughty, hard-working miners, hardy frontiersmen and women undergoing great travail for the building of a great nation. It rarely speaks of the tragedy inflicted on the natural world, the price in human lives and suffering needed to maintain the myth of manifest destiny. Crooked River sits here, hidden from the eyes of this nation. It and other streams like it in Idaho, in the Clearwater Country—Orofino Creek, Red River, the East Fork of the American River—will never be healed in the history of mankind.

Kelley is carsick again. We stop for a brief moment in one of the few relatively untouched sections. I am sick in the walls of my heart.

We camp high on the saddle at Wildhorse Lake. I try to fish. Instead, I see a huge bull moose, big with a large rack, a full-on Bullwinkle, lumber out of the water. My dogs, misbehaving, take off after the moose. I blush crimson-red, embarrassed by their behavior, though there is no one there.

Kelley is cooking dinner when I return empty-handed. No dogs, no fish. I am a poor hunter-gatherer.

Consolation, though, is in the air. The sweet smoke of the Corral Creek fire has blown into the lake basin from McCall and Warren, sixty miles to the south. The breeze has that fall snap again. It is only the end of August, but summer is passing from the high country like a teenage love. The dogs finally come back. Dinner is good. The night will be cold, but Kelley and I will be warm in our hearts. We are just married.

It is a blue sky day today at the trailhead at Wildhorse Lake. Kelley's dog, Tam, is leashed, and Mary is packed. We set out on the trail together. The Gospel Hump Wilderness area, created in 1979, is small by Idaho standards—roughly only twenty by sixteen miles in area. Its saving grace is that it is contiguous to the Frank Church/River of No Return Wilderness, separated only by the Salmon River. Looking at the map, its creation has obviously been gerrymandered too. Sunk deep into its eastern flank is the Buffalo Hump Mining District, and excluded inappropriately because of its timber to the southeast is the Cove/Mallard area.

Looking up the mountainside, the land is rugged: high, granite dome and boulder rock-and-ice. I am subdued at the scale of the country upon cresting the first rise. We had planned to hike to the top of the Buffalo Hump itself today. We will be lucky to make a campsite at Crystal Lake, halfway up, by mid-afternoon.

We run along the ridge, through the whitebark pine and subalpine fir, along the spine of the buffalo, smoky haze below in the valleys from late summer fires, then down the mineshaft off the backside of the ridge past the Wiseboy Mine and out of the wilderness area. The old mine looks as if it has been abandoned for about fifty years. To my right are stacks of mine timbers. To the left and up the hill are the smashed support beams of the mine shaft building. Kelley and I argue if snow or dynamite has caused the collapse. Skewed to the left is an abandoned mine car. Underneath the rubble is a huge steam boiler used to drive the mining equipment. The line shaft drive wheel is sticking up, broken like a compound fracture. On the front of the steam boiler casting is written "Union Iron Works, Erie, Pennsylvania." If inanimate objects have souls, there rests a complex personality in that steam boiler. Drug there by pack train, teetering over the edge of scree slopes, lowered by ropes and sweat down the side of the mountain, it has already known its hell, been stoked and fired, burned from the inside out by hot lodgepole coals. It rests, rusting slowly at eight thousand feet in the Gospel Mountains. There is a slow peace as the mine slumps, collapses, and decays back into the mountain; a small tick on the flank of the Buffalo Hump.

It is a Rocky Mountain fire sky on the Buffalo Hump this evening, fingers of rose running into lavender behind our heads. Slow and methodical, Kelley and I are feeling stately tonight. We walk to the eastern ridge of our granite bowl, examining and crushing conifer needles—this one spruce, another fir, yet another hemlock, and finally whitebark pine—celebrating a silent mass of biodiversity on our hillside. A choir of waterfalls rings down the smooth bell of granite as we watch the strong green river of forest run down out of the couloir at the end of the valley. Designated wilderness is such a relief to my mind—no battles to fight for constancy of the landscape, allowing me the luxury of dismissal of ephemeral nature close to my conscience—I can allow myself the fantasy of this beautiful place lasting forever. Lighthearted, I can feel wind behind my collar, mortal, smoke from the Corral Creek fire lightly in my nose. Fall is approaching.

Kelly Creek vista. *Author photo.*

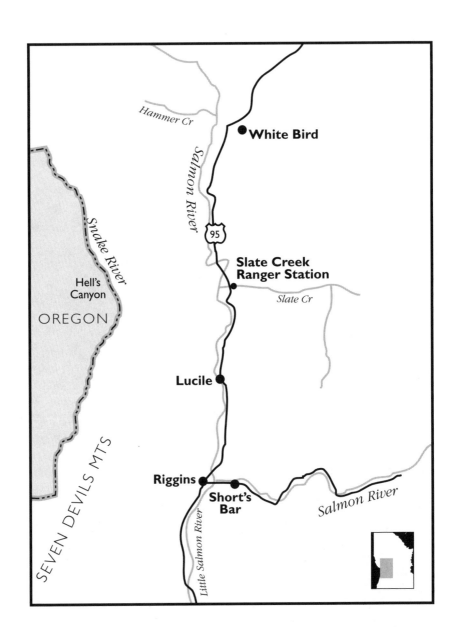

Salmon River

I AM AT THE SHORT'S BAR PUT-IN for the Riggins-to-Lucile run on the Lower Salmon today. It is the beginning of fall. Smoke from the Corral Creek and Chicken Complex fires outside of McCall this summer still hangs heavily in the air. The beach here—long, white, and sandy—stretches down to exposed cobbles of a low-water river along the interface of water and ground. There is a ritual occurring this weekend, an annual rite. The college fraternities and sororities of Washington State University and the University of Idaho have come to trash the river, drink themselves into insensibility, and fuck on the beach.

They are all off the beach now—on the river, I am sure, rafting. They are probably committing the usual sins: drinking on the river, not wearing their lifejackets, yelling and screaming as the slow, autumn flows carry them down the river toward the take-out. LuVerne Grussing, the BLM chief for this stretch, has shown me pictures—eighteen people in an eight-person raft, some hanging onto the outside, not wearing lifejackets. It is a living miracle that a mess of them have not drowned.

The last time I came down here this time of year, the students had knocked over the outhouse and set the waste pit on fire. Having destroyed their privy, they proceeded to shit all over the parking lot. White rosettes of toilet paper were scattered on the grass. Some of the cellulose flowers graced the tops of the piles of defecation, like whipped cream on a fudge donut. About five minutes later, I was getting ready to put my kayak in the water and run the stretch when the Idaho County sheriff pulled up in his police cruiser. We talked, walked around the latrine. He photographed the various piles of defecation. Three bleary-eyed stragglers stumbled to hide half-open beer cans beneath their tent flies. I asked the deputy what he was going to do. He replied, "file a report." He shrugged his shoulders helplessly.

I went home angry and found out the names of the participating fraternities. It so happened that this bunch was associated with the University of Idaho. I called and wrote Bruce Pittman, Dean of Students, about the mess, the disgust, and worst of all, the lessons learned by the students. That was two years ago. Nothing has happened.

I cruise through the impromptu parking lot created by the mob here, set between these tall, dun hills wrapped in smoke. These kids are not poor. There are two new Ford Ranger pickups, an expensive version of a Honda Prelude with a Lynnwood, Washington, license frame. It must be WSU students this weekend. And many other cars—there must be at least forty packed on this small square of sand. In the back of one of the sports cars is a copy of *Glamour* magazine, its cover blaring "Don't have sex until you read this!" I doubt they waited. So much stuff is strewn about here: new tents never before used, barbecue grills, expensive sleeping bags. In the back of one car is a whole makeup kit. Out of one pocket pokes a bottle of "Salon Selectives." Did this woman think that she was going to wash her hair in the river? Did she envision pulling back her locks, stretching her bosom to the sunshine, like some bad version of a Madison Avenue shampoo commercial? I wonder if for a moment she thought of the fish she would kill.

Today, I am taking the local Hispanic college kids rafting. It is a yearly ritual for me also—a small attempt at integrating my wild lands, gaining new allies for my sacred places. They are sweeter and poorer, yet their goals and aspirations are no different than the richer fraternity and sorority students sprawled out on the beaches this weekend. We pass their cars, and the Hispanic students gawk. I think of what my friend Al Espinosa told me: "They want pork in their burrito, too." They have had good families, stay-at-home mothers, yet it has not altered their fundamental direction. I had once relished working for the multicultural agenda, until I realized that the agenda was for everyone outside the consumer society to join that very monster. These Hispanic kids are innocent today. They have no money. But they long for sin.

The raft trip is relatively uneventful. An early flip stuns all of them into wearing their lifejackets. The lecture I gave at the beginning of the day about keeping their feet up while swimming rapids seems to hold. I remind them to look at the scenery just a little bit. They all politely thank me at the take-out, and go on their way, looking for a beach and a party for entertainment into the wee hours.

I am left on the take-out sandbar at Lucile, six miles north of Riggins, thinking thoughts of sustainable economics, with a cold beer, pensive. Riggins seems, in many ways, a model for conversion of a small town with a natural resource economy to that of a tourist economy. Previously, Riggins had been supported by a small mill, ranching along the Salmon river breaks, and small mining operations on the mainstem and a few small tributaries. But the mill burned down and the gold played out. Ranching hangs on in a landscape that makes it tough to support a cow, especially with fluctuating beef prices. An endless stream of rubber rafts, the majority guided by transient labor, has replaced the old rip-and-run industries. But over 50 percent of the students in the Riggins area still receive subsidized school lunch. Things have not changed, nor improved.

The people that live here are like many in small tourist towns, complacent and hateful, alternately despising and praying for the return of their rich patrons from the urban areas. And the tourists are further marginalizing the edge of my wild space, treating it like a playground or summer home construction site when convenient, and a dumping ground when not. From here, there appears to be little hope in the West for a future where community size is defined on a human scale as opposed to a corporate, suburban scale, unless the local population is conscripted into environmental destruction. The challenge of having a sustainable community without growth has not been met in Riggins.

As I sit on the bank today, I am watching my past be pulled into a black hole. Small communities, regional accents, and local food are all vanishing. I think of the tight squeeze of the Salmon River Canyon, US 95 snaking its way along the banks. Then I think of the day that they will pave over Riggins when it finally blocks a straighter shot for US 95, the major north-south route in Idaho. How important will this small town be, compared to the five minutes saved by an as-yet unproposed bypass?

A raft of college kids drifts by me. They are all drunk. Some are passed out, sprawled on the hot, gray rubber tubes. One wears only a single tennis shoe. A lone sailor stands watch, taking slow strokes down the flatwater to the Lucile takeout.

It was cloudy on top, fall-cloudy, with big white streaks spider-webbing across a dull late-fall sky as we dropped down the Kendrick grade. The light improved in the Clearwater valley, but as we passed Lapwai, the dull sunlight returned, first slowly, then in a rush as we climbed up the Winchester grade to the Camas Prairie. I stuck my hand out a barely cracked window, autumn licking my fingertips, as my pickup rolled up and down the slow grades toward Grangeville. "The tamaracks are turning today," I told Kelley. "It's pretty cold." Snow on the Seven Devils—it looks like it is going to stay. No more bright light until March—winter is a close neighbor now. It sure seems like a mighty cold day to go boating, even with my dry gear.

There are many people here today at the Hammer Creek launch site on the Lower Salmon River for a late October day, probably protesting the Nez Perce leveling a use fee on fishermen on the Clearwater. After the tribe closed the river in the middle of September to non-Indians without a special-use permit, the local citizenry is up in arms about being charged an extra ten dollars to fish the Clearwater. Never mind that it costs more than ten dollars just to run one of those fancy jet-boats for an hour, or that ten dollars in gas will probably only get you to Kooskia and back in a brand-new Ford F-150 from Lewiston. Bureau of Indian Affairs police are ticketing offenders, but no violence has been reported yet.

So they have come to my place, the Lower Salmon, for escape from the usurious tax, with their dogs, boats, fishing tackle, and shotguns. There are no drift boats here today, only noisy, screaming jet boats. The drift boats, a graceful way to run easy whitewater, require muscle power in order to safely navigate rapids. Jet boats require gas. Skill too—considering the $20,000+ tag associated with such toys, you don't want to wreck a jet boat on a low water river. But they are noisy, and, equipped with a depth- and fish-finder, they turn the steelheading experience into child's play. The boats can find the deep pools, motor into them, and check for fish. No false alarms, no discovering where the fish frequent, no mystery or cover. People just don't have time. And the shotguns? "Cast and Blast" is the official billing. The chukar partridge season is also open. Motor the jet boat to a beach, blast the birds with a shotgun, and have the dogs fetch them. Easy it is not. Even with such phenomenal physical advantage, chukars are some of the hardest birds to hunt, and the rugged basalt cliffs offer some protection to the hunted.

I have never eaten a chukar partridge, but I have eaten the breasts of mourning doves—slightly smaller, but embodied with the same principle. Shoot the bird, skin the bird, remove the breasts, and throw away the carcass. Two fifty-cent piece-chunks of tasty meat. But worth it for the sacrifice of a life? I understand the poor man shooting a deer or an elk to feed his family. But chukars?

I watched hunters shoot chukars two years ago outside my camping spot up river, on one of my rafting expeditions with my Hispanic students. We had been drinking and laughing late into the night. They had camped on the same gravel bar with their dogs, and had also been drinking. Morning came. I had hiked up the bank to view the river when I heard the dogs bark, the birds flush, and five shotguns go off in rapid succession as the hunters shot at the flock. The chukars exploded into the air. Then the shots hit them. There was a transition, from directed motion and a 45 degree flight path, spreading out toward the sagebrush and basalt, followed by about half of the ten birds hanging in the air, then tumbling and spinning in space. I watched. I could see one wing outstretched, another tucked up against the body. I saw no blood. Then, just as in a shooting gallery, the birds dropped over the horizon of the bank. I did not see the hunters, nor the retrieve, only heard the whoops of success as the dogs busied themselves rounding up the fallen.

My heart as a scientist told me to ignore the moment. Chukars are an exotic. They were never native to the Salmon River Canyon. Ostensibly, they have no place in the picture of biodiversity of the lower river. But the moment disturbed me. When it comes to wild places and wildlife, what is the human right to use?

I do not consider human life first, always. With the needs of every life, it is true that some must live and some must die. But if human life is always first, in the end, when we have consumed all of the fire around us, we will also be last. And I believe that when the last tree falls, the last squirrel is caught, and the last cricket jumps, then we shall be next. But what if this thesis is false? Biodiversity may be unimportant, a discovery only of scientific peculiarity. There is a faint chance that humans might be able to survive without all other beings in the world.

I slip my boat into the water. The river bends through gold hills on its way to Green Canyon and Pine Bar, where Kelley waits for me with the dogs. The day's light stays flat. I paddle slowly, staring at the cliffs. The color is late fall, uniform and brown. As I concentrate, the browns change, hundreds of colors, all of the shades of the Crayola 64 color box from my youth. Green Canyon approaches, only slightly green, dry, adding hundreds more variations of yellows and blacks. The light in the sky changes. I see a golden eagle above, a grasshopper on the lunch beach. Quail and chukars flee up the cliffs. Steelhead and chinook salmon drift below. Maybe a sockeye? Bass, maybe sturgeon, whitefish, suckers, river mollusks also that I cannot see. I see cliffs, waves in the small rapids. My bright red boat is spinning, eddy after eddy as I move downstream. Is that a Cooper's hawk, now a redtail, another golden eagle? I feel the vibrations of the Salmon River elk herd running the Salmon/Snake river divide over my head, trudging through old-growth ponderosa pine, up into lodgepole, near great horned owls, turkeys, and ring-necked pheasants. A spider sits on the sand, a water-strider, mule deer, whitetail deer up the cliff; on the rocks above, a bighorn sheep. A diamondback rattlesnake tucks in between rocks, waiting for warm weather. A small frog, a newt, lizard, or salamander share the edge of water and land. Sagebrush, ponderosa pine, small bushes burn with a dull green fire.

Circling round and round, I am dancing with all of the beautiful life-flames in my world. Gray rock flame, juvenile golden eagle tall brown and yellow flame, a quick streak of maroon redtail flame, patient black spider flame, short sienna cricket flame, silver chinook flame, swirling about my boat, a tornado of spirit, lifting my boat out of the water, connecting me with the white streaks of cloud above. I can see the eye of a rabbit, my kittens jumping after moths in the moonlight, the look of a cutthroat trout flashing the surface of the water, garter snake moving quickly, sinuously off into the grass, fish rising toward mosquito flame in the early morning of a spring day. They look at me with their eyes, all different shapes, butterfly and spruce grouse, mountain lion and pine beetle. "We love our life, too," they say. As they surround me, their flames join mine, all of us, burning up, aspirated by the wind of time. How can I separate my life? Surrounded, how can I claim all of the fire?

I plant my paddle firmly in the downstream current, dipping quietly past the edge of the canyon. The walls open up. I can see green forest high above my head, rimming the edge of the hills, borne on the back of my old friend, Salmon River. I move from swiftwater to slack water beside the river gravels at Pine Bar and the take-out.

The author kayaking in Clearwater Country.

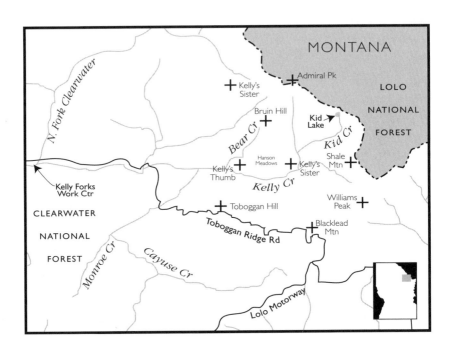

MONTANA

LOLO

NATIONAL

FOREST

Admiral Pk

Kelly's
Sister

Bruin Hill

Kid
Lake

Kid Cr

Bear Cr

Hanson
Meadows

Kelly's
Thumb

Kelly's
Sister

Shale
Mtn

Kelly Cr

Williams
Peak

Kelly Forks
Work Ctr

N. Fork Clearwater

CLEARWATER

NATIONAL

FOREST

Toboggan Hill

Toboggan Ridge Rd

Blacklead
Mtn

Monroe Cr

Cayuse Cr

Lolo Motorway

Kelly Creek

A YEAR HAS PASSED since I started walking, and here I am at the end of my hikes, camped in this wide and long valley, a flat mile by a half mile wide: Hanson Meadows along Kelly Creek. My fish biologist friend Al had told me about it. He talked about the fish, the big cutthroats in deep pools, resting darkly in the cool black water—the present. He also talked about grizzly bears swatting huge chinooks out of the shallow gravels, before Western man came with Sharps rifles and killed all the bears—the past. Al looked wistful, lost, talking about a time before the Lewiston Dam was built, which took out most of the big kings in the Clearwater system, followed by Dworshak Dam, that concrete tombstone hundreds of feet tall across the North Fork of the Clearwater that annihilated the remaining anadromous fish, the steelhead. I saw those pools earlier today, walking up the trail along Kelly Creek, one of the primary tributaries to the North Fork of the Clearwater. It looked more like a river than a creek to me there, with well-defined rapids in a tight canyon, up from its confluence with Cayuse Creek, five miles up the trail. Such a beautiful place, laced with silent tragedy.

I am camping tonight with Craig, an M.S. student in environmental science, working as a summer intern for my small environmental organization, the Clearwater Biodiversity Project. We have hiked to Hanson Meadows, out of the lower canyon, stopping for a short time at a different Kelly Creek. This one is wide and rambling, cutting through glacial moraine, with braided meanders wandering through ceanothus and meadow grasses. After setting up camp, I see three elk. A big bull guarding a cow and teenage calf hangs off the edge of a clearing and watches me bathe in the river after our hike.

There is motion everywhere in Hanson Meadows—ground squirrels tending their vast city among the cottonwoods and lodgepole, deer on the bald overlooking the valley, and Mary on the move, wolf-blood circulating in her veins tonight. Shale Mountain, on the way to Montana and the Fish

Creek Valley, guards the passes above where we camp. I can feel the distance behind these peaks, on further, to Missoula, the Big Blackfoot River, the Rocky Mountain Front, and the plains.

Craig comes from Minnesota by way of Albany, New York. He is a thoughtful young man and a future Peace Corps volunteer, having already signed up to work in Russia cleaning up toxic waste. I have been elected to instill in him his first lessons in governmental intransigence, and maybe, a sense of place. Earlier this summer, I decided that the best method for doing this would be two-fold. The first branch would involve reviewing timber sale contracts, examining places already destroyed. The second branch would consist of hiking through some of the places that we wish to save—White Sand Creek, Weitas Creek, and Kelly Creek. We are out for eight days.

Craig certainly has a mind of his own. He tells me that there is no one place that he has been that he could not leave. As I evaluate his words, I think he is telling the truth. He has lived a similar life to my own—professional student mendicant, going where opportunity and a degree from a good school will take him. But he is diligent—painfully so, an engineer like myself, and upon being assigned a particular task, he pursues it with methodical vigor and technical efficiency. I tell Craig that Upper Kelly Creek, where we sit, has over a hundred mining claims, and the day may come when the miners enter this valley, turning over the gravels in the shallow riverbed, looking for the low grade deposit of gold that lies under these gray and red rocks. Craig is silent. He looks away, down at his feet. On his face rests an expression of resignation. He is twenty-three. He had never seen an old-growth forest until I walked him through the ancient cedar grove behind my house on Moscow Mountain earlier this summer.

This Kelly Creek trip with Craig is my first foray walking in the backcountry this summer. It was only last weekend that I was still enjoying the main part of the kayaking season on the South Fork of the Salmon, flowing into the main Salmon, full from snowmelt from the high mountains of central Idaho.

Paddling out after an eventful run in the last canyon of the South Fork, we made the decision to camp with one of our party's relatives at a small guest ranch. Mike and Lynn, his in-laws, run the place. Mike also represents jetboaters' interests in discussions with the Forest Service, the agency managing the river. He was tipsy that night, arguing with me that the Forest Service was going to ban jetboaters from the river. I told him that he was deluded, that jetboating was a traditional use that extended way back into the past, before the Wilderness Act or the Wild and Scenic Rivers Act. He did not seem to pay attention, instead focusing his comments on Wilderness Watch, a group that monitors management plans in designated wilderness areas throughout the country, with the intent of keeping the areas as wild as possible. When I asked him if he supported the Blue Ribbon Coalition, a "wise use" group that promotes motorized vehicle use on all our national lands, he said that he did. When I told him that their vision for the Frank Church/ River of No Return Wilderness was a grid of roads on every square mile, he yelled that he supported "access." Those Wilderness Watch people wanted to shut him out, he said. I looked down at my plate, filled with baked pork chops from their kitchen.

Mike went on to talk about how difficult the finances of his little place always were, how hard a time he had turning a profit, and how most years weren't good years, only break-even ones, even with a price of $165 per night. All the hay for the horses had to be boated ten miles upriver by jetboat, as well as the passengers, and even before that, anything coming upriver to them had to be hauled up the twenty-some odd miles to Vinegar Creek from Riggins. And even Riggins was in the middle of nowhere. The owner of the ranch, a rich southern California businessman, knew that the operation was a money-loser when he purchased it. In fact, that's why he had bought it—as a tax write-off.

But then the government had changed the tax laws, and suddenly the place had to make money. He had ten staff total, and a maximum of fifteen visitors. The season was only so long, and he needed to run raft trips down the river for his customers. These people were paying a lot of money, and there was other competition. It was a selling point, the whole experience: rafting, horseback riding, volleyball, and fresh milk from their cow, milked by a milking machine. He looked away, quieted down, and said he didn't think much of more roads or timber harvest. It was hard to make a living, that was the main point—he was competing with people's choices for Caribbean cruises, or Disney World. His was a marginal business, and any change in plan might doom the ranch to bankruptcy. He wanted some certainty, some continuity in operation.

Sitting here tonight, looking at Toboggan Ridge and thinking of the road running just beyond my sight, I ponder the fate of Kelly Creek. Recreational development is here in Kelly Creek as well. As Craig and I walked up the trail to Hanson Meadows, we crossed Bear Creek. Sitting up on the rise above the confluence loomed a huge outfitter camp, complete with wall tents, a horse corral, and propane stoves. A small motorcycle straddled the path into Upper Kelly Creek. An older woman dragged a lodgepole pine log down the draw as we passed. She did not even say hello.

Tonight, I repeat over and over to myself that I am in one of the most beautiful places in the world. I wonder if I am just spoiled, feeling my heart sink as I contemplate the fate, past and present, of this landscape. The salmon, steelhead, and grizzly bears are gone—that is a past fate. And as more people come out to this place, I know that it soon will be hauled up in front of some committee of concerned citizens, federal bureaucrats, and local politicians, and the gavel will come down—Disneyland, Logger World, or Miner's Heaven—future fate. I sit underneath the bright stars and pray for respite, for one exception of gentle dignity in the world.

Lodgepole. It's all lodgepole pine, beargrass, and huckleberries, this Kelly Creek country. Steep on the edges, broad, graveled creek bottoms, clean. Craig and I walk up toward the Toboggan Ridge road, the mean man-made divider between Kelly and Cayuse Creek. Craig skips up the steep trail. I plod. He was a former varsity track athlete for Notre Dame. I have always been a slow professor. "Turnover. It's all turnover," he tells me. "You either have the genetic ability to put one foot after the other quickly or you don't."

"Is that supposed to be consolation?" I say, sweating, heaving, as we climb out of Hanson Meadows. Toboggan Ridge is two thousand feet above our heads. At the road, we see trash again, an Albertson's grocery plastic wrapper stuck in a fire pit in a small hunter's camp. As we eat lunch, Mary scavenges a piece of fried chicken from under a rock.

After lunch, we walk up the road another two miles, toward Toboggan Hill. Craig is anticipating a commanding view of both watersheds— Kelly Creek and Cayuse Creek—at once. I am looking at the density of trees in this lodgepole forest. I am not so sure. We wind our way to the top of the knob, basking in the view of Blacklead Mountain to the southeast, and the sweep of Toboggan Creek and Cayuse Creek to the west.

At the top, no view arrives. The knob is closed in with lodgepole. Another hunter's camp, and the roadside trash leave Craig scuffing the dirt with his tennis shoe, making short, sad remarks. As we start down and the biting flies close in, I look off to my side. "Wolf scat!" I exclaim, dropping to my knees and poking the desiccated stool with a small stick, looking for bone chips. I find them. "Maybe that's why we hiked up here, Chuck," Craig says.

Lying in the tent that night, I am telling Craig my banana story. It is a good story, I think, and it gives me an opportunity to be self-indulgent and preachy. Craig listens patiently. The gist of the story goes like this:

I visited Costa Rica a few years ago. I was very excited to go. Costa Rica is billed as the ecological paradise of Central America. The per-capita income there is the highest of any Central American country. The government is a democracy, and there is no standing army. Costa Rica has established the largest park system in Central America, and is often likened to Switzerland. And so on.

The truth that I saw, though, is that Costa Rica has cut down almost 80 percent of its tropical forests, and is rapidly encroaching on the remaining forest and the indigenous people who live in the jungle. One of the main reasons for deforestation in Costa Rica is for establishment of banana plantations, solely for the export crop that they produce. Bananas are a particularly destructive crop. They take nitrogen out of the soil and require a great deal of pesticides to preserve the flawless yellow color upon ripening that consumers in the United States will buy. The bananeros, or banana workers, must place a blue, pesticide-laced bag over each bunch as it grows, to keep the bananas beautiful. A different pesticide is sprayed on the leaves to protect the trees from insect damage. Banana workers in Costa Rica have the highest rate of cancer in the country. The blue pesticide-soaked bags often blow off the trees, then into creeks. From there, they are washed down into the Caribbean Sea. I saw some of the blue bags when I snorkeled the reef off Cahuita, a small seaside town. After the earthquake in 1992, the U.S. Army Corps of Engineers was sent to Costa Rica to help repair roads and bridges. The government instead directed the Corps to build roads into the rainforest for logging and the establishment of more banana plantations.

The litany of sins goes on and on.

"Bananas are the evil fruit, Craig," I tell him. "And to top it all off, I don't even like bananas."

"But I do," Craig replied. "They're a good source of potassium."

I sanctimoniously preach for a little while longer, saying that if you can't give up bananas, what can you give up?

And then I stop, and think to myself, maybe it's not the bananas. Maybe it's a matter of scale. Maybe it wouldn't be so bad if there were only a handful of banana plantations. Maybe if we didn't have to have bananas on our cereal every morning. Maybe if we had bananas once a year, maybe at Christmas. Maybe. I fall asleep.

Craig and I walk up into the headwaters of Kelly Creek today, up the shallow valley of the South Fork, then back over the low divide, across the Middle Fork on a new steel truss bridge, through the lodgepole forest. Huge cedar relics, burnt snags, guard the hills. Scattered on the mountainside, they stand immobile in the breeze, left from the old-growth forest that guarded this canyon before the great fires of 1910 and 1919. The lodgepole up here used to be worth nothing—the mills wouldn't take anything other than old-growth fir, yellow pine, and cedar. To top it off, Kelly Creek is so far away from any mill, the transportation prices to carry logs are just too great. But now there's a mill in Montana that can take lodgepole down to a four-and-a-half inch top and make a 2x4. Nothing is wasted. The remains are chipped for pulpwood. And the timber supply in these parts has gotten tight this year, too. Prices are up. Where once it made no sense economically to access a lodgepole forest, now it does, if the government pays for the roads, and paper pulp prices are on the rise. It's all a matter of scale, this logging. Is there any way we can exercise self-control? Or is that the right question after all?

The lodgepole forest is friendly up here, and flat. I am relieved, or at least my legs are. Craig strides ahead. We pitch our tents in a small, back country hunters' camp. The hunters who use this place are top-shelf. There is no trash, and all their meat-hanging poles are stacked neatly against a solitary spruce. "The harder the road, the nobler the traveler," I think to myself.

As we stop and set up our tent, I glance up the hillside to the man-made salt lick to the north. Bald and dirty, the brown clay has been churned into a small roadcut by the animals searching for minerals. "Nothing is perfect," I sigh, as a moose, a young chocolate bull, wanders into view. He is oblivious to us as he licks the salt on the rocks. He does not ponder the source of the salt, nor the process—the long, slow trip that the salt took on the back of a mule the sixteen miles up this trail. He will not worry about the effort put into the salt, even come hunting season, when the hunter's bullet creases his brow and drops him dead, bloodied in the clearing. There is comfort in ignorance, I think to myself. But it does not last.

I did not think it would rain, as I poked my head out of the tent and glanced up at the sky. Cirrus clouds, mares' tails, swirled in the early dawn, followed by sheep clouds, schools of mackerel, altocumulus scudding across the horizon. There was plenty of blue, too, enough to make a skirt, as my grandma would say. Filled with a rested sense of false optimism, I turned to Craig and confirmed my poor judgment.

Craig and I are hiking to the divide today, the Bitterroot Divide, the ridge between the upper Columbia country and the Clearwater, the Snake and the Clark's Fork. I have stood on other divides before—the Great Divide in Colorado, Wyoming, and Montana, high and craggy, and the Great Lakes and Mississippi Divide in Wisconsin, low and indiscernible. But those places were always roadside, me reading the pithy interpretive signs as I shuffled off to the poured concrete restroom. I have never stood on such divides in wilderness.

Craig and I trip up the trail, him joking about his recent trip to the Cabinet Mountains outside of Libby, Montana. His friends had assured him that Montana was much more pristine than Idaho, and upon crossing the border into the promised land, the problems and contradictions of the West so evident in Idaho would vanish into the ether, magically resolving themselves with the tantalizing homily delivered by a proper noun.

Craig, in his quiet way, tells me how he pointed out clearcuts and roads on the walk into the Cabinets. His friends had not elected to observe these blemishes on previous trips. He said that they were none too pleased with his innate sense of discovery, either. After a while, they asked him to shut up. I assume that he was ruining their fantasy.

Smiling at Craig, I tell him about a favorite singer of mine, Tish Hinojosa, from San Antonio. She sings a song, a catchy number called "In the Real West." The song talks about standard Western themes: prairie moons, tall boot shuffles, clean white shirts, and long cold beers. Tish goes on to talk about "where the spurs that jingle are the working kind." And so on.

God, I love that song, even if I think Tish is a bit deluded about that whole Marlboro man thing. To Tish's credit, later in the song, she does say that she is "a city girl, but I must confess," which makes me think she doesn't have much real experience with life out on the frontier. So I forgive her for her world view, taking this as a confession of ignorance, like the arbitrary, self-appointed god that I am. But I guess that I wish someone would sing about the real West that I know, the world dictated by marginal economies and a culture with a nature-loving facade, backed by a nature-destroying system of earning a living, which ends up justifying any action needed to survive in a land without forty inches of rain a year.

Kill prairie dogs to protect your horses from broken legs? Sure! How about shoot every wolf in the Northern Rockies to prevent predation of a small number of cattle? No problem there either. How about turning over an entire river bed to hunt for gold? Or maybe grinding up a mountain and pouring cyanide on top for a pickup-truck full of gold for costume jewelry? Or running too many cattle over marginal range suited only for pronghorn? Or chopping all the old-growth timber out of an entire river system? Hey, it's the Real West.

The climb up is hard for me. My legs ache from our previous adventures, but I am determined. As we walk up the headwaters of Kidd Creek, Shale Mountain rises out of the foothills behind us. Elk graze on a high meadow above the trees. As the clouds close in, gray and cold, Craig steps up the pace, turning around, swinging his arms and smiling, his scrubby face strangely beatific in the mixed light. "This is the most beautiful place I have ever seen," he says.

We crest the divide and hike up to a small knob for lunch. A heavy wind of an early fall closes the clouds around the top of the high ridges. Summer is going to be short this year, I think. This is only late July. Craig leans against a small marker post on top of a rock. On the cap, an inscription reads "Mont/Id." Craig eats his sandwich in Montana. I eat mine in Idaho. Admiral Peak guards the marches to the north. The Shale Mountain massif fills the view to the south. Looking down in any direction, the lodgepole forest covers both slopes, east and west. Looking down Cedar Log Creek into Montana, or Kidd Creek in Idaho to the west, the forest has no borders—at least not here.

Tish, I want you to know that I dream of Montana, too. I dream of Saturday night music running up against a wall of big silence and sage on the edge of town, of cold stars and two lane roads. I want to dream of friendly people, coupled with an economy based on continuity of the landscape, and space for all living things in the world. I dream of my big forest, my yellow pines and Douglas firs, and lodgepole, too, lasting forever.

Where is this Promised Land, this place of unceasing nobility? I ask myself. As the clouds drop and rain starts falling, I cannot see it from here today. Craig and I run down the trail, back toward the west and camp, alongside clean water tumbling off granite, flowing to the Pacific.

I dreamt of lost friends last night, sleeping with the noise of the river in my ear. I thought I heard the voice of my old friend, Helga, talking and laughing in the creek. My scientific background tells me that the creek makes white noise, a Gaussian signal, containing all frequencies. I can hear the ones I want and make up any words I choose, using selective memory. I am not sure.

I am sitting in Kelly Creek this afternoon. The sun is shining, and a cool, late summer breeze climbs up the canyon this afternoon. The rock I am perched on is slick with algae and thin water, and the current waves my feet like grass in the breeze. Coneflowers, goldenrod, and asters overflow the meadow around the creek, crowding the undercut banks on the water's edge. A four-point buck jumps through the streambed, up into the surrounding forest and history.

I have this theory, that I justify with pseudoscientific fervor, that there are places, refuges that capture sound, hold and focus it. Voices run to these places—mostly rivers, mountain valleys sometimes—where they are recorded on the fluid tape of a summer wind. If I am careful, and listen with a fine ear, I can hear voices of loved ones far away or long past. Today, if I am quiet, I can hear Helga's voice in the river.

Oh, grandfathers, is that what heaven is? A wild place where we can sit in the sun with all our loved ones, tell stories, and know that they will never leave? How close to heaven am I now?

Craig and I pass out of Kelly Creek today, quickly. It is raining, and the weather has turned back from summer to fall. Gray has settled again on the hills. It is Saturday, and we are passing the weekend traffic in to fly fish, all with neat, expensive canvas vests with dozens of little pockets, long, black rods, and ballcaps or porkpie hats. We are sweating in our raingear, walking quickly and soaking our shoes with the brush of vegetation, with dirt running in streaks off our brows and forearms.

It has not been such a good year for the forest, 1994 to 1995, since I started hiking last summer. And it has been tough for me, too, a hard winter and depression, and an uncertain future for my places that I love. But after eight days hiking, I am happy to be moving downriver in wild, beautiful country, following water, like when I was young, my body and mind clean, so clean, oh God, help me. Help me, please.

Erik Ryberg in burned snags. *Author photo.*

Part II

People

WHOEVER SAID THAT PEOPLE have little effect on the fate of the planet has never visited the Clearwater. Humans have made huge clearcuts on the plateaus surrounding the river, turned prairies into wheat fields, expanded those same wheat fields into the old forests, and built colossal spiderwebs of logging roads on the rolling hills. And humans have built dams in and below the Clearwater country: Dworshak next to Orofino, destroying the canyon of the North Fork of the Clearwater and its amazing runs of salmon and steelhead; and the four Lower Snake dams, currently annihilating the remaining runs of chinook, sockeye, and steelhead in the rest of Idaho's wild country.

But humans also left undeveloped parts of the Clearwater Country. And the element of this landscape that is so striking is the result of those human decisions—the juxtaposition of these protected and intact, unprotected places adjacent to the clearcuts, reservoirs, and roads. The contrast marks the consequences of our decisions and lifestyles.

What follows are essays and interviews with the people involved with this place, voices that normally have no audience with the population at large. If past events are any indicator, the majority of people working on issues in this part of the world will leave little mark on the recorded history on Western Civilization. Most of the names of those working on environmental issues even twenty years ago have been lost from the vernacular of those familiar with the issues today.

But the actions of the people in the following stories have influenced the fate of this place, and if their words and deeds have kept one patch of ground from being bulldozed, or have saved even one endangered species from extinction, then they have given humanity a great gift. And because of this, they are important voices to hear.

Brett on Ace. *Author photo.*

Rowdy

"I HATE ENVIRONMENTALISTS," Brett says. "What right do you have to come into our communities and tell us what to do? These edicts just come down out of nowhere, decisions made by outsiders, that radically influence the way we live." Brett is a third-generation timber worker for Ida-Pine out of Grangeville. Ida-Pine is closing its doors in November. Lack of saw logs is the stated reason. Brett—"Rowdy" to his friends—is out of a job in a month.

We are on horseback, riding up a timber superhighway in the Rainy Day country above the South Fork of the Clearwater River, a block of land tucked up against the Gospel Hump Wilderness. The day is clear, cold, blue, below freezing here on the back of Ace, the thoroughbred/quarter horse cross that Brett brought for me to ride. Brett is dressed like a cowboy—no fake, either. He used to rope and ride for a living. With his chaps, weatherbeaten brown felt hat, blue jeans, and black kerchief wrapped tightly around his neck to block the wind, he is relaxed on his horse, with brown and black two-tone cowboy boots poking out of wooden stirrups hanging off a western saddle. Very different from me—I am tense, awkward, sporting my hiking boots, old loose-fitting jeans, a stocking cap, and garish red Patagonia fleece jacket. We are quite the pair, as the horses take off at a gentle clop up the freshly graveled road.

When Ida-Pine announced that it was closing its doors, angry workers blamed the mill owner, Bob Krogh, for not persisting, the Forest Service for lack of timber sales, and of course the environmental community for appealing and suing over proposed timber sales. Brett had been quoted on the front page of the *Lewiston Morning Tribune*, blaming a conspiracy of environmental groups and the Sierra Club for the misfortune afflicting members of cattle, timber, and mining communities across the West in the past four years. He cited the hard times in the ranching business in New Mexico, and the spotted owl crisis in Oregon and Washington as evidence of the conspiracy. From his view, his world was about to end, and I, or others with similar views, were at fault for the end of his job, his lifestyle, and his connection to the land where he was raised.

I took exception to the comment and responded with a letter of my own to the paper, profiling the end of the endless forest. The reason that Ida-Pine was closing, I posited, was because it had cut itself out of a job. Don't blame me, I said. You chopped the trees down. You filled the creeks up with silt. Where were you going to go next, I asked?

Brett and one of his older friends, Gary, wrote back. They were hot, asking questions of me. "How do you know why Ida-Pine closed?" Brett questioned my summer of hiking, saying that there was no way I could have covered the Clearwater and Nez Perce forests in only three months. Gary questioned my judgment, stating that the reason the mill closed was the difficulty in getting federal timber. I responded again in the paper, this time with a challenge: I would buy a beer for anyone who could show me a big stretch of unharvested timber outside the roadless country, including the wilderness areas. There were particulars, of course: no checkerboarded lands, no hammered hillsides, just a lightly roaded area with little or no timber cut. On Sunday night, October 23, my phone rang. It was Brett. "Hell, I don't just want a beer—I'm angling for dinner." I agreed to come to Grangeville Saturday morning. Where were we going, I asked. Brett said "the Rainy Day country."

As an activist, I know how to get information about the country and its status quickly. The word went out over my net of friends. First question—where was the Rainy Day country? Tim Warner of Kamiah responded, steering me to a Forest Service hydrologist, Wayne Paradis, of the Clearwater District of the Nez Perce Forest. I happened to be in Grangeville on that Monday, so I stopped by the district office on my way out of town. Tim had told me the story of development of the road network into the area that Brett had said we would traverse. The Rainy Day country had turned out to be a bench of land buttressed up against the northern flank of the Gospel Hump Wilderness area. The roading necessary for timber harvest in that area had been partially completed, including the Million Dollar Bridge, an elaborate curved crossing spanning the South Fork into an unstable hillside that had resulted in one of the worst sediment sources on the river, as well as The Road to Nowhere, a big bucks logging superhighway into the heart of the country, running all the way to Sourdough Point on the edge of John's Creek, over upland bog and unstable, granitic soils. The trees? Mostly grand fir and lodgepole, some tamarack, punky, ready for the pulper. Some sawtimber for sure, but a marginal sale in a marginal area. I looked at the plan for development for the area we would ride, called the Wing Creek/Twentymile Creek planning unit by the Nez Perce National Forest. The six-mile-wide strip of land, about ten miles long, had been released for logging as part of a deal between Dennis Baird of the Sierra Club, other environmentalists, and the timber industry in exchange for preservation of the Gospel Hump Wilderness Area. Fifty million board feet of timber were supposed to be logged out of a total of four drainages, another last-of-the-big-time timber projects. I stared at my shoes, bitched at Wayne for the sale maps, and walked out of the office with the Environmental Impact Statement under my arm. Didn't Brett know this? More than half the sale was being held up by concerns of effect on salmon—maybe he wanted to talk about this? He was certainly right—there was salable timber in that country. So salable that the Forest Service had sold it.

I called Brett. He first was angry, then frustrated, then resigned. No, he didn't know about the timber sale. "Look," he said, "why don't you just come to Grangeville Friday night and have dinner with a couple of us at the Elks. Some of the guys want to meet you. In the morning, we'll go for a ride. I want to be on the road by 6. I'll jump the stock into the trailer and we'll be on the way. I've got a lot of country I want to show you anyway. Gary Sarbacher wants to meet you; we'll just have dinner and talk. I've never met an environmentalist before. Heck, we have a bet going on down here that you're just an Earth First!er." The conversation turned friendly. I laughed, agreed to arrive at 7 p.m. Brett said, "You probably think all loggers are redneck types, a bunch of hicks." I paused. "I went to school with people just like yourself, Brett."

The Elks in Grangeville. How smoky, I wondered. How old? Like the Knights of Columbus social club back in my hometown of Portsmouth, probably with pool tables, beer by the pitcher, popcorn shrimp, and bite-size steak. My friends had a pool on whether I would get back alive. My mother was not pleased either. "Be careful," she admonished. I called up Al Espinosa, my fish biologist friend. "You've just bought yourself a one-way ticket to Logger World, Chuck." LeRoy Lee, another of my mentors, was more encouraging. "Loggers, though having the characteristics of a unique species, have been known to interbreed with other humans, and their offspring are not even sterile," he joked. I asked him if he thought it was a good idea. He said yes. I asked him if he wanted to go. "I'll be visiting Logger World soon enough, Chuck. This time, you're on your own."

Kelley and I drove to Grangeville on Friday. As we pulled into the parking lot underneath Brett's apartment, I saw darkened faces pressed against the window of the second floor apartment. I knocked on the door, and met both my antagonists. Brett, a little shorter than me and about my age, greeted me with a firm handshake, wearing a black felt cowboy hat, a mustache, and a big smile. Gary, older and more tired, also shook my hand. He was missing two fingers off his right hand from two sawmill accidents. We exchanged formalities, then headed to the Elks.

The mill in Grangeville, according to Gary, closed for a lot of different reasons. Bob Krogh, the owner, had decided that he had no desire to pay higher stumpage prices, that timber on-the-hoof was expensive enough. Timber was harder to get, the uncertainty in the timber supply had made it harder to justify capital investment to improve the facility, and he had simply felt that his money could make more money elsewhere. Bob Krogh had married into the timber business—his wife's family had owned the mill in Kooskia, Clearwater Forest Industries, and had bought the Grangeville mill from the Wicks family to show his in-laws that he could make money milling trees. He had completely revitalized the decrepit mill, installing a state-of-the-art sawing facility, computer-controlled and laser-guided. He had cut the payroll by more than half. But he had grown tired of the business, having originally bought three mills, so that he could leave a mill to each son. Two sons had opted out of the business. Only one wanted to run a sawmill, and there was the business in Kooskia for him. He wanted to race cars with his other sons and enjoy life, instead of spending long days at the mill. Never mind that the community depended on the income. He had put the mill up for sale a couple of years ago, but it still had not sold. Buyers had been located for the mill equipment—the edger, the planer, the computer control. The mill would be taken apart and auctioned, piece by piece.

"When I saw your piece in the newspaper, I went through the roof," Gary says. "Here was a guy telling us why Ida-Pine was closing. You never visited our mill, never saw our production. You couldn't know what was happening, and here it was in the paper. How could you know? We didn't just run out of timber."

When we get on the trail the next day, Brett tells me his family history. "Grandfather came out from Iowa to Grangeville with a stake truck in the Twenties. They were all flat broke, had nothing. What money they had, they had made running moonshine. Granddad was a logger, my dad was a logger, drove a logging truck. We moved to Missoula for a while, where I completed high school. I came back to this country. Faller, worked on a logging crew, loaded spray planes over by Craigmont, helped run cattle, farmhand stuff. I competed in high school rodeo—I rode bulls. I'm pretty well rounded. Here in Grangeville, there were always two kinds of people. You went to work, or you went to college. I went to work. You asked me on the phone if I traveled much. I've never wanted to go anywhere but here. The Nez Perce Forest, this is my country. I've ridden most of it, spent a lot of time up in the Selway/Bitterroot, up Mocus Point, Eagle Creek, Split Creek. I've hunted all over the country. I spend my weekends riding my horse. Sometimes I can get someone to go with me. Most times, I go alone. There are three guys at the mill that also ride." I ask him about ATVs and snowmobiles. "Never liked 'em much. Never been on an ATV. I'm a little hard of hearing—most guys in the mill have some degree of hearing loss. When you're on a horse, you can hear everything. Sneak up on elk, deer. Can't do that with a trail bike."

We talk about Bob Krogh. "Bob Krogh always paid us an honest day's pay for an honest day's work," Brett says. I asked him how much he makes—a little over $11 an hour after ten years of working there. When I asked him how much severance the workers at the mill were getting, he held up his hand, forefinger touching the tip of his thumb—nothing. "Hell, I had to get on the phone with Senator Larry Craig to get any retraining money at all. We finally got a deal—two years tuition and books from the Job Training Partnership Act—the JTPA. Of course, that's only good for one year—there's no guarantee that we'll get money for the second year, even if they promised." Unemployment? "Six months. I'm entering a two-year program, welding, up at North Idaho College in Coeur d'Alene. After that, I might go to an underwater welding program in Bremerton. But that's a long way off. One thing for sure, I'm getting out of the timber business. In a way, I understand why Bob Krogh got out. He gave that mill ten more years than it would have had otherwise. But in another way, I don't. We were making money. Others that have mills a lot less modern are still in business, and they're paying the higher stumpage prices. In Grangeville, you only do a couple of things—ranch, farm, work in the mill, or bag groceries. That's about it."

The tamaracks are turning, bright yellow patches burning up the sides of big rounded hills. We talk about streams, road condition, look at some parked logging equipment. The air is cold. I look out over Wing Creek, up into the Gospel Hump. Medium elevation timber country—there are trees here, the punky white firs, but some good sawtimber too. We examine a tamarack stand. I talk about successional forest progression, how tamarack comes in after a fire, grand fir comes up underneath the tamarack on the boggy ground, overtaking the older trees to become the old growth for this forest type. My expertise is confirmed—Brett rides over to the stand where the ten-year-old grand firs flank the tamarack. "Yep, burned underneath." I explain the necessity of not managing everything, the ignorance of man, letting some fires burn and some beetles eat some trees, letting natural processes take their course, the need to set aside low-elevation land as well as high-elevation ground for wilderness. I talk about forestry as a young science—trees have only been logged and regrown twice anywhere in the Northern Rockies.

"Precluding options. You don't want to not give future generations options." Brett is quiet. I think that I reach him. "But," he says, "you environmentalists always talk about future generations. I'd like to think that we've got to support the children of the people that are working right now, too. You've got to consider that." We both complain about the Forest Service. "You know, I've ridden over hundreds of miles of roads. I never thought about erosion—it was just the way things are. You guys have got us by the short hairs on the salmon. The Nez Perce is an island, surrounded by rivers. Anything we do up here is going to end up down there, in the South Fork, the Clearwater. There's nothing we can do. That fish is going to get us." We talk new forestry, and I explain understory removal. Brett informs me that his mill could take lodgepole with a six-inch top. "Heck, our mill runs close to 20 percent lodgepole—2x4s, 1x3s, 1x2s. We have one of the highest recovery rates of any mill in the area. Quality product, that's what we turn out." Brett's conversation topics are industry related— getting fast-growing trees on the site, log utilization, timber sale contracts, different operators and the jobs that they do. Mine are biological, forest history, needs of the ecosystem. "Call me Rowdy," he says. "No one that knows me calls me Brett." I ask him my favorite question—how does one instill a land ethic in someone who has none. He has no good answer.

We eat lunch, mine a cold roast beef sandwich, his a ham croissant wrapped in plastic and foam, picked up at a convenience store. I feed Ace my apple. The road back is quick, up six miles to a saddle and back down into Golden Canyon on the South Fork. I ask him what he plans to do with his horses. "I'm going to sell them both. Ace, there, is going to my brother-in-law. Not going to have much money or use for them while I'm in college. He's worth $1,800, but I'm going to sell him for $600, same as what I paid for him." I am sad for him. I tell him about my economic redevelopment plans, computer networks, and moving light industry to Grangeville. "What about the air?" he asks. "I know, I know, you can't have your cake and eat it too. Is Idaho going to become just like all of those places back East? Dirty air, dirty water? I know things are going to change. Progress." I have no answer.

Back at the truck, I help Rowdy load the horses. I put my borrowed rain slicker back into the toolbox in the bed of his pickup. A huge paddle rests on top of wrenches and sockets. Slogans are written on the face— "Earth First!, This One's for You." I am laughing as Rowdy turns a little red. "One day, we heard a rumor that Earth First! was going to come and vandalize our mill. Well, I've been in enough fights in my day. We made us these sticks. We were ready for 'em." I am laughing now, roaring. I tell Rowdy that the biggest threat from any Earth First!er is getting too close and being forced to smell the garlic stink and sweat. Rowdy breaks out in a big smile. We drive away from the landing, down the road to the South Fork, and across the Million Dollar Bridge. Kelley drives up to take me home. Rowdy and I shake hands. I thank him for the ride, give him my best wish for luck, and wave as the big white trailer fishtails around the corner, out of sight, down the river.

As Kelley and I drive down the road, cold and sore from the long ride, I ponder the circumstance that as an environmental activist I have to bear the news to Grangeville that the indecency and uncertainty of modern society have finally reached this small Idaho town. Grangeville has been through boom and bust before. But this bust is different. The economy will never be ruled by timber again, and for better or worse, the people of Grangeville will have changed forever. Small houses and trailers are being replaced by 4,000-square-foot monster homes; $5000 per acre prices and an expanding national population are preventing all but the rich from land ownership on this edge of the Big Outside. I wonder whether it will be even remotely possible to foster a land ethic in a society doomed to transience by the whims of a changing job market. Rowdy and I discussed at length the creation of a sustainable timber industry. I told him that if he wishes that environmentalists not interfere with the affairs of the Nez Perce Forest, then people on the inside like himself must police the industry themselves. But it's not easy to police the man who provides your paycheck.

I can still see Rowdy, erect in the saddle. He is losing his job, his horses, his place, his attachment to the land. More difficult, he is riding with a man that a part of him blames for the loss of his job. He is listening to me, asking me sincere questions, straining to keep an open mind about my concerns. As the day fades to dusk, I wonder if I could have been as gracious. If my wildlands are preserved, the next major challenge of the environmental movement is to worry about sustainable economies. Social justice and environmental ethics must go hand in hand—the wild country will never be safe unless I consider the livelihoods of these people and enfranchise them into the cause.

Charlie (I)

İt is a long drive back from the Idaho Rivers United (IRU) board meeting in Boise to McCall with Charlie Ray, the wild salmon advocate for IRU. I like talking to him; that's not the problem. But I only grabbed four hours of sleep last night at my friend Whale's house, with both of us moaning about the usual—women, the environmental movement, and not enough time. I don't do well without eight hours of sleep. I know that day spent in the meeting was my one opportunity for exercise this week. I am filled with a feeling of slipping, of losing control over my life.

Traveling down the road, we pass Banks, Smith's Ferry, Cascade, Donnelly, Lake Fork, then the outskirts of McCall, past the lumber store, the cineplex, and new mall rising on the outside of this little ski/lake town on the shores of Payette Lake. Condominiumization is happening to McCall. We turn down the road toward Charlie's log cabin, then up a snow-covered street. It's late, 1:45 in the morning. His black lab, Olive, greets us as we stumble toward the front door.

Charlie has work experience with all the traditional industries of the West. He started off as a timber faller with Columbia Helicopter, just outside of Lowman, Idaho. After a brief stint in Portland, he ended up working construction at the Lucky Peak powerhouse for the dam outside of Boise. During a lapse in work at the dam, he worked as an electrician at the Newmont-Maggie Creek Gold Mine, a huge heap-leach operation outside of Carlin, Nevada. But mining didn't suit him, and soon he was cutting logs in Lowman again for a gyppo outfit. "Mining, logging, dambuilding— I did all the sins of the West," Charlie says.

One winter day in 1990, Charlie was reading the legal notices in the paper, and saw that Idaho Gold Corporation, based in Vancouver, British Columbia, had applied for a permit for a heap-leach gold mine on a series of small creeks on the South Fork of the Clearwater—Buffalo Gulch Creek, Whiskey Creek, and Maurice Creek. "You know, I had never read the legal notices in the paper. But that's where I liked to fish for steelhead," Charlie says.

The heap-leach gold mining process involves grinding up a mountain, then pouring liquid cyanide over the crushed rock to separate the gold out of the rock. When the vein of ore is played out, the mine is abandoned. Recovery of the pit is not even required by law in Idaho because the destruction is so extensive. Charlie knew about gold mines, having worked at Newmont. "I kept thinking about the water management problems that the Maggie Creek mine had, with cyanide leaching into the ground and contaminating surface water. And that was in a desert. What kind of problems would a mine have in an area that had about thirty-five inches of rain annually, like Elk City?" he says.

"That was back when I thought the regulatory agencies actually regulated. I was sure that once the agencies—the Idaho Division of Environmental Quality (DEQ), the Bureau of Land Management (BLM), and the Forest Service, in particular the Nez Perce Forest—became educated to the problems, they would put a stop to the mine. I found out pretty quick that the BLM, which actually owned the land where the mine would be built, was encouraging them."

After talking to the agencies, Charlie was ready to quit. But his wife Leslie gave him the number of Ed Cannady, an activist for the Idaho Conservation League (ICL). Ed, from Oklahoma, used to work on the oil rigs and at mines. "Ed and I hit it right off—we both had southern accents. Plus, he knew what mining was all about. He had a job as a wilderness ranger, and was packing up to leave. But he gave me the name of someone else that he thought could help." That person was Will Whelan, a water policy analyst for the ICL. Charlie stormed into the ICL office in Boise one night and spilled his story about the mine to Will. "He didn't know who I was. I couldn't believe that he would just take my word for this kind of thing." Will asked Charlie if he thought a public hearing would help. Charlie yelled "Hell, yes!" So he typed up a request for a public hearing to the DEQ on ICL stationery, ripped it out, and handed it to Charlie. "I was so impressed," Charlie says. "Here was someone who knew how to use the system to get something accomplished."

"It didn't take long for it to sink in after I sent in that letter that having a hearing meant that I was going to have to testify at that hearing. I had never spoken in public before." Charlie returned to talk to Will about his dilemma. Will leaned forward in his chair, opened up his top desk drawer, and pulled out a booklet of about a hundred pages, Idaho's regulations on ore processing with cyanide. He handed them to Charlie, and remarked "I think you might get familiar with these."

Charlie plowed through the document several times, each time making notes. "I started to notice that I saw the phrase 'plan of operations' over and over," he says. "So I decided to call the DEQ office in Boise and asked them if they had a copy of the plan of operations for the mine." They told him that it was available for his examination, Monday through Friday during office hours. Charlie had a job and had to work, but if he wanted to see the plan, it was 8 to 5. When he finally arrived at the office, they pointed to a stack of four-inch ring binders full of information. Charlie gasped.

"But when I opened the binders, and started looking through the pages, I relaxed. They were full of engineering drawings—real information, just like I had used in my whole career, working on power plants. I knew that I could understand that stuff. It was really similar to the mine I had worked down in Nevada. Same plan, same bad assumptions," he says. He took another day off from work to examine the entire plan, made a sheaf of comments, and went back to visit Will.

Will liked Charlie's comments. Sitting at his desk, he casually suggested that Charlie call up the staff at Idaho Fish and Game. "These mines kill a lot of birds and terrestrial animals," Charlie says. "I've seen ducks floating in the barren solution ponds, where the cyanide is diluted before being sprayed onto the unprocessed ore. A songbird needs to dip its beak one time into the pool for a small drink of water and it's dead. There were mornings at the Maggie Creek mine where we would see deer lying still around the edges, poisoned by the solution in the pond."

Charlie contacted Idaho Fish and Game. A fisheries biologist there who shared Charlie's concerns traded information on the project with him. "He didn't just blow me off, like the folks in the BLM and the Idaho DEQ," he says. Meanwhile, the public hearing Charlie had requested was drawing close. It was being held in Elk City, a six-hour drive from Charlie's house. He took another day off work and drove to Elk City. The closer he got, the closer he came to returning home.

At the bottom of the Mt. Idaho grade, just outside of Grangeville, Charlie started feeling nervous. When he crossed the South Fork of the Clearwater, he stopped his old pick-up truck, got out his fishing rod, and walked down to the riverbank. It was March, and the South Fork was running low, the canyon gray with clinging fog. Charlie took a few casts and hooked a steelhead. After he landed the fish, he released it back into the river, conviction restored. When he arrived at Elk City, he stopped off and bought a Coke. At that moment, the Fish and Game fish biologist that Charlie had talked to on the phone walked into the store. Looking around, he spotted Charlie, walked up, and shook his hand. "Are you Charlie Ray?" the biologist asked. "Do you mind if I walk in with you?" he asked Charlie.

The hearing was being held at the Elk City school. Thirty people were there. The mining company went first, giving its testimony concerning the benefits of the operation. The Idaho DEQ was next. Charlie was surprised and irritated that its show was almost the same as the miners. Several citizens testified in favor of the mine. On the last call for testimony, Charlie finally mustered his courage, walked to the front of the room, and sat down in front of the microphone. He laid out his entire case why DEQ was compelled to deny the operation permit. "You could have heard a pin drop when I finished. And when I finished, I got the hell out of there." As Charlie was leaving, four people came up and cornered him in the back of the room. They told him that they lived in Elk City, and that they were really glad that he had gotten up and spoken against the mine. "For the first time in the conservation movement," Charlie says, "I was empowered." Charlie got their names, and for every future piece of correspondence he sent to the government agencies, he sent them copies and encouraged them to do the same.

Directed by his wife, Leslie, he contacted the Mineral Policy Center in Washington, D.C., an organization dedicated to fighting mining. They sent him some literature, which had good bibliographies. Charlie went digging in the library. He made short presentations at both the Audubon and Sierra clubs in Boise. "I was totally surprised again. Here I was a complete stranger walking into a roomful of people, and they were concerned with everything I was telling them. They agreed to help me—I made some more friends that night. People are willing to help if you ask them." Charlie also went back to visit Will, who opened his top drawer again and pulled out a copy of the National Environmental Policy Act (NEPA). He handed it to Charlie, and said "I think you might find this useful."

Charlie began lobbying the BLM to do a full-blown Environmental Impact Statement (EIS), required when a project will significantly alter the physical environment, which the mine would certainly do. The BLM refused, wanting only to perform a shorter study, an Environmental Assessment (EA). In the end, only an EA was produced. However, Charlie notes that it was one of the most complete EAs he has ever seen. "When the EA came out, I sweated blood over that thing, making comments, looking for weaknesses." When Charlie had completed the analysis, Will took Charlie's comments, incorporated all the appendices full of information that Charlie had gathered, and mailed it to the BLM.

One of the biggest problems with the mine involved the road access. Idaho 14, the slow, winding road for the forty miles up from Kooskia to Elk City, had a bad accident history, and the possibility of a chemical or fuel oil spill into the river was significant. Will and Charlie were informed about an Interagency Transportation Task Force being formed by the Nez Perce National Forest, which surrounded the BLM land where the mine would be built. The Forest Service, the miners, the BLM, as well as the Idaho State Police and others were all going to be involved. Will wanted Charlie to be on the task force. It was another huge educational process. At the first meeting, the organizers trotted out all the Department of Transportation regulations, as well as information on the Emergency Response Network, along with accident frequency rates, similar scenarios, and research on moving hazardous materials.

"Think about all the diesel fuel moving up Idaho 14, to the mine, fuel for all of those huge dump trucks" he says. "Think about what would happen if one of those tanker trucks ended up in the river, and what that would do to the fish." At the next meeting, held in Grangeville, Charlie started going down the list of hazardous materials with the task force. "Ammonium nitrate, for example," he says. "They'd tell me that it was just fertilizer. But they were going to use it as a blasting agent. Just a touch in the water is deadly for fish. Hundreds of tons would move up and down the river road. The miners on the committee told me that I didn't need to worry—DOT regulations had that kind of thing covered. Do you know what the DOT regs for ammonium nitrate are? You can haul ammonium nitrate in paper sacks on top of wooden pallets on a flatbed truck." Charlie shakes his head.

Sensing that things weren't going their way, the miners brought in consultants from DuPont to a meeting of the task force in Lewiston. DuPont, which would be supplying and transporting the cyanide, had prepared a presentation concerning the safety of hauling the chemical. "The DuPont people were pitching the idea that their special Flo-Bin containers could withstand 'damage.' I stood up and asked them 'You mean to tell me that if a cyanide truck moving upriver at forty miles per hour has a head-on collision with a log truck moving downriver at forty miles per hour, that no cyanide would have a chance of spilling and ending up in the river?' The DuPont representatives said 'no problem.' But the Idaho State

Police representative stood up, pointed at me, and said 'This guy's right.' After that, the task force never met again. I had a hard time coming to terms with the fact that everything that the agencies did was to grease the skids for the mine."

Charlie went back to visit Will for the third time. Will pulled out a copy of the Clean Water Act, pointing to Section 404D. According to it, the mine owners would have to replace any wetlands destroyed by construction of the mine. In the meantime, the BLM issued a Record of Decision to proceed. Will enlisted the help of a University of Idaho law professor to determine whether they could sue the BLM and stop the mine. The law professor reviewed the document, and said no. Charlie, disappointed, was ready to give up the fight. But the Nez Perce tribe appealed the project and won, temporarily stopping the mine due to the lack of mitigation efforts for the certain destruction of fish habitat. Additionally, the Army Corps of Engineers, involved with the project because wetland destruction was an issue, did not find that the substitute wetlands to be created would be adequate compensation for the lost habitat.

Out of the blue, the BLM announced a fish habitat enhancement project on tributary streams to the South Fork of the Clearwater in the area where the mine was to be sited. "They saw that the project was going down the tubes, so they tried to grease the skids again to get it going—compensation for lost fish habitat was a definite issue with the project," Charlie says. Meanwhile, the operation permit that the mine held from the state was about to expire. The day that the permit expired, Charlie wrote a letter to the DEQ, asking it to revoke the permit. The DEQ replied quickly, telling Charlie that it had forgotten to tell him that the mining company had reapplied for the permit, and the DEQ had given the company an extension of six months. "Forgot, nothing. Why would they 'forget' to tell an involved citizen?" he says. Six more months passed, and the mine was still having problems with its replacement wetlands. Finally, in September 1994, the DEQ revoked the mine's permit.

"The mine is done for now, for the time being," Charlie says. "But it is public land, and they still hold the trump cards. They hold the mining claims. It could come back at any time."

I ask Charlie about a new mining project that is being started up on some small tributaries of the Upper Salmon River that I know he's examining. He laughs and stretches his arms behind his head. "One day, I was reading the legal notices for another mine on another salmon/steelhead river. Now, I never read the legal notices, Chuck."

Charlie (II)

I BELIEVE THAT THERE ARE TIES that bind, truths that string together a people and a land. Back in southern Ohio, I can remember sitting out under the oak trees after a new snow, during winters that never did get cold. I remember coal dust, gray skies, the closing of fall and the deer hunt in November, though I never carried a gun or shot a deer. There was a web of memories there, and while I was a child, my world did not change. I thought that it would run forever, with the same winter skies and summer heat, the same beautiful earth and tall summer thunderclouds, and I would always remain a child.

I have moved out west now, displaced. My old community has collapsed, a ghost town along the banks of the Ohio. People have tried to fix things up back there, trying to compensate for the loss of their false god—a steel mill, which led to a wrecked environment and lost jobs when the mill finally closed. The last time I visited my mother and father, we went down to the floodwall to look at the historical paintings on the face of the rough concrete. Manifest destiny history for sure: baseball, peaceful Indians, and strange showbiz heroes like Roy Rogers and Jerry Lee Lewis, the rock star who married a thirteen year old cousin. The main street runs through a ghost town now, with spray-painted graffiti on the strange cement park outside the bank building. The carcass is there, and the buildings are still intact from when Portsmouth used to have a population of a hundred thousand people. But the land screams as the remains are consumed by the vagaries of the local economy, reverted back to logging and mining, while the farm economy plods along in the background. I can see that the web, the thread of this place, has been broken. I do not know if it can recover again.

It is hard to discern those links in an unfamiliar place, and for my first five years in the Clearwater Country, I could see no ties that bound. I think that I was self-absorbed, involved with my rivers and explorations in the summer, and skiing in the winter. But the land talks, whether one listens or not. The stories of past events, successes and tragedies, can be heard as the rustle through the branches of an old-growth grove, or the boom of a landslide down a clearcut slope.

My first trip out of Pullman after arriving from North Carolina was a Labor Day whitewater expedition to the North Fork of the Payette River. I had driven up through McCall on my way here, and rushed down to jump on that stretch of whitewater along Idaho 55 because of some strange, self-selected rite of manhood and passage upon arrival in this place. The flash and the memories of paddling the river have faded. It was not that the weekend was uneventful. I was paddling some of the biggest whitewater of my life, and a young man rowing a raft was killed on the second day I was there, in a rapid called Jacob's Ladder. I can barely remember his pretty girlfriend standing with her face in her hands, crying alongside the bank as the helicopter came to take him away.

But a different picture stayed with me—a gathering of Native Americans around Amphitheatre Hole on the Little Salmon River, some twenty miles south of Riggins on US 95. I can still see it as if the events occurred just yesterday. They were standing on the riverbank, surrounding this small place in the sunshine, cars pulled off on the road underneath the trees. More than twenty of them were holding nets. I slowed down for just a moment, then saw a flash of red and green jump up over the three-foot-high falls. A chinook salmon, I thought to myself, Indians catching chinook salmon. This was the Pacific Northwest, home of anadromous fish, after all, and both elements I took for granted.

The sockeye, chinook, and steelhead are almost gone from Idaho. Idaho coho were declared extinct in 1987. In 1994, only two sockeye returned to Redfish Lake outside of Stanley, named as such because the lake during the sockeye run would turn red when the fish moved out of the river into the lake. The chinook have almost vanished, with the runs of spring and summer chinook down to combined levels of only twelve hundred wild fish each year. I fear for the loneliness of extinction for the chinook, swimming all the way from the ocean back to this beautiful land to love, then die. Fish biologists will tell you that populations reach a point where the migrating fish cannot find mates, because there are too few spawning fish spread out over too great a geographic area. The steelhead population is decreasing so rapidly that this last year was a catch-and-release season on the Clearwater, home of some of the largest steelhead in the world. All of this is so hard for me to accept: the idea that my rivers were once so incredibly alive, that high mountain lakes and streams once boiled over with salmon and steelhead fire once a year, that people could once walk over creeks on the backs of the great fish. I cannot come to terms with the loss of a species.

I am on the Salmon River today, outside Riggins, up the Big Salmon Road, with Charlie again, along with his young son Alex. It is late October and cold as he slips his drift boat into the water at Island Bar. We are fishing for steelhead, huge sea-run rainbows, some of the best game fish on the planet. Idaho also happens to have some of the biggest in the world— the run over on the Clearwater, the famous Clearwater Bs. Some also run up the Salmon. The season on the Clearwater is only catch-and-release for both wild and hatchery stock this year, the fish numbers are so low. There hasn't been a salmon season for almost twenty years.

There are hordes of other boats on the river, looking for that wild connection in the cold, and lots of money—jet boats, regular outboards too, with big Mercury engines zooming up and down this quiet stretch of river. All the boats are made of aluminum, belonging to these lovers of fish—products of the aluminum industry, one of the main beneficiaries of the cheap power from the dams that are busy killing the fish. I cannot decide if there is fundamental hypocrisy afloat here or not. But lack of choice runs modern society. My fish biologist friend, Al Espinosa, always said "smolts or volts—give me a choice" when I would tease him about having dam-generated power running his household. "I'd burn candles if it would mean I could have fish, Chuck," he'd say. "But what is the point of my sacrifice if the dams stay in place?"

Alex and I hop in, and Charlie grabs the oars, pulling the boat out into the mainstream. We drift down the current, Charlie explaining steelhead fishing philosophy as he back trolls his dory across the fast water above a short pool. Alex is holding on to his rod, a bait casting reel, with a silver HotShot coated with herring oil tied on the end of his line. "There'll be a fish right behind that rock, Alex," Charlie says, swinging the boat around toward the right bank. The HotShot drifts out of the main current, across the eddy line, then WHAM, a steelhead takes the lure and runs line off his baitfishing reel like no tomorrow.

Alex's small arms strain against the fish. Charlie coaches and chases the fish downstream with the boat, Alex reeling in line. The steelhead surfaces next to the gunwale. "Now guide him into the net, Alex," Charlie says. He scoops the sea-run rainbow into the bottom of their craft. "Looks like a two-ocean fish, Chuck," he says, untangling the net off the fish. It must be a twenty-eight incher, a Clearwater B run hatchery fish. Not only is the adipose fin missing, but the main dorsal fin has probably been worn off on one of the concrete raceways. "Two oceans?" I ask Charlie. "That means it has two years at sea, Chuck. This is a Clearwater fish, though, and must have got lost being up here on the Salmon. Just took a wrong turn in Lewiston."

Charlie asks Alex if he wants to keep the fish, and Alex says yes, his first fish of the season. "We'd have to keep it anyway, Chuck. It's bleeding from the mouth. It would die anyway," he says, sensing my uncertain demeanor. I have never seen a live steelhead, blunt rounded head, hooked jaw, and sleek, silvery body. Charlie whacks the fish on the head with a small baseball bat. I move to the back of the dory, and Charlie removes his camera from his front compartment. He hands Alex the fish. "Tilt your hat back, Alex. I can't see your face," he says, as Alex smears on his picture-smile, and the camera starts clicking. Afterwards, he plops the fish in the fish box under the seat.

"Salmon and steelhead, Chuck," Charlie drawls. "Sixteen million each year historically in the Columbia River run. Three hundred million pounds of biomass up into this granite country, this Batholith country of sterile soils. Salmon are the fiber in the web of this country. Think of all that fertilizer. What is going to happen when all the fish are gone?" We talk about keystone species, the organisms that all life in an ecosystem depend on for survival. In the clear, nutrient-poor waters of the Clearwater Country, salmon and steelhead are the thread that runs so true.

"Who fell asleep at the wheel, Charlie? How could things have gotten so bad, so quick? Didn't people know what was happening?" I ask Charlie as the drift boat slides down the river. Alex looks distantly off the bow of the boat, bored. His father is talking fish again. "Who was asleep at the wheel?" he replies. "That's a long story." Charlie sighs, and rows his boat across the current.

No one was asleep at the wheel. People were always active in trying to protect and save the Idaho salmon runs. But the dams were built with the pretense that they would not hurt the fish. At the beginning of the construction of Bonneville Dam, the first of the Columbia River dams, the Army Corps of Engineers, which built Bonneville, and the Bonneville Power Administration (BPA), the government agency in charge of managing the hydropower system on the Columbia and its tributaries, promised Congress and the Columbia River tribes that the salmon runs would not be affected. But Grand Coulee Dam, completed in 1941 without fish ladders, annihilated the entire upper Columbia run. The construction of the dam at The Dalles on the Columbia destroyed the historic Native American fishing spot at Celilo Falls in 1956. And finally, the lower Snake was dammed in the '60s and '70s, with the construction of Ice Harbor, Little Goose, Lower Monumental and finally, the coup de grace, Lower Granite Dam, which made Lewiston, Idaho, a seaport 450 miles inland inside the United States. The combination of the four dams on the Snake, coupled with the four dams on the lower Columbia mainstem, broke the ability of the salmon to reach the ocean and return home.

The problem with the dams is not so much the upstream passage problem. The big fish have some difficulties with the fish ladders, to be sure. The trouble revolves around the baby salmon and steelhead, the smolts, and their passage downstream through the gauntlet of dams and pools. Besides the huge turbines, which suck many of the smolts down through and kill the fish by impact with the turbine blades and pressure drop across the huge machines, the pools behind the dams cause some of the largest problems. Smolts move downstream tail first, with heads constantly pointed upstream. They use the current for direction to the sea. With no current to guide them, the smolts first get lost. And because the dams have created unnatural habitat, which harbors many exotic predators, such as small-mouth bass and walleye, they then get eaten. Though all the dams on the Snake and Columbia take their toll, the large pool created by John Day Dam on the Columbia and the four dams on the Snake are the worst. By the time the smolts finally reach the Columbia River estuary, past Portland, more than 80 percent have been killed.

In 1977, two years after completion of Lower Granite Dam, both the salmon and steelhead runs collapsed. "Makes sense, you know. Understand that the fish spend a year or two in the ocean. So two years after you kill all the smolts going out, the run dies," Charlie says. The result of that was that the steelhead season closed in 1978 for two years. The salmon season was closed, and never reopened. People knew that Lower Granite Dam was the straw that broke the camel's back. Clippings from the *Lewiston Morning Tribune* from that time show people talking that Lower Granite would be the death of the fish. The National Marine Fisheries Service at that time began a status review of salmon to determine whether listing was warranted or not, under the Endangered Species Act of 1973 (ESA), which had only been used prominently once, in the case of Tellico Dam and the snail darter.

At the same time that the fish populations were collapsing, another cohort of the BPA was also running into difficulty. The Washington Public

Power Supply System (WPPSS), known to the public as "Whoops," was building a number of nuclear power plants along the Columbia River, and approaching financial default. The nuclear plants were ostensibly designed to meet supposed increasing power needs in the region through the next millennium, and were financed with what WPPSS termed virtually "zero-risk" bonds. But the plants were never finished. When the projects folded, the bonds were worthless, and the bondholders—many retirees—faced ruin.

Congress got very upset about WPPSS. After examining the whole debacle, its solution was to pass the Northwest Electric Power Planning and Conservation Act, known popularly as the Northwest Power Act, to straighten out the way the BPA was being run.

At the same time Congress was looking into the financial problems at BPA, NMFS started a status review on salmon in the Columbia system. Because of declining fish stocks, it appeared that the ESA was going to come into play at the same time as the financial mess with WPPSS. BPA had blown it monetarily. Now they were blowing it with the fish .

Congress started working on a piece of legislation to straighten out the BPA. They attempted to fix both the WPPSS default and the salmon collapse, so they put the fish and wildlife provision in the Northwest Power Act, which stated that the fish would be considered equitable partners with the other users of the hydropower system. It also said that the fish would be restored to the extent that they had been affected by the development of the hydropower system. The fact that the Northwest Power Act specified that salmon would be restored was especially important. Unlike the ESA, which only supports maintaining species at a population bare minimum, the Northwest Power Act promised restoration.

"Everybody that was upset about the fish run collapsing here in Idaho, as well as concerned that the USF&WS and NMFS were conducting the status review, breathed a sigh of relief when this gift from God came down in the form of the Northwest Power Act," Charlie says. "Most activists forgot about the fish, dropped the status review, and went on about their business, appealing timber sales or whatever they were doing before the Northwest Power Act, because they thought it was fixed."

"But it was not fixed," Charlie drawls, leaning forward and pulling both oars out of the water, "because no one thought to watch the keepers of the river, which was the Northwest Power Planning Council. And they were immediately captured by the BPA and the aluminum companies."

Things have been going downhill ever since—except, initially the steel-head run. The numbers in the steelhead run started going up. At the same time that Congress was coming to terms with the WPPSS debacle, it also realized two things. First, that the Corps of Engineers had lied when the agency told Congress that it could build the dams without affecting the fish run; and secondly, that Congress realized it had misled the public in authorizing the dams under the promise that the fish runs wouldn't be destroyed. So in 1976, Congress passed the Lower Snake River Fish and Wildlife Compensation (LSRC) Plan. The LSRC Plan appropriated money to build a series of upper river hatcheries, which would flood the river system with hatchery fish. The mortality caused by these dams would be compensated for by hatcheries.

It was a classic case of destroying habitat and mitigating by building hatcheries, a fix that has failed in every situation that it has been tried. For Idaho sockeye and chinook salmon, hatcheries just don't work. No one is sure why, but returns of hatchery fish are substantially below returns of wild salmon. Steelhead, being more disease-resistant and a tougher fish in general, fared only slightly better. After the steelhead facilities were built, steelhead populations in Idaho jumped. And appearances were such that the entire population was on the rebound, because prior to 1985, hatchery managers didn't mark the hatchery fish, so that fishermen and fish scientists alike couldn't tell the difference between the two. But after hatchery smolts started being marked by clipping of the adipose fin, fish counts showed that the wild population was decreasing. And because hatcheries cause genetic narrowing—too many children from one parent fish—you can't keep a run alive on just hatchery fish. Wild fish are necessary for the infusion of new genetic stock.

The people who fished for salmon had been promised that the closure of the salmon season in 1978 was only temporary. Once the hatcheries kicked in, they planned on fishing for salmon again. But that hope was never realized. "For example," Charlie says, "the McCall salmon hatchery has been turning out hundreds of thousands of salmon smolts every year for at least ten years and dumping them in the South Fork of the Salmon, at a cost of tens of millions of dollars, from taxpayers and BPA ratepayers, and we have yet to catch the first adult produced by that facility. That's because the product of the hatchery is slaughtered downstream—by the dams. We spend millions of dollars, make a lot of smolts, then slaughter them." The results of these failures are now history. Sockeye were listed under the ESA in December 1991, and chinook were listed in May 1992.

Charlie came into salmon activism through a connection with an old enemy—the aluminum industry and the public power agencies. One of his favorite rivers in the east, the Little Tennessee, has five Tennessee Valley Authority (TVA) dams on it, built to supply Alcoa Aluminum with power in Alcoa, Tennessee. "I was heartbroken when they closed the gates at Tellico," Charlie says. "One of the first camping trips my wife and I went on was on Rose Island, a thousand acre island in the middle of the Little Tennessee. There was a Cherokee village on the island that had been continually occupied for eight thousand years. Now it's a hundred feet underwater."

While Tellico was being built in the mid-'70s, Charlie was canoeing and kayaking the Little T that was scheduled to be flooded by the Tellico project. But because of the snail darter controversy, the dam was sitting out in the middle of nowhere for four years with the river diverted around it. "To be honest, I just didn't believe that they could close the gates—the whole project was such a colossal boondoggle," Charlie says. "When the ESA kicked in, the dam was 90 percent complete. And the benefits of completing the final 10 percent still didn't outweigh the costs. But the federal government was paying—it didn't matter."

"I wasn't active on the issue of anadromous fish in Idaho in the late '80s, but I had already made the connection that what was killing salmon would eventually kill steelhead," Charlie says. "One day, I casually mentioned to Wendy Wilson, executive director of Idaho Rivers United, that the salmon petition for listing under the Endangered Species Act had been filed by Oregon Trout and the Shoshone-Bannock tribe, on sockeye and chinook. I mentioned to Wendy that if she wanted to do something on steelhead and salmon, I had a fair amount of experience being an activist, what with my personal jihad against the gold mine in Elk City. I also knew fish—I had been studying them systematically for the past twenty years, because I liked catching them. With my knowledge of fish, and a modicum of expertise working the process, Wendy asked me to work twenty hours a week on contract, working on fish. So I put together a slide show and hit the road."

Charlie has driven a lot of miles all over Idaho and showed a lot of shows, to mainstream organizations like chambers of commerce, county commissions, and the Kiwanis. His angle was to enhance each county's understanding of the issue, since the fish would affect everyone in the long run. Idaho did not get the benefit from the dams, and the fix was also going to hurt Idaho if the wrong fix was implemented. "I met with a lot of disbelief, suspicion, and disinterest," Charlie says. "In Challis, they just couldn't understand how salmon were going to affect logging, mining, and grazing." At that time, salmon advocates still had good cooperation with the governor, Cecil Andrus. The state legislature also endorsed the Idaho plan, which called for reservoir drawdown—basically eliminating the long slackwater behind the dams during the times salmon were in the river by dropping the water level behind the dams and making them more like a natural river, to help fish passage.

"The job gradually consumed me from there," he says. "I traveled 24,000 miles last year. I don't get to spend a lot of time fishing. I sure catch fewer fish now than when I wasn't trying to save them. The job's taken away time from my family, and I took a cut in pay by working for Idaho Rivers United. Working construction or logging, every job I ever took had a beginning and an end. This job, though, just seems interminable. But I'm in it for the long haul. All I've ever wanted to do is go fishing. I'm just trying to make sure that I'm going to be able to go fishing ten years from now. The alternative to doing this is trying to tell my two boys, Alex and Andrew, why there's no salmon in the Salmon River. And that alternative is much more distasteful than doing this."

It is late at night, and I know that I am reading something written by Charlie when he had to be all whiskeyed up. It's not hard to imagine Charlie a little high on booze—he's got that truckstop look to him, with his jean jacket, motorcycle boots, and pointy Van Dyke beard. But I've never seen him even tipsy, and he won't drink in front of his kids. It's not a good example, he says, and Charlie's probably one of the best dads I've ever met.

It's his press release to the news media in the spring of 1994 that I'm glancing at, and I can remember the timing. It was looking like we were going to get our asses kicked in trying to influence the operation of the hydropower system again, if I remember correctly, and I think he was a little frustrated, to say the least. Charlie had this to say:

> For three solid months earlier this year, the biggest story coming out of the Pacific Northwest, covered ad nauseum by the national media— was every minute wrinkle and crease in Tonya Harding's tutu. There's a lot more here than tawdry Tonya, guys.
>
> This is the calculated, systematic destruction of what once was the world's largest run of anadromous fish (salmon and steelhead entering the Columbia River, representing an annual supply of 300 million pounds of protein) by the self-proclaimed "most environmentally friendly nation on earth."

The Pacific Northwest is on the verge of a major public policy "trainwreck" and the most profound environmental, social, and economic tragedy to ever hit the region.

Would it be big news if the federal agency in charge of bald eagle protection ruled that it would be O.K. for other federal agencies to kill 80% of juvenile bald eagles this year? The same thing is happening right now on the Snake and Columbia Rivers.

Doesn't this story warrant more national coverage than the occasional 10 second sound byte or back-page filler? It looks like there could be a Pulitzer Prize here for the journalist who can (if humanly possible) sort out this biological Bosnia.

Charlie and I talk about the fact that the Clearwater steelhead run was limited to catch-and-release for both hatchery and wild fish this year, for the first time. It looks like the beginning of the end for the steelhead now, too. We talk about the eventual ESA listing of steelhead, and hope that the high flows this year will help bring back the fish.

It's getting late; 3:30 in the afternoon, and I can already feel daylight slipping away from us. Charlie says that we need to move downstream quickly. Charlie is going to take his wife to a Halloween party tonight. "It's been a long time since Leslie and I have been out, Chuck. Can't remember when," he remarks. We pull the boat up at the Riggins boat ramp, Alex jumps out and ropes us up to a rock, and Charlie and I walk up the steep hill to his beat-up old Ford pickup. We drive upstream to my car, then return to load his drift boat.

I want to take a quick paddle, and ask Charlie if he wouldn't mind running my shuttle, dropping my truck down by the fruit stand on U.S. 95. He assents, and we are off. Before I know it, we are back at Short's Bar, me walking down to the water with my kayak on my shoulder. "Sure you'll be O.K. by yourself, Chuck?" Charlie asks. "Don't worry about me. I've been here a thousand times before," I reply. I shove my boat into the water. I leave Charlie on the beach with his young son, handing out information to other fishermen, pressing the flesh, like a bankside minister extolling the path to salvation through anadromous fish. I start thinking about the past, present, and uncertain future for the fish that has, as a relative newcomer to this place, been present mostly in my mind's eye.

And then, I finally get tired of thinking about anything other than the now. My boat slides down the tongue of the first rapids, my arms insistently stroking for the take-out. Though I cannot see from down inside this inner, narrow gorge, the sun is setting up on the prairie above. The water turns slate black from the canyon walls. With only the reflection of the sky running across the ripples along the banks, I am breathless, like a salmon, a stranger to the air, along an unsure path into a darkening future.

Reed

Piano teacher and salmon advocate Reed Burkholder and I are talking about paradigm shift—removal of the four dams on the Lower Snake. Reed and I spend the first ten minutes chatting about his wife. Just two weeks earlier, she was diagnosed with liver cancer. Monday she goes into the hospital for chemotherapy. Reed tells me this, falsely energized, staring upstairs toward photographs of his children. They have three kids. And then, a switch flips, and Reed starts talking about fish.

In the summer of 1991, Reed, his wife and young children went camping on the South Fork of the Salmon River campground near Warm Lake. After breakfast one morning, Reed, glancing at his Forest Service map, saw a notation on the map about a fish trap a mile below their camp. He loaded the family into the car and drove to the access gate, but found it locked. "I tend to be a little aggressive toward these things," Reed says. "It was just a single wire. So we walked on down about 300 yards, and there was this concrete thing that I had never even dreamed of in my wildest dreams. Holding tanks, a fish ladder, a scientific work area, and Idaho Fish and Game employees, netting chinook, measuring them, inoculating them with erythromycin, and tagging them with yellow tags about an inch and a half across. They would release every third fish into a tube, back into the river, where they would spawn. The other two would be kept in the holding tanks to be artificially spawned so that they could release their smolts next year."

In the course of the conversation with the Fish and Game workers, Reed got two very distinct impressions: the first was that the survival of chinook salmon in the South Fork of the Salmon was a highly questionable proposition; and secondly, there was nothing they could do to help these fish—it was a downstream problem. He didn't know what they were talking about. What did they mean, a "downstream problem" on this pristine river running through central Idaho? But he dismissed it. For the rest of the summer of 1991, he hardly gave it another thought. On his second camping trip to Coeur d'Alene at the end of the summer, he stopped at the

Rapid River Hatchery outside of Riggins, Idaho. Out of curiosity, he talked to the manager there, too, and saw the big chinooks rotting in their holding tanks, their noses going white.

"What I had done in that camping trip of 1991 was return to a river where I had caught two chinook in 1962," Reed explains. "I hadn't been there in twenty-nine years. In 1962, I went on a camping trip with a Boy Scout buddy, Ricky Furniss and his dad, Malcolm. Malcolm was a state entomologist, and he always camped at Camp Creek on the South Fork and did his Douglas fir beetle studies. He always attended the opening day of chinook season. I had heard these stories for years as a kid, so I begged to go with them. I was in ninth grade."

"I was the only guy in the family that caught chinook that summer, the worst summer for fishing in a lot of years. I remember that Ice Harbor dam closed the year before, the beginning of shitty salmon runs in Idaho. But none of us knew that. Ice Harbor's a long way from here. I had never been to Pasco, Washington, nor heard the words 'Ice Harbor Dam' at that time. That was the seed, this flashback to this childhood fishing spot. It was like coming back home."

About eight months later, a friend of Reed's from church, Bud Knickerbocker, handed Reed a book that he had checked out from the Boise Public Library. It was *The Columbia River Salmon and Steelhead Trout, Their Fight for Survival*, by Anthony Netboy. Reed says "They knew what they were going to do to the salmon runs, and they built the dams anyway. The priorities in the early '60s and the late '50s were such that economic development of the human variety was all that mattered. I learned that we had a chinook run, right here, in Ontario, Oregon, just downstream. No one had any idea how big it was. Well, they finished Brownlee Dam in 1958, and all these fish came back to spawn. The run was monstrous. Then they hit the dam."

A big project of Reed's had just failed, a music game that he had invented and marketed. Since he is a piano teacher—he starts teaching at 3 in the afternoon, with open mornings and early afternoons—he had no project to fill his time. In the spring of 1992, he started making a few phone calls to find out about these "downstream problems." What Reed found was there were four dams on the Snake that he had never heard of, for a total of eight dams on the lower Snake and Columbia system that were blocking the salmon. He called the Port of Lewiston. He told them that he was trying to learn about the waterway. Reed asked questions like, "What's your budget?" And they'd tell him. Then he would request hard copy. After using this technique for about six months, he had built a huge file of information. He did the same thing with electricity—he called the stockholder office and the shareholder services, and asked for annual reports. The secretary would pop it in the mail, and then Reed would get his electricity numbers.

Reed came out of the closet on June 30, 1992, when he testified in Boise in front of the Northwest Power Planning Council, the body in charge of management of the river system formed by the 1980 Northwest Power Planning Act. Reed says, "I didn't know a soul in salmon recovery. I just laid out the case for tearing out the lower four Snake River dams. Mitch Sanchotena, from Idaho Steelhead and Salmon Unlimited (ISSU), shook my hand and said 'Good job!' Tom Stuart, from the board of Idaho Rivers United, walked up to me outside in the parking lot, and said 'You know, Reed, you really need to be connected to some of the salmon folks here in Boise. We have this meeting every other Wednesday. Why don't you come?'"

"I was thrilled," Reed says. "I've been attending ever since. I joined the Mainstem Flow Coalition, which represented ISSU, the Idaho Conservation League, Trout Unlimited, the Boulder/White Clouds Council, IRU, and the Idaho Wildlife Federation, and a few of us hangers-on. Salmon recovery became my personal project. I'm a teacher at heart. I teach every day, and the idea of presenting stuff to people who don't know what I'm talking about is very natural to me. I started typing out flyers, writing little things down that I would pass on to these Mainstem Flow Coalition guys. With regularity, I would give them my latest research. It turns out that it would fall pretty much on deaf ears, because these people were locked into the spillway crest drawdown scenario. But it did give me an outlet for my work. Bert Bowler, salmon recovery chief for Idaho Fish and Game, also attended those meetings. About November of 1992, the Sierra Club had a salmon meeting in Boise. I got wind of it through a friend. It was an all-day salmon meeting, and we decided to start meeting as a salmon workgroup. For two and a half years we've been meeting. I pass them all of my stuff. We discuss strategy and facts."

The facts are damning. The navigation structures on the eight dams originally cost $591 million dollars to build. Considering the time value of money to be 5 percent, and spreading the cost out over fifty years, that makes the cost just for the structures $32 million a year. Dredging, an annual cost, was approximately $8 million in 1992. The Lower Snake River Fish and Wildlife Compensation program, funded by Congress to mitigate for the loss of habitat, cost $27 million.

Reed examined shipping. Out of the Port of Lewiston, approximately two million tons of freight were shipped at the cost savings over rail transportation of $4.60/ton, for a total savings of $9 million; a $9 million subsidy for $67 million cost. Even if you added in savings from other ports on the lower Snake, the costs of maintaining the inland navigation system outweighed the benefits. Reed says "I finally had to quit studying the Port of Lewiston, it was so stupid. The story of building the waterway to Lewiston centers on this very influential special interest lobby group, called the Inland Empire Waterways Association, centered in Walla Walla, and its executive director, Herbert G. West. Herbert West was a genius of persistence. West got turned down for authorization in Congress year after year. Ten years after he got started, these dams got authorized on the basis of electricity generation, in 1945. After that, he tried to get them funded. Lower Granite went in finally in 1975. Not just money—these dams cost me my salmon."

Reed went on to study electricity, the supposed driver of the economy of the Pacific Northwest. The eight dams on the Columbia/Snake system provide only a fifth of the Northwest's energy, and of that, the four dams on the Lower Snake provide only 4 to 5 percent of the Northwest's total. Since 1992, when Congress deregulated the generation of electricity, independent power producers have flooded the market in the United States with natural gas-fired combined cycle combustion turbines, selling electricity at about the same rate as the BPA. Reed stops, waves his hands in the air. "From the customer's point of view, the dams become almost valueless. They're no longer assets. They have now become a clear liability. They don't give our society anything that we can't get somewhere else."

Reed points at me. "Your power company, Washington Water Power, got 89.5 percent of its power from free enterprise, and only 10.5 percent from the system of socialized dams, all of which can be easily replaced. The public doesn't benefit from Bonneville Power. The aluminum companies do. You get 10.5 percent of your power from BPA. My electric company is Idaho Power. I get 1.4 percent of my power. They literally can go to hell in my mind. They are truly expendable. That holds true for 80 percent of the people in the Northwest."

"One of the reasons that I have been so active in salmon," Reed says, "is because I have this dear close friend from my church, Bud. We have talked about everything I have done. I have always done salmon recovery with a sense of community. It wasn't on my own. It undermines your program if you are trying to save the world by yourself."

Reed's face turns from a smile to a frown of frustration. "One of the things that has undermined salmon recovery in the Northwest is that environmentalists feel that they have a need to cooperate. It almost seems like they want to be liked. I've seen enviros drinking whiskey until 3 in the morning with Corps of Engineers and Bonneville Power guys. They want to get along, as if they're nice enough to Bonneville Power, then the BPA is going to treat them right. We've got to shut down Bonneville Power. We've got to change their charter in Congress, and say 'OK pal, you've got six less dams to deal with.' We can't get along with the BPA. Their motives are totally different. What I see with so many environmentalists in Boise is that they're all politicians. They've got a few connections with former Governor Andrus, and they will never step out on a limb. They will never say the truth. They'll never say 'The fish need fewer dams. So we're going to work for a river with fewer dams in it.'"

Charlie Ray has a term for this—he calls it the Patty Hearst syndrome, a case of victims falling in love with their captors. Many enviros in Idaho can't break the fascination of a dance with power. The messengers who are supposed to bring the bad news to the people have been diverted.

"Something that I'm seeing in the environmental movement is that it's a hierarchy," Reed continues. "The attitude is that 'OK, you guys are the grunts, you're the volunteers, and we're the decision-makers. You carry out our agenda.' I've felt that. It's undermining the cause because it's not developing divergent thinking. We need people to use their brains to solve these problems, and this approach is not encouraging brainwork."

My head is swimming, listening to Reed. Yeah, hell yeah—dam removal. But then again, this nation cannot even remove two dams on the Elwha, a small river inside Olympic National Park, a removal project that has popular support from almost everyone involved. What a wild, wonderful thing, removal of Lower Granite, Little Goose, Lower Monumental, Ice Harbor, restoring that big, wild river, flowing past the low hills of the Palouse. Taking out the dams would make the Salmon/Clearwater/lower Snake system the only free flowing big river system in the Lower 48. I remember scenes from a trip down the lower Salmon and Snake River to Heller Bar, outside of Lewiston, down the undammed section of the lower Snake—the power of the water, the wide rapids, the river almost a mile across at points in the canyon. Then I think of sitting at a meeting with the Northwest Power Planning Council and the port managers of Lewiston and Clarkston, who won't support anything except business as usual, which means eventual salmon extinction. I think of the effort in convincing the mainstream environmental community to support dam removal.

Reed talks about the feasibility of removing the dams. All four Lower Snake dams are cookie-cutter dams, meaning that they are basically the same design, assembled out of identical parts arranged to match the contours of the stream channel at each dam site. Each dam has a section easily breached, leaving the structures in place in the river bed. It is all so possible, if we can just change our minds to accept a new paradigm—a free-flowing river that benefits humanity more than a dammed river. I sigh, and think about restoring a river doomed by a series of thoughtless acts. Any way you look at it, Reed is swimming upstream.

Al and Dan

SNORKELING IN THE ST. JOE RIVER is going to be chilly, in this deep, shady, pool. It's been getting down to below freezing every night. The temperature gauge on my watch says 40 degrees when I dip it in the water. I have my drysuit, but I forgot to bring a skullcap. My jaw is going to freeze. But the pool's only sixty feet long, and it can't take that long to float the length of it .

I wade into the current, water seeping into my neoprene booties. I have put on extra socks, but that's not how these things work—a thin layer of water warmed between me and the rubber. It takes time for that water to heat up. Al is fishing downstream in the eddy, laughing at me. "Over there, Chuck. Up by the rock. Just drift down next to the cliff. You'll see plenty of fish." Al waves his fly rod toward the cliff on the far shore. The water is crystal, obsidian in the waning, afternoon sun. I squint. I see nothing on the surface. "This is a Class 9 pool here. Lots of big fish. Check out that white thing." Something barely visible flashes from the bottom of the streambed. I spit into my mask, strap it on my head, and put the mouthpiece from my snorkel in my mouth.

Clouds of cutthroats surround my mask. It is unbelievable. I have fished these pools for a day for two bites. But underwater, more than a hundred fish surround me. A school of mountain whitefish dart across the bottom along the wall. White spots on a dark background, big head—is that a bull trout? My mystery fish vanishes under a cobble. The instant emotion passes. I feel the sharp acupuncture needles of cold penetrate the pinholes in my collar. My drysuit is leaking. I hear only the noise of bubbles and clear water bouncing over rounded cobbles. I see a flash of color below a black eye, a twist in diffuse light. Hundreds of cutthroat part the inland sea in front of me. My hands and wrists, aching from tendonitis, demand their removal from the water. I comply, a huge blue clown coasting down the St. Joe River on my stomach, chin frozen and hands over my head.

I jump out of the water at the end of the pool. "There are hundreds of fish in there, Al!" I shriek. Al is smiling. He cocks his fly rod, drops a nymph at the top of the bubble line, and hooks a sixteen inch cutthroat that immediately dives under a rock. He plays the fish for five minutes, dragging it slowly into the eddy. Finally, the fish tires and swims closer. As Al reaches out to release it, the cutthroat, with one last fish-gasp, jumps and throws the hook. Al shakes the water off his hand, grinning.

I had always wanted to get to know Al Espinosa, former fisheries biologist with the Clearwater National Forest. His reputation preceded him in our circle—he was THE combat biologist, the man who coined the term. He was the guy on the inside, the one responsible for the salvation of the Cayuse Country in the '80s. For myself, an activist with no victories, he was an uncertain hero. I knew that Al had fought the good fight. While he was on the watch, he stopped many plans for roading and logging pristine country. But he lost his job in the end, before the permanent victory of declared wilderness could be achieved for the Clearwater.

But "permanent" victory in most environmental battles never seems to last, and is perhaps a poor goal to set. Permanent victory is a fundamentally human concept. But victory for two years is the life of a chipmunk or gopher. Victory for ten years is the life of a goshawk. And the goshawk, if it is saved, never knows that the fight occurred at all, nor cares. Al fought for twenty-two years—multiple generations of bull trout, goshawks, and pocket gophers.

I met Al at a Clearwater Forest Watch meeting, while I was busy grilling the Lochsa District silviculturalist, Kris Hazelbaker. The Lochsa District was up against a wall. The stream condition summary for the Clearwater had come out, and the Lochsa had major problems in most of its primary timber-producing watersheds. They were trying to avoid the whole road construction issue, the primary cause of stream sedimentation, by proposing a pick-and-pluck helicopter logging operation, called North Lochsa Copter. I was deconstructing the argument in typical engineering fashion, when I noticed an older man sitting in the back, watching me. I figured him for a local "Wise-User." We don't have many older environmental figures, and he wasn't one of the ones that I recognized. My friend, Gerry Snyder, introduced me after the meeting. I shook his hand. So this was Al, I said to myself.

"There are five types of biologists in the Forest Service," Al says. "There are the combat biologists, the lap dogs, the diplomats, the career managers, and the displacement experts. Combat biologists stand up and fight for the resource. Lap dogs sell out to their timber masters. Diplomats are all happy talkers—no matter how bad the environment is being damaged, they've never seen a bad situation. Career managers are biologists who are in the right place at the right time. They'll stand up for the resource only if it won't cost them any progress in their careers. Displacement experts avoid conflicts. While the timber beasts are down raping their district, they're up in a wilderness lake collecting aquatic insects. Only one is reproductively isolated from the rest: the combat biologist. And they're gradually going extinct."

Born in Fresno in 1939, Al grew up hiking and fishing in the southern Sierras. He got interested in fish after doing a high school civics and conservation project. "After reading some books, I decided that there wasn't a conservation ethic in this country. The fundamental American philosophy of the West has always been to exploit, develop, and move on."

After graduating from Humboldt State with a B.S. in fish biology, and earning a master's degree from the University of Nevada-Las Vegas, Al supervised a baitfish rearing program for five years with his advisor. When the project was about to fold, Al sent out his resume. A job on the Clearwater National Forest came back. He had never been in northern Idaho before arriving in Orofino. "Hell, I probably would have kept going if I had come through Konkolville, outside of Orofino. But I didn't have a job, so I had to stay." Upon arriving, he found that not only was he the lone fish biologist on the Clearwater, but he had also been appointed to be a zone biologist, covering both the Clearwater and Nez Perce national forests. "It was the pinnacle of tokenism," Al remarks. "I would work one month on the Clearwater, then one month on the Nez. Two forests and no budgets." The situation only lasted about two years before he was assigned to the Clearwater full-time.

One of Al's first experiences on the Clearwater was meeting the timber sale planner, a famous "timber beast." The planner introduced himself and told Al that he had given a former fish biologist he had worked with the nickname "Sticks," because whenever he needed to cut trees, his fish biologist buddy had always obliged him with a lush riparian area. Al looked him square in the face, and said "Look, you can call me 'No Sticks' Espinosa, because that's how much timber you're going to get off me." After a few years, that same sale planner had nicknamed Al and his fellow biologists the "Yeahbutts": "Every time I've just about got a log on the truck, you guys come up and say 'Yeah, but,' and the sale goes down the tubes."

After Al was assigned solely to the Clearwater in the late '70's, the Central Idaho Wilderness fight commenced. RARE II (Roadless Area

Review and Evaluation), the Forest Service inventory of all the roadless areas on the national forests, had just been completed, and Al was intensely involved with land use planning on the Clearwater. "Back then, before the National Forest Management Act (NFMA) was passed, the emphasis was on unit plans. These plans carved the forest up into hunks for development," Al says. "There was lots of work that never went anywhere. Dennis Baird and Mort Brigham, both local environmentalists, stopped a lot of roadless entry during that time."

Then the NFMA was passed. All unit planning ceased, and the specialists in the Clearwater started working on the larger, more complete forest plan. Al noticed that they didn't have any information on roadless watersheds, so he initiated and completed surveys on Cayuse and Weitas creeks, the Upper North Fork of the Clearwater, and Fish and Hungery creeks. In the pristine drainages on the forest, and especially Cayuse Creek, he found big cutthroat trout, a wild strain of monsters compared to others in the Clearwater Country. He assembled all of the data and reasons for preservation in a database to be used for the upcoming forest plan.

But Ronald Reagan got elected in 1980, and with Reagan came a no-holds-barred attitude toward development of the remaining wild country on the Clearwater. Previously, Al had convinced his superiors on the Clearwater to stay out of the roadless areas. "The country was roadless for good reason," Al says. "Marginal timber, poor soils on top of the granitic Batholith, some very remote country. They would have needed a lot of road just to access the timber. From a rational perspective, it was simply impossible to justify."

Al remembers a day down on the Lochsa District when he was trying to teach the district ranger, Jon Bledsoe, about riparian area management. They had been looking at a planned timber sale in the headwaters of Pete King Creek, a steep tributary of the lower Lochsa. They stopped at the Canyon Meadows Work Center off the Smith Creek road and were eating lunch when Al noticed a seasonal employee shooting baskets at the small basketball court attached to the Work Center. "He was a big Indian guy," Al relates. "We had been fighting with Bledsoe all morning about those harvest units. He wanted to chop them down. We wanted to keep them intact. By lunch, I was just exhausted. I was sitting next to a friend that I played ball with, Hudson Mann, a watershed technician. I told Bledsoe that I would take Hudson and the big Indian. He could pick his two best guys, and we'd go three-on-three basketball for twenty-five points. If we won, the riparian areas would remain uncut. If we lost, they could do whatever they wanted."

The district ranger wouldn't take the bet. Al ended up losing half the units on that Pete King sale. "Pete King is now a degraded watershed," Al says, "but it just doesn't matter to those guys. I have never met a single forester that would be so taken aback about the condition of a particular watershed that he would say 'I'm out of here for twenty years—no more trees out of this watershed.' There's just no land ethic in the Forest Service on the timber side of the agency. And the reason is because the incentives to behave and care for the land are just not there. The incentives are to cut trees. The problem is what I call 'the career cookie.'"

The problem was bigger than just the desire to road the roadless lands. The Clearwater started running out of timber. "The lack of good places to cut trees in the roaded front started to drive the timber program into the remaining backcountry," Al says. A new forest supervisor was appointed, John Hossack, with a get-out-the-cut timber mentality. The regional office had told Hossack before he arrived that Al was running a bunch of renegade biologists who were ruining the timber program. Hossack was instructed to go for the most controversial roadless areas in the Great Burn Country first: Cayuse Creek, Toboggan Creek, and Weitas Creek. If the timber program could fold those areas into the timber base, the loggers could go anywhere.

The timber staff first wanted to log Toboggan Ridge and Toboggan Creek, a primary tributary of Cayuse Creek. "But the trees just weren't there to justify the necessary road construction and sale administration," Al says. "Most of the stands were very young. But the country had a large elk herd, and the fishery was just outstanding. When you looked at timber values versus wildlife values, there was simply no comparison. And cutting the trees would have destroyed those other values." Cayuse Creek and its tributaries were also Al's favorite place, and he didn't plan on losing that watershed. "Once the timber people enter a watershed, even if it's just for a small initial cut, you can be sure they will be back. One road is all that it takes. Before you know it, the area is nuked."

In order to save Cayuse Creek, Al had to involve people outside the agency. Going public with differences is especially taboo in the Forest Service, an agency that has a long history of keeping its conflicts and problems out of the public eye. He enlisted Bert Bowler, the regional fish manager for Idaho Fish and Game, who put on a road show with data, information, and slides provided by Al and took it all over Spokane, Boise, and Sun

Valley. The resultant media created a firestorm of protest among anglers and outdoors people across Idaho. More letters were written to the Clearwater Forest about Cayuse Creek than any project up to that time. Hossack retired before the end of the controversy.

Hossack constantly tried to get rid of Al during his term as forest supervisor, to the point of attempting to cancel his position in 1981. One day, the staff officer, Dick Thompson, walked into Al's office with a sardonic smile to tell Al that his position was being eliminated. Hossack also called Al into his office two days later. He told Al that he was going to upgrade the position and get an elk biologist with a little fisheries experience to replace him. But Al was prepared. He told his Idaho Fish and Game friends that the Forest Service mafia was coming after him. Al also called Mike Schlegel, a wildlife biologist for Idaho Fish and Game out of Kamiah. Mike vowed to expose the whole thing if they canned Al. "They never pulled it off," Al says. "They were trying to hire one of my friends for the job. After six months, things got quiet. They figured out that if they fired me, I was going to take them all down with me."

After Hossack's retirement, Jim Bates, the next forest supervisor, still persisted in attempting to log the Kelly/Cayuse Country. In the end, the entire area was allocated as roadless lands and included as such in the Forest Plan. In response to Kelly Creek and Cayuse Creek being preserved, though, Bates combined the Kelly Creek District and the Canyon District into the North Fork District. "This was a lost opportunity for the Clearwater National Forest to really shine and manage the Kelly Creek District for values other than timber," Al says. "Instead, because commodity production had stopped, Bates had to come up with a new scheme for a new 'multiple use' district so that the foot of the timber beasts could still be in the door."

Fred Trevey followed Jim Bates as forest supervisor. Sensitive to environmental issues, Trevey saw that overcutting on the roaded lands in the Clearwater was going to lead to a collapse in the timber program in the not-too-distant future. After Trevey transferred to the Coconino National Forest in Arizona, Win Green, a biologist and friend of regional forester John Mumma, also a biologist, was appointed to the job. "No biologist can ever be accepted into the club of foresters and engineers that composes the Forest Service elite," Al says. "Green wasn't on the job six months when they greased Mumma. Mumma's mistake was that he actually believed that he was accepted into the hierarchy. But biologists in the Forest Service have always been looked upon as lepers at a cocktail party." Mumma was fired from the regional supervisor's job for not getting the cut out. "If they wanted real criminals, they would have gone after those boys in Region Six, the Washington and Oregon forests, who screwed up the whole spotted owl thing. But George Leonard, deputy chief forester, and Dale Robertson, the chief of the Forest Service, needed a scapegoat for timber supply problems to feed to the industry at that time. They sacrificed Mumma, a biologist. He was convenient."

Al also saw the train wreck in the timber program coming. In the spring of 1992, the cut on the Clearwater went from 140 million board-feet to 26 million board-feet. An Idaho Conservation League suit against the Clearwater concerning old-growth was also settled in '93, restricting harvest of old-growth on the Clearwater and capping the timber program at eighty million board-feet, as opposed to the old ceiling of 178 million. The salmon/endangered species issue hit, which led to PACFish, a strategy to protect the fish's spawning grounds by stopping timber cutting and the resulting sedimentation along creeks and streams. Since much of the volume of timber on the Forest was along streams, taking out these areas had a large effect on the sale program.

Win Green asked a regional study team to evaluate why the Clearwater wasn't getting the cut out. Al, Bill Wulf, the forest silviculturalist, Steve Petro, the timber sales group leader, Dan Davis, the forest wildlife biologist, and Dick Jones, forest hydrologist, were fingered as the players who had paralyzed the different districts because of infighting. Forced reassignment was the solution promoted. Al was going to be sent to Atlanta. Steve Petro was going to go to the Gallatin National Forest in Montana. In the end, though, the only person to take the fall was Al. "The districts and the management team were trying to use the whole scenario of paralysis in the timber program as a masquerade. They fingered all five of us to get rid of me." Instead of moving to Atlanta, Al took an early retirement. The rest kept their jobs. After losing his job, Al went public with his allegations of mismanagement and overcutting. The regional office was being pilloried in the papers. One more head had to roll. The regional office reassigned Win Green, and selected Orville Daniels, supervisor of the Lolo Forest, as interim forest supervisor.

Losing Al in his position as fisheries biologist on the Clearwater has been a fantastic loss concerning safeguarding the remaining roadless areas and native fish populations. The strong voice of resistance from the biologists on the Clearwater has been weakened—maybe critically. Al works outside the agency on anadromous and inland fish issues on the forest now. I ask him how he feels about losing his job. Al has a strong identity with his work. He is succinct. "You have to adapt or die. Humans are the most adaptable of all animals. If we can't adapt, what species can?"

Dan Davis, the Clearwater forest biologist, and I are talking about managing fear, driving along the Lolo Motorway towards Hemlock Butte, on the edge of the Weitas country. We are coming from the south, through Pierce and around the headwaters of Lolo Creek. Dan reflects on the warzone environment on the Clearwater National Forest that ended up with Al Espinosa taking a discontinuance retirement. "Biopolitics, that's what it is. The biologists are politicians, decision-makers," Dan comments, driving his small, green pick-up through the woods. I ask Dan how secure he feels about his job now, after the battle. "I probably have as secure a job as anyone," he replies. I ask him about his effectiveness as a biologist. He tells me about picking the right fights. "I know the minefield." We talk about fear again. Dan has a wife, two children—one is in college now. He is active in the Kamiah community. "You can't let fear get to you. You have to manage it. Weigh risks, fight for the country that is most important for you. It's the classic battle of good versus evil."

Dan was raised in Massillon, a small, neat farming community in Northeast Ohio. He attended school at Kent State during the National Guard massacre associated with the anti-war protests against the Vietnam War. Dan ended up out West as consequence of the massacre—after that event, they shut the school down. Dan was going to lose all of his college credits, as well as his draft deferment, so he opted instead to go to summer session at the University of Montana. He gathered up his high school sweetheart, drove to Montana, and got married in Missoula in 1971. May 27, 1972 marked his start on the Clearwater, with a job offer as a seasonal worker on the Pierce District. Dan remembers the day. "I was hired as a brush piler. I got there late, driving from Montana, and showed up on the job at 11. I didn't even last a day. I met Lawrence Clark, the district hydrologist, who hired me away as a watershed technician. I wanted to stay on the brush crew, figured I'd learn about sawing timber, using a chainsaw, all of those things. Lawrence set me straight." Successive summers, Dan worked timber, fire, and watershed jobs.

Because of his biology background, Dan was having a hard time getting part-time work. But in 1974, a wildlife technician position opened in the supervisor's office. Motivated to apply for the job, he had also met Al Espinosa and Don Jenni, the fish and wildlife specialists on the Clearwater. Dan had earned a reputation as a rabble rouser, and had managed to annoy Tom Blunn, then district ranger on the Pierce. Al was impressed that he had managed to irritate Blunn, and hired him for that reason. Living up at a small Forest Service cabin on Mex Mountain in the lower Lochsa country, he conducted field surveys for Espinosa and Jenni.

We stop at the trail for the lookout on top of Hemlock Butte. It is a gray day. The walk up to the lookout is covered with snow, four inches deep, coming over the top of the laces of my brown hiking boots. We climb to the top of the knob and up the stairs of the lookout. I am scuffing my boots on the sand laid into paint on the steps. "This is the Forest I have always wanted to work on," Dan says. "This is my place." He points out the geography to me: Weitas Creek, the North Fork of the Clearwater Canyon far in the distance, the ripped hills of Sheep Mountain, and the industrial timberlands bordering Dworshak Reservoir. Dan's prize elk herd is in Hemlock Creek, the biggest in the Clearwater. He points out Cook Mountain, place of my wolf response. Clouds and fog close in. Dan gestures, using the cottony wisps as reference markers as he orients the map on the stair rail. I recall past summer hikes, orienting myself. Dan bugles for elk. No call returns.

After graduation, Dan ended up with a position on the Clearwater Forest planning team as a Forest Service biologist, the only one on the team who had actually worked on the ground in the Clearwater. Eventually, he was promoted to the job of forest biologist. Although controversial, both he and Al received national and regional awards in 1990 and 1991. "Sure, there was lots of conflict," Dan says. "But I was flown back to Washington, D.C., to shake [head of the Forest Service's] Dale Robertson's hand."

Six months later, the Association of Forest Service Employees for Environmental Ethics (AFSEEE) newspaper headline blared, "Award Winning Biologists Get the Axe." The cut on the Clearwater had dropped from more than 100 million board feet to 26 million. The collapsing timber program resulted in a regional office review of the Clearwater. Win Green, then-forest supervisor, said that the sub-staff of resource specialists, namely Al Espinosa, Dan Davis, and Dick Jones, the forest hydrologist, would not compromise with Steve Petro and Bill Wulf of the timber staff to get the cut out. "Compromise what? Resource values cannot be compromised to the point where you're breaking the law," Dan says. "We were painted as non-team players, needing directed reassignment."

Directed reassignment—transfer to another national forest. "That's the nuclear bomb in this business. I knew it was true when a fellow biologist called me up and told me that he had been offered my job." The case ended up attracting national attention. Win Green was transferred to another position, and Orville Daniels, the forest supervisor from the Lolo National Forest in Montana, was appointed temporary forest supervisor of the Clearwater. Dan, Dick, Steve Petro, and Bill Wulf managed to keep their positions on the Clearwater. Al Espinosa was forced into retirement.

The truck stops again, overlooking upper Canyon Creek. Dan looks out over the breaks of the lower Lochsa, stops, then shuffles his papers, reading his motivational sheet. It says,

> The battle of good vs. evil has been here since time immemorial.
> Good shall prevail.
> Attack ideas, not people.

He laughs nervously, fidgeting and staring out across the clearcuts. The shrubs dotting the opening are turning to autumn oranges, yellows, and reds. We are quiet for a moment, looking out across the expanse, the dramatically man-altered landscape. Dan rolls down his window. I feel the wind blow as small cumulus clouds scud in under the ceiling of gray, borne by a breeze from the sea coast four hundred miles away, with cold drops of rain on my exposed cheeks. The rainy season has arrived.

A year has passed. I am talking to Dan on the phone. I ask him about the situation after the forest salvage rider. "There's nothing the biologists can do to stop timber sales," Dan says. "It's like the '60s again. They don't have to follow any laws. We just write a paragraph about wildlife to tack on the end of each project."

Kovalicky

I THOUGHT WITH A LAST NAME like Kovalicky, Tom would look, well, Polish—short, round, and balding. I am greeted by a tall man of gentle stature, with slumped shoulders, wearing wire frame glasses. He has a friendly, unbalanced smile beneath a mop of silver white hair. "Don't forget, Chuck; the Swedes invaded Poland more than once," he says. So this is the forest supervisor with the discretion to leave Meadow Creek unlogged, I think to myself, as Tom waves his small hands with long, skinny fingers over his head. In charge of the Nez Perce National Forest from 1982 to 1990, he kept the industry from logging this roadless area in the face of continual industry and congressional pressure.

Tom talks about his career with the Forest Service, a succession of two- to four-year stints across the northern Rockies and the intermountain West. He started out temporarily working on the Beaverhead National Forest as a forestry technician, filling the remainder of his time on a private cattle ranch out of Wisdom, Montana. After six months, he finally found a permanent job with the Bridger National Forest in Pinedale, Wyoming. The first clearcut controversy began on the Bridger, when the Forest Service started planning thousand-acre clearcuts. He remembers the people: "Tough, with a definite user mentality. I can remember when ranchers started shooting fifteen or twenty elk at a time for eating their hay. They just left the meat to rot. The elk situation was so tense in Pinedale, we had to build a twenty-mile fence to keep elk off private land. That fence is still there today. The people felt that they had the right to do whatever they wanted with the natural world."

Tom stayed in Pinedale from 1962 to 1966. However, the advent of a possible national park around the Flaming Gorge of the Green River sent him down to live in Rock Springs, Wyoming. His first line officer job, a district ranger position for the Stanley Ranger District of the Challis National Forest, moved him to Stanley, Idaho. After the Sawtooth National Recreation Area was established in 1972, Tom moved to Sun Valley as assistant superintendent for administration. After four years, he was sent back to the Region One office in Missoula as the regional wilderness management specialist. In 1980, he went to the Flathead National Forest in northwestern Montana, and then finally in 1982, he was given the job as forest supervisor of the Nez Perce National Forest. Tom has had what many consider to be the classic Forest Service career.

A dizzying progression of moves—Dillon, Pinedale, Rock Springs, Stanley, Ketchum, Missoula, Libby, and finally Grangeville. I have traveled across the West for most of my adult life, and have sat in deserted cafes in all of these towns; they are all spectacular, picture-postcard pretty. I can remember stepping out of my truck at the big gas station in Stanley on a storm-clearing day, watching sunlight and clouds on the Sawtooths, and literally gasping, forcing myself to remember to breathe. But it has taken me seven years of hiking, of sitting, of watching and kayaking, of sleeping on hard ground on narrow river bottom land and mountaintops to begin to develop a sense of place here in the Clearwater Country, to engender the notion that there might be a place I would die for.

But what of his sense of place? What ideals are we attempting to inculcate in our line officers in the Forest Service? I have talked to many, and their careers have followed similar tracks. Like the military establishment, every four years they move—a new post, new job, and new friends. And like the military, they are expected to do their job and obey. Tom has survived the system, and has still done good work. Most do not. The legacy of this on the Clearwater and the Nez Perce forests is checkerboard clearcuts for miles.

In many ways, it is the reenactment of the old argument regarding whether it is better to love many places once, or one place well. Tom is a pro at the interview business, hiding his true feelings about all those places and times behind a breezy, storytelling facade. But how does he really feel about all of those lost loves, big skies, and gray peaks? On a lonely day in Grangeville, with slate gray clouds hanging five hundred feet above the Camas Prairie, does Tom cry for Pinedale, for a cold, clear Wyoming sky? He must remember the high steppes when he smells burning sagebrush. Do the Beartooths hang at the edge of his dreams?

The local community apprehensively greeted Tom when he arrived as the first supervisor with a non-timber background on the Nez Perce National Forest. The forest had also been selected as the first in Region One to undergo the implementation of the Forest Planning Process, as specified in the National Forest Management Act of 1976. For the first time, an entire spectrum of public opinion would be considered in developing the management strategy for public lands. The biggest controversy involved the Allowable Sale Quantity, or ASQ, the amount of trees to be cut each year on the forest. Tom studied the situation and took a figure of ninety million board feet (Mmbf) to Tom Coston, the regional forester at that time. Coston informed Tom that there was political pressure to round the number off to one hundred Mmbf. Tom knew that he could compromise. The ASQ was supposed to only be a target anyway. His staff had told him in 1983 that he would never be able to harvest more than sixty Mmbf off the Nez in a particular year anyway.

Senator Jim McClure wanted even more for a target, and one hundred and twenty Mmbf was set as the paper figure. Tom would not budge. McClure tried intimidating Tom with frequent congressional staff visits to Grangeville, as well as conferences by representatives of the Idaho Forest Industry Association (IFIA), the industry lobbying group. Regional supervisors changed. Jim Overbay assumed control of Region One and immediately changed Tom's protection prescription for the west side of Meadow Creek, putting the area into the timber base. McClure told Tom he would withdraw funds for forest operation if he would not give in. McClure brought in Senator Steve Symms and Representative Larry Craig for meetings in the supervisor's office. Group meetings were set up between the congressional delegation and representative of the Clearwater, Idaho Panhandle, and Nez Perce forests to discuss ASQs for the forests. McClure then started threatening Tom's job verbally, and Tom soon thereafter received a letter implying the end of his tenure on the Nez Perce Forest.

Events came to a head in 1986. McClure, Craig, and Symms stopped the publication of all forest plans in Idaho. The plans had passed all the way up to the chief of the Forest Service, but the Idaho congressional delegation would not permit the Forest Service to issue them because the ASQs were not high enough. For almost two years, the plans were held hostage. Carl Haywood, one of McClure's Washington office staffers, indicated that if the Nez Perce Forest would increase the ASQ by 20 percent, the forest plans would be released immediately. At this time, Tom and Bob Abbott, the Slate Creek district ranger, discovered evidence that Carl Haywood might have stolen trees off the Nez Perce Forest on land next to the Salmon River. Tom and Bob put the case together in 1987 and forwarded it to the regional forester, who gave it to the office of general counsel, then the U.S. attorney. The case was never prosecuted; shortly after, Haywood declared bankruptcy. In 1987, the Nez Perce forest plan was finally released, with an ASQ of 105 Mmbf. In the forest plan, the east side of Meadow Creek was not to be developed. The west side was to be entered only under the discretion of the forest supervisor.

The stress, the harassment, the pressure that Tom had to cope with during that time was certainly intense. But Tom got his share of the cut out on the Nez Perce forest. Up in the country around Dixie, the area is still covered with forty-acre clearcuts, still bare, cut in the mid '80s. They are more widely spaced, for sure, and maybe represent a better job than the Forest Service did previously. But a new course? Tom's ASQ for the Nez ended up being 105 Mmbf, for a forest that I estimate can sustainably produce around thirty Mmbf. Tom fought the good fight. But one man can't change a corporate culture.

Tom's manner, once light-hearted, turns deadly serious when I bring up the Jersey/Jack sale, the original version of the Cove/Mallard timber sale planned after the passage of the Central Idaho Wilderness Act. He leans forward, tossing off my comments, intent on establishing his version of the historical record. Jersey/Jack was the first confrontation with the public on how to manage the controversial area on the Nez Perce Forest dissected by Big Mallard, Little Mallard, and Noble creeks, sitting between the Selway/Bitterroot, Gospel Hump, and Frank Church/River of No Return wilderness areas. "I came into the Jersey/Jack sale in the middle of the game. The original lawsuit was over lack of public participation in the planning process. They wanted to build a road right in the front of Harold Thomas's property. Thomas owned the Cook Ranch inside the Jersey/Jack. The Forest Service engineers would not move the road a single inch, so Harold sued. The momentum in those days in the Forest Service was to do an end run around any process, get into the roadless areas, log them, and get out." The sale was appealed twice, and was finally lost by the Forest Service in the 9th Circuit Court of Appeals on cumulative effects from the sale.

The Jersey/Jack package was taken back to the planning stages, and the name was changed to Cove/Mallard. "Steve Williams, the district ranger on the Red River District, did a very thorough biological analysis," Tom claims. The only reaction at that time was from Emmett Smith, a local outfitter, and Ron Mitchell, of the Idaho Sportsmen's Coalition. "It was a trade-off for the Gospel Hump and the Dixie Tail. We were obligated to do the analysis. We were trying to follow the intent of the court, direction of the forest plan, and trying to honor the political trade-offs made in both the 1979 and 1980 wilderness bills," he says. "We believed that the EIS for that area should be written with the maximum amount of flexibility, and it should leave options for the future open. It was never mandated for us to sell every sale. It was O.K. to not develop the area. We were trying to reduce political pressure on the outside and still not give away the farm." Tom sighs. "Then I retired, and I transferred Steve at his request. The two people that were the architects left the project. I can't say things have gone so well since we left. The Forest Service should not make a battleground over Cove/Mallard. They should just back off for ten years and let things settle down."

"The Forest Service needs to be sensitive to the fact that what people think is important in their life changes with time," Tom says. "It also needs to answer the big question of level of preservation between wilderness designation and full development. Cove/Mallard is an indication of that value shift."

I ask him if he, or anyone else, dealt away Meadow Creek in return for the Frank Church or Gospel Hump, like what was done for the Cove/Mallard. Tom leans forward again. "No deal was made."

Dennis

I T IS EARLY FALL on the Palouse, and Dennis Baird and I are walking through his garden, picking tomatoes out of the small patch for spaghetti sauce. We are both scooping the small red and yellow fruit into our respective brown paper sacks. Dennis is a long-time activist and avid promoter of wilderness designation in Idaho—he sat at the table during the negotiations for the Gospel Hump and the Frank Church/River of No Return wilderness, and he is imparting personal history mixed in with political philosophy to me. Dennis saw combat in Vietnam, moved out to Idaho, discovered Meadow Creek, and fought to keep it unroaded and unlogged.

Dennis is still an active environmentalist after some twenty years of working on issues. He is president of the local chapter of the Sierra Club. But he's older, quiet, and doesn't talk to folks outside his circle much. He's a librarian, and bookish. Dennis doesn't believe in fads involving people or land management.

Dennis is very political. Some activists don't think much of his friendship with Larry LaRocco, former United States Representative from the first district of Idaho. Some call him a sell-out for supporting LaRocco's last wilderness bill—only one and a quarter million acres of designated country—that never went anywhere. One and a quarter million out of five million—I think that it was hard for folks to swallow. He doesn't have a problem with negotiating, can compromise and has compromised. But Dennis is really from another generation, and sometimes activists more recent to the battle are separated from him by a generation gap. And maybe that gap is close to irreconcilable, because Dennis belongs to that group of people in the environmental movement that has actually known long-term success.

Dennis and I move inside and leave our bags of tomatoes on his kitchen counter. He pours us both a glass of wine and drags out his corrugated cardboard container of information he has gathered on Meadow Creek, full of maps, letters, and comments through the years. I start leafing through the top. "You can take the box home with you, Chuck," he says. "There's a lot of information in there." Dennis is giving me his Meadow Creek box, detailing all of his fights to keep that place, his place, intact. I am taken aback, as if he had bestowed on me an undeserved honor. Dennis is a librarian, and librarians prize information.

I continue digging, looking down. There are nasty letters in here from him to Don Biddison, forest supervisor of the Nez Perce in the early eighties, as well as nicer ones to Tom Kovalicky, the supervisor who followed. Technical information and maps surface, landtype maps documenting soil types, as well as stuff only a hydrologist would love. Dennis talks about Dick Bennett, the lumber king, setting up the organization "Save Elk City," sending a big delegation of citizens to D.C., as well as hiring a professional to lobby then-Senator Frank Church in 1980 to exclude Meadow Creek from wilderness designation, opening it up to logging. Meadow Creek was left out of the 1980 bill. "But there was no deal made giving away Meadow Creek to be logged for the rest of the River of No Return Wilderness," Dennis says.

Dennis is leaning forward, talking about politics. "We have to support Larry LaRocco in the coming election. Do you have any idea what it is like to not have a single friendly face in our congressional delegation from Idaho?" He talks about the importance of politics in environmental activism. Everyone can have access to the political process, if they want, he says. "You do it the old-fashioned way. You work on someone's campaign. You fold chairs, put up tables, talk to the candidate while they're a candidate. This country is a democracy. But the responsibility to make it work is up to us."

I sit in the library this evening, holding a heavy debt in my hand: the hearings held by Senator Frank Church that preceded the enactment of the bill that created the Gospel Hump Wilderness. Evidence of Dennis's work is here: there are pro-environmental signatures in the hearing minutes from Dennis and Mort Brigham, another elder in the local environmental community, along with Doug Scott and Dan Lechefsky, who negotiated the boundary for the Gospel Hump Wilderness Area. But the document is loaded with hostility. There is no happy consensus written in the pages. Most of the testimony concerning the bill is negative—unhappy locals protesting the lack of a government giveaway, no federal money to build a road network into the high country of the Gospel Mountains to log and mine across the fragile land.

Representatives of the Grangeville Chamber of Commerce, those representing the resource-extraction side of the equation—Jack Olson, Jack Marek, Herb Blewett, and others—in due course endorse the compromise, on the principle that certain lands will be made available for timber harvest immediately. Many of the citizens testify that they feel that the chamber was forced into the decision, that the environmentalists used economic blackmail to get land designated. Many trumpet their right to snowmobile and ride motorcycles all over the high country. Geologists complain about the fact that mining will be severely curtailed by the Wilderness Act. One person said that the task force was only timber-oriented, that the compromise committee didn't consider his access privileges. It seems that nearly everyone is sullen.

But only 10 percent of the timber base of the area ended up in the Gospel Hump—and most of that in isolated mountain valleys, inaccessible for all intents and purposes. The soils in the area are so unstable that it is unlikely that anyone could build a road, even if they wanted to. In Dennis's testimony, he uses Howie Wolke's phrase, "wilderness on the rocks," and having spent time up there, it is just that. Up on the Buffalo Hump, the forest canopy is barely closed. The wind blows through the trees, not over the top, providing no thermal cover. The angry locals, the dissenters, may be pleading a noble cause and a threatened way of life. But they might just be arguing for perceived loss of benefit because they do not truly know their own backyard. Gwen Shearer, then-owner of the mill in Elk City and future benefactor of any sales in the area, says that the whole area will be good timberland in the future, and that he would have no trouble processing seven-feet-in-diameter ponderosa pine; no problem sawing up five hundred to one thousand year old trees.

Nothing changes. Their hearing in 1977 over the Gospel Hump is similar to the 1992 hearing in which I testified over the Clearwater Country's Wilderness Bill that faltered and was withdrawn. Senator James McClure grills Dennis over high-elevation lake fish stocking. Dennis, voicing then the position he still holds today, says that the Sierra Club will not move to prevent stocking of high-elevation lakes.

I talk to Dennis later, ask him about the hearing, and tell him I think all the battles are the same, and basically endless. He agrees. "What you don't see in the hearing minutes is that half the sheriff's department of

Idaho County was on stage with Senator Church. There were armed wacko, Militia-types outside the building, and other locals with a gallows for Frank Church on the back of a pick-up truck."

A year has passed. Larry LaRocco, Dennis's moderate Democratic friend, has lost the 1994 election. North Idahoans have elected in his place an extreme right-wing candidate, Helen Chenoweth.

Chenoweth's various goals include gutting the Endangered Species Act, removing the public participation process in managing our national forests, and undesignating wilderness areas. She is my worst nightmare, financed by the timber and mining industries. She panders shamelessly to the fear running through small communities around the edge of the national lands, towns already in economic transition, talking about the outside destroyers of "custom and culture," those environmentalists. She writes legislation to increase logging in the national forests. She sees no future for Idaho except more logging, more mining, more destruction. She is the worst, paranoid incarnation of federally subsidized frontier entitlement mentality come to roost. She is one of those Westerners who argue that the government owes the people a living while demanding that the government get out.

I talk to Dennis for a moment in his office. "I told you, and you didn't believe me," he says. "We should have all supported LaRocco's wilderness bill. That would have been 1.25 million acres of country that we wouldn't have to worry about now."

Dennis, by anybody's book, is a mainstream, moderate environmentalist. Maybe Dennis's real point is not to compromise values on the land. Maybe we must look for different ways to protect landscapes other than the Wilderness Act. Maybe the real lesson is that the environmental community has spent too much time in the courts over the past fifteen years, and hasn't organized enough, led hikes, moved the people to want to save these places. Maybe the fight isn't going to be over whether we ever get a wilderness bill for the Clearwater Country—it will go on all our lives. And maybe the real message is this: without influencing the people who make the law, seeking justice under the law only leads to power-brokers changing the law.

Meadow Creek Canyon.

Unless otherwise noted, all photos are by the author.

Fishing in the cool waters of White Sand Creek. *Gerry Snyder photo.*

The meandering Hoodoo Creek in the high mountains of the Powell Ranger District. *Gerry Snyder photo.*

Lodgepole snags on Cook Mountain.

Ranger Peak on the Bitterroot Crest, overlooking White Sand Creek.

Black Lake in the Mallard-Larkins Pioneer Area.

Lodgepole, hot in the summertime.

Vanderbilt Gulch, headwaters of the North Fork of the Clearwater River.

Kelly Creek through Hanson Meadows.

Weitas Creek, looking up toward burned highlands.

Potlatch Corporation lands adjacent to Dworshak Reservoir.

Sheep Mountain clearcuts on the North Fork Ranger District of the Clearwater National Forest.

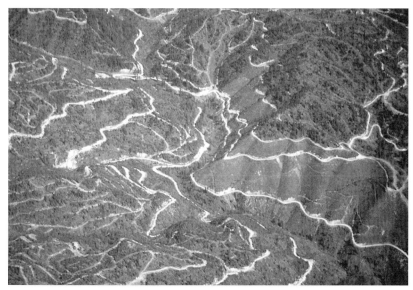

"Subdivision" roading on Potlatch Corporation lands adjacent to Dworshak Reservoir. *Gerry Snyder photo.*

Dworshak Reservoir in winter, with clearcuts covered in snow. *Gerry Snyder photo.*

Hidden Creek fire salvage project on the Upper North Fork of the Clearwater River in the North Fork Ranger District. *Gerry Snyder photo.*

A Plum Creek Corporation timber harvesting clearcut within the mixed ownership of the Powell Ranger District. *Gerry Snyder photo.*

Logs from the North Fork of the Clearwater River destined for the mill. *Gerry Snyder photo.*

Plum Creek Corporation clearcuts on lower White Sand Creek. *Gerry Snyder photo.*

Plum Creek Corporation mile-square clearcuts on the northern edge of the Mallard-Larkins Pioneer Area.

Bald Mountain "nuclear zone" on the Palouse Ranger District of the Clearwater National Forest. *Gerry Snyder photo.*

Stony Creek landslide on Potlatch Corporation lands adjacent to the Floodwood State Forest. *Gerry Snyder photo.*

Road blowout on Isabella Creek, down from the Mallard-Larkins Pioneer Area.

Landslide-scoured streambed and debris dam. *Gerry Snyder photo.*

The author and Ponderosa pine on Meadow Creek.

Good Old Bill Bob

Every species makes its own farewell to the human partners who have served it so ill. I...will finish with a Brazilian parrot, Spix's macaw. It is the most endangered bird in the world, and one of the most beautiful: totally blue, darkest on top, with a greenish tinge on the belly, black mask around the lemon-yellow eye. The species, *Cyanopsitta spixii,* is so distinctive that it has been placed in its own genus. Never common, it was limited to palm groves and river-edge woodland across southern Para' to Bahia near the center of Brazil. It was driven to extreme rareness by bird fanciers, who near the end, in the mid-1980's, were paying up to $40,000 for a single bird. The Brazilians hunting Spix's macaw say that the decline was hastened by imported Africanized bees, whose colonies occupy the tree holes favored by the macaw. Their claim is self-serving but has the ring of truth. It is plausible natural history and therefore too far-fetched for the ordinary imagination. In any case, the collectors and their suppliers were the killing force. By 1987 four birds were left in the wild, and by late 1990 only a single male. This last Spix's macaw, according to Tony Juniper of the International Council for Bird Preservation, is "desperate to breed. It is investigating nesting holes and showing all the signs of breeding behavior." At last report, the male has paired with a female Illiger's macaw (*Ara maracana*). No hybrids are expected.

-E.O. Wilson, *The Diversity of Life*

IT IS MID-SEPTEMBER, and the air—cool, clean in the morning, hot in the afternoon—feels like fall in the evening. I can even see the days shorten from more than sixteen hours of daylight in July down to only twelve. I am meeting my friend Bill Haskins, a fellow environmental activist, founder of the Ecology Center in Missoula, on the North Fork of the Clearwater this weekend. He is driving over from Montana, the long way through Superior. We are going to do a clearcut tour from hell. And if we have time, we may take a little hike.

Beyond Orofino, I drive along the twisty road along the Clearwater River to Greer, then up the Greer Grade to Weippe, by Lolo Creek. The drive fades into slow misery as the well-tended wheat farms give way to poorly managed timberlands and worse, on the road to Pierce. One mauled farm/woodlot has roads lacing a small stand of timber, with dirt and slash everywhere. God, those trees couldn't be more than sixty years old, I think. The skidder operator wasn't careful. He just drove his old D-8 up to the downed trees and dragged them in a straight line to the waiting semi.

I drive through Pierce, a true timber town, ringed by clearcuts, big ones, with one of Potlatch's running about two miles. They have a nicely printed sign in front of the clearcut, giving the date and some bizarre description of silvicultural practice, similar to others I have seen in timber country. Lately, the bigger corporations seem to have dispensed with the beauty strip, the artificial belt of trees running along the highway that hid the clearcuts from the insulated motorist. I am sure that the beauty strip was not popular with the absentee landlords. The media campaign mounted by most of these big operators—Potlatch, Boise-Cascade, Plum Creek, whose corporate slogan is "Where every day is Earth Day"—was probably a cheaper way to fool the public than leaving a little timber. But it could also be that they ran out of old-growth trees, and suddenly those big pickles by the roads mattered to the corporate bottom line. To hell with illusion—this is money. The sign on this back road into a forgotten part of America will most likely be read by few who are not already receptive to the message. Potlatch knows that this spot is way off the interstate, and the sign weakly justifies the management. But the only effort required to make this monster cut was someone to direct the surveyors who laid out the plot, the loggers who cut all of the trees down, and the burn crew who came in with their drip torches to burn the slash. The only forestry done was by accountants with a timber stocking survey.

Pierce passes quickly, mostly bars and a small grocery: a coal town without the coal. I smell no soot in the air, just a passing breeze of pine, or maybe cedar bark fallen off a logging truck, remnants of a recent sale. Maybe the trees surrounding Pierce are putting off the scent, but I am inclined to believe that it is the smell of loss of place, of quiet catastrophe abandoned now by humans for another sixty to eighty years, save maybe for a brief episode of replanting and thinning. There are many other living things starving and dying tonight, even though they cannot scream.

Headquarters is next, old timber sheds, the Clearwater Timber Protection bunch, a little Forest Service activity, and signs noting the twenty-some odd mile drive through the Beaver Block to the North Fork. The Beaver Block, rich forest in times past, is hammered now, an island of

Forest Service land surrounded by the Potlatch nuclear zone. There is a sign back at the Jaype mill, outside of Pierce, that I remember at this point, saying something to the effect that I should be thankful that this forest has been destroyed, because now there are roads here. As I drive by the Forest Service cuts, I am not even shocked by the clearcuts further on down by the river. I have seen too many, have become inured. I sometimes look at places, forests lost, and smile, as if holding the higher moral ground on any issue is the same as winning.

It is dark by the time I reach the North Fork and the Aquarius campground. Bill corners me with his junky four-wheel drive rig, smiles, and shines his brights in my face. We drive down the river road, pull off on a turnout, and drink beers across from the Aquarius Research Natural Area. Big green, even in the dark, and God, it is beautiful. The stars are out tonight, and I like watching them from my lawn chair with a beer in my hand. The corporate powers-that-be may deprive me of my forest, but they cannot take the stars above my head.

Morning comes, along with a quick breakfast. We have a long day planned. The first stop is across the river from the Aquarius campground. I walk over to a logging landing for the just-cut Steep Creek sale on the North Fork District of the Clearwater National Forest. Bill accompanies me. "Here, look over the edge," Bill says. "I want you to tell me where you think the edge of the creek starts."

I look over the berm of slash, disposed asphalt, and fill dirt. A small secondary channel flows at the foot of the landing through a bog filled with the scent of butchered cedar and leaded gasoline from Bill's twenty-year-old four-wheel drive.

"In the environmental assessment for this project, they said they would use existing landings 100 feet from streams," he says, as he scuffs the dirt below the heel of his black logging boots. It is late September and a dry year. Water is lapping the tips of our toes, eroding the bottom edge of the platform. "Kind of makes you think they don't give a rat's ass, doesn't it." Bill is quiet as he dons his camera, an old medium-format Pentax, around his neck. He looks up at me with bright blue eyes, burning intelligence behind a facade of shabby flannel and denim. We lock up the rig and walk up Road 6061 for a top-view of the sale.

The Steep Creek sale was first proposed in 1990 with an extension of a Potlatch road across Steep Creek, a small tributary of Beaver Creek adjacent to the North Fork of the Clearwater River, to access a stand of big, old-growth timber. Steep Creek lies in a valley-pocket of coastal disjunct habitat—wet, maritime weather supporting species isolated from Pacific cousins by dry desert and geologic time. Two places left in north-central Idaho contain these types of plants: here, and at the bottom canyon of the Selway River. There used to be much more, running along the banks of the North Fork down into Orofino, but most of that coastal disjunct habitat type was taken out by Dworshak Reservoir. Here, in these isolated pockets, bank monkeyflower, California sedge, western starflower, and crinkle-awn fescue still maintain a foothold. Coastal disjunct areas also grow huge trees, brothers of Cascade mountain giants. Towering cedars, grand fir, Douglas fir, and larch shelter the forest floor from the sun, retaining moisture late into the dry fall. We walk silently, down off the road. The ground under the trees is spongy, thick with humus and decayed matter, but clean—everything always seems clean in an old-growth stand. We then walk to an adjacent clearcut, part of an older sale across Beaver Creek from Steep Creek.

"This is a good place to stop," I remark. Bill laughs, says that this is not a good place at all, but it is *the* place to stop. We are in the middle of a clearcut, a forty-acre checkerboard square, tip-to-tip against another clearcut up the hill. The National Forest Management Act's text states openings in the forest canopy can be no larger than forty acres total. The Forest Service abides by the letter of the law, but not the spirit. These openings are neatly catty-cornered together, a vicious tic-tac-toe game sprawling across a muddy hillside.

We move on and stop when we have a view across Beaver Creek. Bill comments that the size of this facing unit is at least twice what was specified in the environmental assessment. The cutting units were supposed to be strips, not apple-pie shaped units. Bill props his hand-me-down back pack between his ankles and sighs.

The son of a professor, Bill grew up in Lincoln, Nebraska. After graduating from the University of Nebraska, he worked in Lincoln, followed by a move to Berkeley, California, where he met Mike Roselle, co-founder of Earth First!. Intrigued by the rainforest issue, he started giving large amounts of his salary as lab assistant in the molecular biology department to the Earth First! Direct Action Fund.

After leaving Berkeley, Bill moved to Missoula and attended the University of Montana, studying for a master's degree in environmental studies. He joined the Environmental Studies Advocates, a group of students, closet members of Earth First!, who had control of a small portion of student funds from the University of Montana. He also started associating with other Missoula grassroots groups—the Alliance for the Wild Rockies and the Native Forest Network. In 1989, he founded the Ecology Center of Missoula. Based on the Ecology Center at Berkeley, the Center served as a clearinghouse for all sorts of environmental issues. He also started Recycle Missoula, driving the garbage truck through the university neighborhood once a week, providing Missoula's first curbside recycling service.

Sara Seeds, a peace activist and one of the organizers of the group, Seeds of Peace, once told me "there's no better way to get the FBI interested in you than to get in the way of money." Bill found this out the hard way when his house was raided in 1989 by the FBI searching for evidence in a tree spiking incident on the Clearwater National Forest. The incident involved the Post Office timber sale, where several dozen spikes and nails were pounded into a few dozen trees scattered around a small amount of acreage. Bill believes the reason for the raid was connected to a trip to the Powell Ranger Station, where he, John Lilburn, and Jennifer Johnson had asked questions about old growth within a few days of when the ranger district had received a typed letter notifying it of the tree spiking of the sale. John and Jennifer's house had been raided as well. Bill had no connection to the tree spikings. "They put two and two together," Bill says, "came up with five, and kicked in the door." The FBI took books, diaries, and shoes. At the end of the raid, the house was a mess. The FBI and Forest Service team, supervised by special agents Mike Merkeley and Tom King, found nothing. Their household possessions were returned three years later.

That spring of 1990, the University of Montana's School of Forestry had its annual Boondocker's Day, a local logging celebration, replete with ax throwing, spur climbing, and log sawing competitions. The environmental studies group decided to put on its own version of the event, though its individual competitions were decidedly different. Slogan chanting, letter-writing, survey-stake pulling, and tree-spiking provided the main venue, causing the competition to play larger-than-life in the state's right-wing newspapers. Boondocker's Day coincided with the time the state legislature scrutinized the university's budget. Alternate Boondocker's day wasn't popular only with students—the other primary attendees were FBI and Forest Service law enforcement. The "suits" with dark glasses and shoulder holster bulges were everywhere, obtrusively taking everyone's photograph and recording license plates. Even special agent King was there, in his bright yellow suit.

Soon after, nine people attending the event received subpoenas from a grand jury in Boise, investigating the Post Office sale spikings. The activists, besides being fingerprinted, were forced to write slogans like "Hayduke lives" in print and cursive twenty times each for handwriting analysis, even though the comparative evidence for the spikings was a typed letter and phrases spray-painted on trees. The official harassment of the Ecology Center ended with the subpoenas. The Post Office tree-spiking was traced to a young man named Scott Spicer a number of years later, found guilty only after testimony from his common-law wife.

The U.S. Forest Service has always attempted to appear as a progressive agency. Throughout its history, the USFS has allowed administrative appeals, whereby citizens who did not agree with its land management decisions could ask for review of these decisions by a level of management higher than where the decision was made, all the way up to the chief forester in Washington, D.C. Additionally, there was no charge for filing an appeal—anyone could state their case and have the possibility of justice, or at least review. Until the mid '80's, the appeals process was relatively unused. When the process was starting to be used effectively, in the early '90s, to stop hundreds of timber sales that violated the National Forest Management Act (NFMA) and the National Environmental Policy Act (NEPA), congressional delegations from Western states and individuals inside the Forest Service called for abolition of the administrative appeals process. The end result was not quite what was expected; where formerly the appeals process had been a statute enacted by the agency, Congress responded by revising and formally enacting an appeals process for Forest Service activities.

Even with formalization of an appeals process by Congress, the system has fallen on hard times. More and more citizens are writing appeals and criticizing Forest Service opinions. However, appeals are now only heard on the regional level, and cannot be carried to the office of the chief forester. This change in process has effectively silenced the concerns of citizen activists. Of 586 appeals submitted in the first six months of 1994, only four were upheld by the appeals officers nationwide, and only one involved a timber sale. The rest involved protests by off-road vehicle users denied access.

It is not that the appeals don't necessarily have merit. Instead, the Forest Service has decided to tell the citizenry of this country to sue it in a court of law if the people don't like what it is doing. This of course puts justice out of the hands of most folks. It costs approximately $25,000 to take the Forest Service to task in the Ninth U.S. Circuit Court of Appeals.

Bill used the citizen's administrative appeal process four times to attempt to stop the Steep Creek project, a classic "zombie" timber sale—one that keeps coming back from the dead. His first appeal, as well as the following three, raised the issue of sensitive species and survival. One of the goals announced in the environmental assessment for the timber sale was to conduct "experiments" on the coastal disjunct sensitive species to determine the effects of logging on these plants. Bill objected to the thought of subjecting the area to a formal experiment on rare plants found only in one other place in northern Idaho. Bill noted that besides the unethical notion of doing experiments on rare plants, the procedures were set up poorly. There were no control groups, and the logging prescriptions for the sale called for dramatic modification of the environment by virtual clearcutting. The heat and dryness alone, noticeable even as we walk into the opening, would preclude survival of most of these plants, even without the catastrophic influence of felling trees and stamping the soil into oblivion.

Bill won the first appeal, on the basis of a lack of analysis on how the sale would affect the surrounding area, a procedure called cumulative effects analysis. After some small revision, the Forest Service resurrected the project and resubmitted it for public scrutiny. Bill appealed this version and won, because of a change in forest supervisors and the emergence of the old-growth issue on the Clearwater. The Forest Service modified the sale again, and released another final environmental impact statement (EIS). Bill appealed again, noting that an expanded sensitive species list had been released by Forest Service biologists, and crinkle-awn fescue, a recent addition to that list, had not been surveyed on the sale site. By the time the Forest Service released the fourth version of the EIS, Bill had, in effect, worked all the legal deficiencies out of the sale document, and the sale went through.

Before Bill appeals a sale, he always walks the site, making notes for the legal document to follow. Bill was out on Steep Creek when he heard in the distance a pileated woodpecker. He followed the call, running through the woods, finally spotting its ancient pterodactyl head flitting on top of its huge, prehistoric body. Bill was tracking with his camera, closing for a shot when he heard, then saw, a pair of goshawks flapping back and forth in a big Douglas fir in front of him.

Goshawks are large accipiters, stubby-winged, long-tailed birds, the fighter-bombers of the hawk community. They do not cut lazy circles in the sky above expansive prairie and mountaintop. Instead, their niche is pulling tight slalom turns through thick forest, using their exceptional senses to locate prey on the forest floor. Black masks across their eyes, they have pearly-white and speckled breasts, with light gray backs. Goshawks nest halfway up large Douglas firs, above the bole in the first huge branches needed to support their twig and straw homes. During nesting season, late June to August, they will dive-bomb an approaching person's head. The birds will keep this up for a while, attempting to drive the transgressor away. They abandon their nest eventually, only if pressure and the immediate threat is too great.

Bill saw the band across the eye, the light underbelly, and stopped. He tried to take photos, but feeling intrusive, left and recorded the finding in the third appeal. Goshawks are rare and belong on the sensitive species list. They are not. They are, however, listed as an indicator species. Where one finds goshawks, one finds intact old growth, remnants of the continuous forest that used to roll over the hills of the lower Clearwater country.

Bill traveled again to the site before writing his fourth appeal of the sale. He was walking a sale unit when a goshawk went after his hat. Excited, he took pictures during the goshawk's alarm call. Upon returning to Missoula, Bill sent a letter to Dan Davis, forest biologist, and Art Bourassa, the district ranger in charge of the North Fork District. He informed them of the goshawks, and because the timber sale contract stipulated that any goshawks noted would result in a five-acre patch around any nest site, he wanted to know what they were going to do to mitigate damage. Incidentally, that summer, the Forest Service had contracted with an ornithologist to perform a neotropical migratory bird census. Piggybacked on top of that was a goshawk survey. The ornithologist put out 500 calling stations to locate goshawks. The expert, working mainly from roads, had located none. Bill, after a short walk into a sale unit, had located one in thirty minutes.

Johnna Roy, the district biologist, promised that she would look for the sighted goshawk. Dan Davis went with her. The pair found nothing. Bill insisted on his sighting. To appease him, both Dan and Johnna offered to go out with him on a Saturday. Bill and the biologists climbed to the top of the ridge and sale unit boundary, and activated a tape recorder with an attached bullhorn playing a goshawk call. A goshawk called back immediately. Dan made a remark that it was probably a jay. At that moment, a large goshawk swooped into view and perched on a low branch twenty yards from the trio. Dan and Johnna, excited, tried to find the nest. However, there had been a storm recently—it was August and nesting season was past. The nest had probably blown down. The conclusion, though, was the same—no nest, no foul, no provision to protect the habitat. The trees fell to the chainsaw the following winter of 1994.

We are looking at the clearcut now. Bill tells me they call this an irregular shelterwood cut. Clearcut, shelterwood cut, the trees are gone. All I can see is spindly trees dotting a clearing, bright sun on red soil, and logging slash, ugly against the green ridge. One thing is certain: no goshawks will nest there for a long time. I stand on my feet, staring, my eyes burning. I am watching extinction happen.

We return to our car. There is a dead coyote, freshly killed, lying in the road. Mary barks as Bill flips the carcass. No bullet hole. It must have been hit by a truck. Bill drags the body into the bushes.

We drive up the Smith Ridge Road to the next stop on the clearcut tour, the Lower Salmon sale, high on top of Smith Ridge crossing Salmon Creek. The drop is precipitous, 1,500 feet down to the North Fork. The clearcuts are near vertical, cut and burned almost down to the river. We arrive at the gate to inspect the sale. It is locked, so we defer the hike. Bill tells me the story.

The Lower Salmon sale, all fourteen million board-feet of it, was nearly cut by the spring of 1994. Then, in late May, weather patterns produced a microburst, a short violent windstorm localized in a few hundred acres in the bottom of the North Fork of the Clearwater Canyon. Bill describes it as if the jet stream dips down to the earth for a few minutes. It made one hell of a mess, starting on the south side of the river, jumping over, and knocking down 150-year-old grand firs like jackstraws. The burst flattened more than fifteen acres. Bill could barely walk through the jumble of trunks surrounding the clearcuts.

Bill had found out about the blowdown by his standard monitoring of timber sale contracts. For some reason, the Lower Salmon sale contract had mysteriously been sent back for revision. Bill traveled to the sale site in early August, 1994. The sale was an old-fashioned volume grab that had been prepared in the mid '80s with plenty of clearcuts—the logging operators were working away cutting trees right down to the banks of small streams flowing through the cutting units. Scars raked the land where logs had been yarded through the creek bottom. The plan to salvage the blowdown timber had been arranged in secret between the logging operators and the Forest Service. The Forest Service had claimed no additional impacts for the sale of the blowdown, even though the microburst had knocked down timber over a number of small creeks in the sale area. Bill had previously requested the contracts for the sale, but there was no contract. He looked at two of the units, determined that trees had been cut directly out of the bottom of two streams, and discovered one stream where logs were laying in the muddy creek bed. One quarter mile away, the same streams were carrying eroded soil straight down into the North Fork river.

Upon returning to Missoula, Bill wrote a long letter to the District Ranger, requesting any documents relating to revising the environmental assessment for the sale. Months later, Bill had yet to receive an answer, only a cryptic message from Art on the Ecology Center answering machine, from a field telephone, saying "ZZSZTZZ, Art Bourassa, ZZTSTSZ, can't talk now, ZZTSX, fires."

After lunch and a beer at the Lower Salmon gate, Bill and I decide that we are tired of clearcuts today. In our separate trucks, we bounce down the road, dodging rocks on the right-of-way thrown from mini-road blow-outs. Once at the bottom, it is a short path back up Isabella Creek, land of the giant uncut cedars, and only a short road to the edge of the land and a hike into the Heritage Grove. We will walk in two miles to spend the night. Unlike the desertified checkerboard, the magic has not run out of the land here.

Packs on, we hike the two short miles from the trail head, with Mary, my border collie, carrying a bottle of sour mash whiskey in her panniers, safely wrapped in a raincoat. We make camp under the big trees. The sky is gray. I pitch a tent and fly. We cook dehydrated refried beans, spicy pintos with Swiss cheese. Stars come out with the sour mash. We drink, talk about trees, then women, then trees again. We sink into the thick duff on the bottom of the grove, lower body, torso, then shoulders and head, fading into slow conversations. Isabella Creek rumbles in the background, on her way to the North Fork of the Clearwater and the sea.

Bill and I are up early today. We pack and eat quickly. Soon we are out of the grove, back at the rigs. We drive up the river to Weitas Creek, home of the largest elk herd on the Clearwater, and penetrated by only two marginal roads, unused except in hunting season. We have planned a short hike up the creek before parting, and it is a good day for it—fall, yellow sun, small white cumulus, a cool, terrycloth breeze to wipe the sweat on the uphill climbs.

We start. The signs are not good. The trail is broad enough for a four-wheel all-terrain vehicle. There are tire tracks. We make the usual jokes about motorized trail use before bursting out of the entrance grove onto the creek. The east side is burned, scrub ceanothus and regenerating white pine. The west is dark and cool, forest reaching up to weathered highlands, sunshine resting on the backs of grand fir. Bill notices them first: red flash against smooth burnt sienna. We scramble down the banks for a closer look. The kokanee, a landlocked version of the sockeye salmon, have come up into Weitas Creek for shelter in cool waters during the middle of the day. With green parrot faces and slick red backs, they waver like kelp in a rising tide, dormant behind rocks in schools of forty fish. Bill, in the natural world, is smiling.

We walk along, up the trail, away from the creek, stopping at a small opening in the thick forest canopy. The water, now below us, is a braided meander, stretching its shoulders a hundred yards from side to side of the U-shape canyon. I remark to Bill on the relative difficulty of even seeing a stretch of water like the one below us. Most rivers with this type of canyon and level gradient are buried now beneath the country's innumerable dams. Bill, winsome, nods. After the trail drops down off the mountainside, we stop for lunch. Bill and I are talking about the kokanee again. I tell him about my thousand-year plan.

We stare at the water as I spin my thoughts, braiding them with the story of the creek. Two hundred years from now, Dworshak Reservoir will be filled with silt. Cascading down the front of the dam is the North Fork, clear, powerful, and erosive. Cracks open. The river, knowing only its own mind, picks one. The crack widens, urged on by hard winters and ice. Four hundred more years pass. Soon, the river is at the toe of the dam. The concrete is cold and solid. The river uses an abrasive cutting edge—six hundred years of silt, mica, and schist. Trees are growing on the bank again; the bathtub ring left by the reservoir is visible only behind moss on the Belt Rocks.

A spring flood, the two-hundred-statistical-year-visitor, arrives, child of a large snowpack on Windy Ridge, Weitas Butte, and the lower Cayuse Country. It screams, hissing, rolling down the canyon. The adult kokanee cling behind their rocks, a restless sleep on the river bottoms. Their smolts are blown out to the Clearwater, then down the Snake, Columbia, and out to the sea. Many die; two return, transformed into sockeye, kokanee no longer. They swim up Weitas Creek, spawning in the gravels of a new, small lake in Hemlock Creek. Salmon have returned to the Weitas drainage.

Bill smiles, unkempt whiskers sticking out above his beard, off his cheekbones. "I see," he says. "Alright, Chuck, what about the king salmon?"

"Ah," I exclaim. "Let me tell you about the ten-thousand-year plan." Bill leans back on a rounded rock and laughs.

There in the sunlight above is an osprey, creamy white, with a brown mask and sharply cut dihedral wings, medicine man of the fish. He circles a shallow pool. The fish wave like flags in the liquid breeze. Then splash, the contact of talon to red scale, with sharp claws slipping under backbone. The fish's mouth gapes reflexively as the osprey is airborne, carrying an orange marker of a successful catch to roost.

Uncle LeRoy

"Now this is an example of good forestry," LeRoy says as we walk through a recently logged stand on state ground outside of Deary. "They make this kind of showpiece so they can bring the dignitaries out here. Be nice if they left this alone for twenty years, maybe underburn it to take out the understory grand fir that's going to come up. Either that, or murder all of them with a chainsaw. No way that they will, though." We walk through wet November snow on a site logged twice in its short, white man history. "They'd probably call this a selective cut, though I think I'd call it a pure shelterwood." We move further back in the stand, and see a marker for an adjacent University of Idaho study site. The canopy overhead, once open, is now closed. On the previous site there was open sky all the way up. Here, tree branches touch tree branches twenty feet above. "Now this is a truer version of what I call a selective cut." The trees are much thicker, continuous. There are hardly any signs of activity. "I don't mind this logging job at all." When I ask him what he means, LeRoy slings an imaginary cable over his shoulder. "This guy didn't just drive his log skidder all over the place like a lot of them do. He kept it on the road, and dragged the cable from the winch by hand to the downed logs, then winched them out. That's hard work. See, no tire tracks." That means no soil compaction, no tamping down the earth to the consistency of asphalt. Trees can grow here again.

Back on the state sale side, LeRoy gets out his increment borer, a small, sharpened, narrow pipe of surgical steel used to pull out a tree ring core, and takes a sample from the tree. "Some renewed growth here from this thinning." He twists the borer in another tree. "I've bored over 20,000 trees in my lifetime." LeRoy's wrists and elbow are swollen with tendonitis from cruising timber all summer. He grimaces, turning the borer, waiting for the Ibuprofen to kick in. "A stable configuration for this stand would be cedar, larch, maybe some ponderosa pine, with an understory burn every ten years." Young grand firs are shooting up around us. "If they don't do anything to take care of these, we'll have a replay of the Blue Mountains—a trash tree like grand fir taking over the stand. Normally, fire moving through here would take out these." LeRoy points out blister rust on a white pine, showing me a red flag branch, burnt-orange needles on a dead stem, twenty feet up. We walk back to the truck.

LeRoy Lee, Uncle I call him—my term of endearment for anyone attempting to educate me—has been one of my teachers in forestry. He is an unlikely sort—late thirties, two kids, and two black pigtails. Every time our circle talks about the beginning of anything having to do with the environmental movement in the late '70s and early '80s, LeRoy was there. Big Mountain on the Navajo Res? Some of the first Earth First! actions in the Kalmiopsis? Herbicide spraying in North Idaho? LeRoy was there.

"I was a hippie road dog," LeRoy says. "When I got out of high school, I hitchhiked all over the Lower 48, eating out of garbage cans and sleeping in the bushes." After a stint in a Texas community college, where he got married and had his first child, LeRoy dropped out, sold everything, bought a bus, and headed for Idaho. There, he hooked up with the Rainbow Family, a New Age movement forming at that time. He traveled around with them for a while, until 1980, when his school bus/home broke down in St. Maries, Idaho. "No brakes going down the Thorn Creek hill with twelve hippies—lucky there wasn't anyone on the street when we hit the middle of town." At the Rainbow Gathering, he met people fighting the widespread spraying of herbicide across sixty thousand acres for brush control outside of Avery, Idaho. LeRoy, the Rainbozos, and the Rainbozettes occupied the site in protest. "We were Earth First! before Earth First!" he says. After the action, they got the bus fixed and camped out in the woods, eventually finding a piece of land where they could permanently park the bus.

But LeRoy soon parted company with the Rainbow Family. "The last Rainbow gathering I attended was at a Native American sacred site. Representatives from the tribe came to us and asked us not to have the gathering there. As far as the organization went, it would have been very difficult for us to change our plans. There were twenty thousand Rainbows on their way. The natives then asked us to have the gathering at least the very best way that we could. There was one particular ridge, connected to a peak that they had used for vision quests and other ceremonies that they didn't want us to occupy. During the gathering, a peace sign was spray-painted on the peak, and one of their fasting pits was used as a latrine. After the gathering, I was on the clean-up crew. Twenty thousand 'ecologists' left twenty-five people to clean up after them. As far as I am concerned, we took the very worst that our culture has to offer to that sacred place." LeRoy never went to another Rainbow gathering again.

After his falling-out with the Rainbows, LeRoy started spending more and more time on reservations across the West. LeRoy was at Big Mountain on the Navajo Reservation when Peabody Coal was forcibly relocating the sheepherders off their ancient grazing lands. He spent a winter helping out the tribe. "I was pretty popular," he says. "I think that I had the only chainsaw for a hundred miles."

"All my environmental activism has been driven by spirituality," LeRoy says. "The woods have taught me, and Native American words have guided me. I lived for ten years with no electricity or running water. For two winters, I had to walk four miles from the nearest road to get to my teepee. When you live like that, you get a lot of respect for a cup of water, a stick of firewood, or a bowl of rice. Without that connection, it is hard to have a real appreciation for clean water and a warm house. When I was living out there in the woods, all of the time I would hear the trees talking, the creeks singing. We're taught to discount that. When I hear Indians sing, I know where their songs come from."

Driving down Idaho 8, just before Bovill, we turn left at the sign for Moose Creek Reservoir. Surrounding us is a second-growth lodgepole forest, maybe seventy years old. "Bovill lodgepole," LeRoy says. "This site used to be all white pine and mixed conifer. Then they cut the big old forest down—the timber volume was thirty thousand board-foot per acre, maybe more. Now the only thing that comes back is lodgepole—maybe seven thousand board-foot per acre, probably a little more." We are looking out over five square miles of lodgepole seedlings. "Did they replant this with all this lodgepole?" I ask. "No, they probably planted white pine, but the blister rust came in and knocked them off. They might have planted Doug fir. I'm not sure. Frost causes top kill for all the other species: grand fir, Doug fir, tamarack. There is a huge frost pocket here—lodgepole are hardier, and aren't affected. Without the protection of the overstory, the other species die."

"You'd think that the timber folks would learn. The same thing happened in the 'teens and 'twenties, as part of the Marble Creek gold rush up on the St. Joe. They chopped down the big, mixed conifer forest—lodgepole came up. Now they cut all the lodgepole, hoping for better things, replanting different species, but another lodgepole plantation just returns. "We are standing in the center of a section of state ground. Looking at the map, there are a variety of timber ownerships within our purview—Bennett tree farms and a little Potlatch ground—but similar stories. The state ground has been recently thinned, LeRoy comments. This is better in a relative sense. But to me, it still looks like five years after a nuclear explosion. Second growth tamarack covers the hillside in the distance. I ask LeRoy why tamarack, why there? LeRoy shrugs. "There are so many variables, we don't even know what they are."

"So what do you say, Chuck? What do you even do with a place like this? Do we say 'go ahead' with the bug infestation and eventual catastrophic fire? Do we thin and let grand fir come up? The system's been tweaked so bad. Is preservation even an option?" I shrug my shoulders. "I don't know either," says LeRoy. "My gut reaction is to save as much as possible for as long as possible, for watershed and wildlife if nothing else. Maybe some harvest. The average environmentalist would see trees here, and want to save it all. But you can see that it's a long way from being an intact forest—it's a single species monoculture. We're paying the piper for past bad land management practices. Our practices have reduced the ability of the land to grow trees."

The trees at the edge are thick—lodgepole. "If it were me, I'd nurture the ponderosa pine. They're frost resistant." LeRoy kicks a stump. A deer rifle shot rumbles in the distance. LeRoy is carrying his gun. We have coupled a little hunting with this outing. If we can get meat for the freezer this winter, we will.

After his arrival outside of Santa, Idaho, in 1980, LeRoy got jobs planting trees and working as a sawyer for Plum Creek, Potlatch, and various small gyppo logging outfits, small independent operators that contract to the bigger companies for jobs. He also started his career as a forest activist in North Idaho. He met John Osborn of the Inland Empire Public Lands Council in Spokane and started feeding John information about what was really going on in the woods. LeRoy also started working the NEPA process and commenting on timber sales.

One of the first timber sales where LeRoy went toe-to-toe with the Forest Service involved Dennis Ridge, a large sale on the St. Joe National Forest in 1983. The Forest Service had completed the NEPA process for the sale completely out of view of the public eye. LeRoy got almost every logger and farmer in Benewah County, about as rural and backcountry a county as there is in Idaho, to sign a petition against clearcutting in that timber sale. He had a newspaper letter war with the Forest Service in the St. Maries *Gazette*. The Forest Service had official press releases. LeRoy had his letters-to-the-editor. At the beginning of the fight, the Forest Service swore it would never change a sale. Because of LeRoy's pressure, it ended up eliminating some of the clearcutting and left buffers around the creeks in the cutting units. But negotiating with the Forest Service left a bad taste, compromises LeRoy later regretted. He let himself be talked out of more radical sale modification, both for future goodwill and also out of intimidation. "I found out later that the goodwill was worthless. The same problems surfaced in the future," he comments.

"Often, the small communities are not happy with the way that the big operators or the Forest Service run their operation in the woods," LeRoy says. "The gyppo loggers, who work primarily on contract for the big corporations, realize that they're getting ripped off every day—they're underpaid, or their logs are scaled low. Every now and then, the resentment reaches a boiling point," he comments. The scenario is always the same, and repeats itself. The small loggers hold public meetings, lobby the state for reforms, and apply public pressure by showing discontent to the company.

But, inevitably, the big corporations break the leaders of these revolutions. The companies won't buy their logs, or they will apply pressure to log truck drivers to refuse to haul the gyppos' timber. "The little guys get starved down to the point where resistance collapses. No one can afford to not work for very long," LeRoy says. "It so happened that the Dennis Ridge timber sale coincided with one of these revolutions."

After that timber sale and LeRoy's relatively successful protest, LeRoy was approached by a group of local loggers, and a committee was formed: Citizens for Future Forests. "We're in the Tensed Grange Hall," LeRoy says, "which was just about filled with loggers and farmers. At the table in the front were the officers in the group. One was a founding member of the Grange. Another was a small mill owner, one the president of the local cattlemen's association and a respected gyppo logger, and of course, myself. We agreed to restrict the group's mission to eliminating clearcuts—it was the only thing we could agree on. We got the local loggers bitching about the big companies overcutting, as well as clearcuts. We created an environment where all the loggers could stand up at one time and face down the big boys."

Though they managed to pack the Grange Hall a few times, in the end, the movement disintegrated. The group lost momentum over the winter and never regained it, and LeRoy still has regrets to this day. "The next summer, Bruce Vincent formed his 'Wise Use' group, Citizens for a Great Northwest, and they had their log caravan across the state," he remembers. "I keep thinking that if we could have made our group work, we could have replaced the 'Wise Use' movement."

In order to perform the task of planning timber harvest on the national forests, the Forest Service conducts inventories of available trees on all its lands. Surveys for all the parts of the national forests are routinely contracted out; such things as fish and stream surveys, bird studies, and timber assessments require a specialized staff that can only be employed during the summer months. LeRoy had started his own company, Tree Talk, to perform stand exams, which involves "cruising" a stretch of ground and estimating the amount of timber, as well as its condition, age, and species mix. The telltale sign of a timber cruiser is a vest covered with pockets and filled with tools such as an inclinometer for measuring slopes, an increment borer, a compass, a measuring tape, and a notepad.

Such work is not easy. Cruisers must walk cross-country across rugged terrain, much of which is filled with tangled second-growth timber and brush fields. The on-the-ground data gathered by a stand examiner is then correlated with other information, such as aerial photographs and old records, to estimate the volume of timber actually on the forest.

In many ways, the job of the stand examiner is one of the most important in the forest. His estimates determine the true productivity of the land and set the volume of annual cut to be allowed. The stand examiner's estimates determine if the national forest is managing its resources wisely, as well as whether the forest is operating under the principle of "sustained yield," which implies that the forest can continue producing a set volume of timber forever. The most important manifestation of this information, though, resides in a single number—the Allowable Sale Quantity, or ASQ. The ASQ is "the number" in the forest plan, the guiding document specified by the National Forest Management Act (NFMA) used to dictate how the land will be managed and how much timber will be cut in the ten-year period that the plan is supposed to be in effect.

Unfortunately, during the first round of forest planning, in the early- to mid-eighties, setting the ASQ primarily revolved around politics and local mill capacity. Instead of being a scientific estimate of a forest's productivity, it too often turned into a football tossed around in the small communities surrounding the national forests, as well as the corporate boardrooms and Senate offices in the far-off halls of Seattle, San Francisco, and Washington, D.C. A higher ASQ meant more trees to be cut now—more money, more jobs in the woods, more new pick-up trucks, and more profits for both the small mill operators in the local area as well as the timber megamagnates of Potlatch, Plum Creek, and Boise Cascade. Unfortunately, too many trees cut at once would also have greater environmental consequences—more silted streams, less old growth, less wildlife, more impact on sensitive species, and of course, more effect on long-term job prospects for the loggers in the small towns.

LeRoy was performing stand exams on the Avery District of the Panhandle National Forest when he started noticing discrepancies in volumes of timber between what the Forest Service officially said was there and what was actually on the ground. The Forest Service was listing "phantom forests" in their inventories to inflate harvest targets. Inflated inventories could be used to justify a higher level of cutting in the present—though it was obvious that such "cooking the books" would result in timber shortfalls in the future.

LeRoy showed that the national forests were keeping two sets of accounting documents: one involving FORPLAN, the predictive computer model that tracks current forest condition and estimates how much wood a given site would grow over time, would set the ASQ and ask Congress for money for appropriations (the more timber ostensibly produced, the greater the congressional appropriation for management); the second, the Forest Service Timber Stand Inventory database, actually indicated what trees were standing. Hundreds of clearcuts and reforestation failures across the Clearwater, Panhandle, and Kootenai forests—the entire Inland Northwest—were shown as either mature stands of timber ready to be cut, or successfully growing trees in the FORPLAN-generated estimates. The real amount of timber present, though, was much less, and this, recorded in the Timber Stand Inventory database, was used by the Forest Service for laying out timber sales.

LeRoy testified concerning his findings on February 27, 1992, before the House Appropriations Committee's interior subcommittee. "I walked every acre of that mountain [Pegleg Mountain, on the Avery District of the Panhandle National Forest], and I figured seven to ten thousand [board] feet of lodgepole pine per acre," LeRoy said. "When I was in the district office, I saw a map and what they said was there was twenty-two thousand board feet an acre—about two times what I told them." He rolled out his maps, his overlays, and his inventory data. By his estimates, many districts on the national forests would soon experience shortfalls in annual timber yields, measured in decades. For example, on the Palouse District of the Clearwater National Forest, the estimated shortfall was more than twenty-six years of output of timber.

In his testimony before Congress, he also spoke fair words about our responsibilities to our children:

> I am submitting this in the belief that the truth stands on its own. We need to confront the reality that we are not competing with "environmentalists" or with Japan for our timber. We are competing with our own children. It is a competition they cannot possibly win. It is my hope that when we as a nation see the situation in this light, we will be willing to make the sacrifices in our own lifestyles that will enable our children and their children to have a decent world to live in.

When LeRoy returned home to St. Maries after testifying in front of Congress, our activist community was buoyed. There was word of a General Accounting Office investigation. But this was followed by the news of suppression of such an investigation by Representative Larry LaRocco, who, later that year, would start the "Forest Health" ball rolling.

After backing down the slush covered road toward the reservoir, we let our dogs run behind my truck. We drive up the Vassar Connector road past a landowner whom LeRoy implicated in timber theft from state lands. The state just slapped the person's hand, LeRoy says. After passing a small divide, we walk back into a Forest Service irregular shelterwood cut. The area is ringed with blowdown. LeRoy says "This is the New Forestry." I smile, and say "meet the new boss, same as the old boss." "This is a mess," LeRoy says. "This is not a good job. See where they ran their skidders all over the place? Come over here. Look—see how bunged up their 'leave' trees are." I walk over to a red-barked larch in the center of the site, one of the trees left to reseed the area. I step over another downed larch laying next to it. The bark has been stripped off the standing tree on one side from someone felling another tree into it. Around the site is lots of logging damage. "See, another skidder trail." LeRoy points at the ground. "Bring your compact-o-meter out here, Chuck, and check soil compaction of the ground. If they leave this place alone for twenty or thirty years, it might recover. Not a chance, though." LeRoy sighs. "They'll be back in ten years," I say. "Maximum," LeRoy responds. "I'm not impressed. And the irony is, they're just doing this to please us, the 'progressive' community. The logger that did this is probably pretty proud, telling himself, 'I left some. I didn't take it all.'"

We move out of the cut, into the uncut timber around the opening. The stand is a mix, but barely: mostly grand fir, Doug fir, lodgepole, and the occasional larch and spruce. What would LeRoy do differently? "Not take out so many trees. The forester that laid out the sale was saying that in that last logging unit the species mix was unacceptable. The consequence was that he ordered all the trees chopped down." LeRoy pulls out his increment borer again. He looks up while he cranks the long slow draws into the center of a grand fir. "Ah ha!" he exclaims, glancing at the crowns. "Indian paint rot. See the conks?" I look at the shelves of fungus growing out of the tree. "From a logger's perspective, these trees are worthless. If we agree that we want to manage these for timber, the grand fir's going to have to go. Sixty-year-old stand," he says as he pulls another core. "What place on the planet do you want to grow wood for timber harvest? This is a good spot, close to the mills, next to a road, moderate gradient, no salmon, no live water, no grizzly bears, and no wolves. Just deer and loggers. Here, I would cut trees. I'd come in twice. Take the big stuff first. All the grand fir. Keep that spruce, here. It's got a lot of years left in it. We'd like to see more of these. All this grand fir, on the other hand—a trash tree, a legacy of past logging and fire suppression. And not only here, but all the way up to St. Maries and the Coeur d'Alenes."

We cross a small draw, into a stand of lodgepole. "It's easy to see how this kind of stuff gets perpetuated. If a guy comes in here and wants to make some money and not clearcut, he'd probably leave these big old rotten grand firs and take the smaller stuff. But if you just took the smaller trees out, you'd end up with a bunch of pure grand fir, and perpetuate this stand conversion problem. Plus, now you're genetically selecting for grand fir that is prone to rot and disease, because you're leaving behind the big ones with the Indian paint. Replanting would help, but you just can't replant and walk away. It would just get swallowed up by the grand fir."

We climb back in my F150. LeRoy points his finger out the window at a seed-tree cut—scattered small trees in a large opening. "The guy that did that probably called it a select cut. It's what I call cull-tree release. They leave the worst genetic stock to reseed the site and run down the gene pool. They took the best—if you keep doing that, you end up with the worst possible trees on the site after just a couple of generations." LeRoy talks about the Torrey Pines in southern California. The Torrey Pines were located on the coast, famous for their height and straightness for ship masts.

Ships damaged at sea would stop at the harbor, cut the straightest, tallest trees, strip them, and store them for masts on deck. After a couple hundred years, the straight and tall genes had disappeared from the gene pool, leaving only small, gnarled trees clinging to the coastline. "It's so picturesque, little Bonsai, Zen trees. We're doing the same thing to the grand fir in this country today. What is our forest going to look like one hundred years from now? A lot of rotten grand fir. Except around Bovill, we'll have lodgepole," LeRoy laughs.

This loss of biodiversity in this section of forest has real economic consequence to human communities. It is true that Doug fir, larch, and white pine are not going extinct in a global sense. But by depleting the genetic resource in this stretch of the land, the mixed conifer forest being annihilated and replaced with lodgepole and grand fir, money is lost over the long haul. Timberland that used to be capable of producing 30,000 board feet per acre is now reduced by a factor of two or even three, for hundreds of years.

We drive up Mica Mountain, looking for one of the few small groves of old-growth forest left on the Palouse District. We go in four-wheel drive, until the snow is so deep the center strip brushes up against the underside of the truck. We cannot find the big, old trees, but crest a rise to see the second-growth forest of the Palouse country stretched out beneath us. There are visible clearcuts below, but by and large the spaces have filled in from the destructive cutting legacy practiced by Potlatch and the Forest Service in the first part of this century. As LeRoy said, the system is corrupted: the species mix is wrong, the ecosystem unstable, the creeks barren of fish, and many filled with silt from decades of bad land management. But the forest is still here, even if it is mostly only grand fir and lodgepole.

The drive down the mountain is filled with cedar and larch. LeRoy waxes philosophical, tells me about his plan for the four revolutions to restore the earth. "We need four simultaneous revolutions. The first revolution needs to be the design revolution. Cars, houses, the way we make everything, the way we get energy—stupid. We do not need the materialistic concept of the highest possible standard of living to be happy. Which leads to the second revolution. An economic revolution. There have to be economic incentives for loggers to leave trees standing, for people to stop driving their cars, for McDonald's to wash plates. All the incentives are for people to consume. We need incentives for people to save."

"But in order for the economic revolution to happen, we first need to have the political revolution. The powers-that-be will never sit still for economic change because the status-quo favors them, even if there is no long-term future in it. But we're never going to have a political revolution, though, without the fourth, a spiritual revolution. We have to change our basic values to where our obligation to posterity overtakes our obligation to our present comfort level. Environmentalists, in all of our illustrious history, have only focused on the political revolution, which has only shifted the impacts away from the place we have concentrated on, and moved them to a place where we weren't watching. We have to change ourselves. It's so convenient to point the finger, to blame the loggers. How many of us have changed our lifestyle around? Someone's got to go first."

Doc

"HEY, UGLY," DOC SAYS, leaning out the window of his truck. "You ugly too," I tell him. I have come to the south side of Moscow Mountain to spend the day with Dr. Art Partridge, of the University of Idaho College of Forestry, the resident expert on forest pathology. This is field trip day, and Doc has brought his students along to dig through the soil, examine tree roots, and chop at log decks to increase their understanding of ecosystem function. Doc starts rambling down a small skidder trail in the U of I experimental forest. It's hard covering any distance with Doc. Though he is spry for his age, he has a detail man's eye for forest function. Wielding his pulaski, with the head painted day-glo orange, it isn't long until he is on his knees, chopping at a downed log.

"People cruise timber and make diagnoses about root rot by looking at the tops, the crowns of trees. I was flying over a stand of Doug fir with a Forest Service official, and he was looking down at the crowns. He turned to me, and told me that the trees below us were dead and dying, and would have to be cut down. At first glance the crowns were brown. But I looked a little harder. The reason that the crowns were brown was because the Doug fir had a huge cone crop that year. The brown was the cones. The trees were having one of the best years of their lives." Doc looks up at his students. "If you want to diagnose root disease, you have to dig in the ground." He takes a few more swipes at the roots of a grand fir. "No root disease here," he says.

The students gather around a log deck. Art is not just teaching ecosystem function today; he is teaching how to make a living. He digs at a pocket of rot in the heart of a cedar log, laying skewed in a pile. "Log landings are good places to diagnose stand condition. You can see many things inside a tree by looking at these cross-sections." He pulls out a handful of brown rot, crumbling into cubes in his small, rough hands. "Brown cubical rot," he says. "This stuff goes inactive when you cut the tree down." He grabs another handful of rot, this time whitish and stringy. "White laminate rot. This stuff stays active. Doesn't matter if the tree is chopped down."

We wander past the log deck, into the forest. Doc stops at a downed log, covered with rainbow conks. He points to lichens growing on a tree. Pale green and lacy, they cover the outside bark. I ask Doc if they hurt the trees. "Nope," Doc replies. "Lichens are nitrogen fixers. They help the soil. They're also an important food source for deer and many other wild animals. Clearcutting kills lichens. They're also very sensitive to air pollution. Lichens tell you something about the true health of the forest. If you have lots of lichens, you have a healthy forest." Art grabs a huge hunk of wet fungus from the outside of a dead trunk. "*Phaeolus Schweinitzii,*" he pronounces. "Look at how wet this stuff is. This holds the water up here, in the mountains. It lowers the chance that the wood will burn in the summer, and holds the rain on the ground. It breaks down the wood into the soil, the major recycler up here." Doc tells his students, mostly future silviculturalists, to consider how the whole ecosystem works. "Think, dammit, think!" he yells.

Doc chops away at the midsection of another grand fir, this one sickly and obviously not thriving. His first swing takes away a chunk of bark, exposing a set of insect channels, a fir engraver beetle gallery. "I'll bet that you students think that the beetles are killing this tree. Well, I can guarantee you, 97 percent of the time, when you see bugs, you'll also find root disease. Bugs hardly ever kill trees. They're weakened by disease first." He is down on his knees again, chopping at the root. The first root is clean, bare, white against the dirt. He digs further. White fungal fans cover the surface of the next root down. "See," he says, laughing, jabbing his finger at a student. "Root rot."

Doc goes on, a small troll, yelling at his students, telling them to get down in the dirt, take pictures and collect specimens. He is stressing identification and taxonomy. "Are you going to buy this sale, this lot of wood?" He points at a stand of larch. "What do you think?" One student looks at the swollen knots on the side of a young tree, and says no, the correct answer. Doc takes a swing with his pulaski again. The knot flies off, exposing a pocket of rot. "Lose your shirt on this one. All this wood is cull."

"You can't get rid of root disease," Doc says. "Direct intervention never works. What you can do is understand the ecosystem and look at natural trends." He points to the stand of larch. "What was probably originally on that site was Doug fir and white pine. But over time, root rot eliminated the Doug fir. Blister rust probably got the white pine. Now what you have growing up is larch, which is very root disease resistant. Going through and chopping everything down just makes things worse. Just because Doug fir gets root disease doesn't mean you want to go through and chop every Doug fir out of the Inland Northwest. Most Doug fir can live anywhere from 90 to 120 years with root disease. Healthy trees keep such diseases at an endemic level. What you can do is mimic mother nature and harvest those trees at just the right time, right when root disease would kill them anyway. Maybe in the long run, you might want to push that stand toward being primarily composed of larch, or cedar. But gentle manipulation is the key."

Doc is doting on his students again, yelling. "Needle problems—do you think needle problems show you any clues about whether trees will die? They're very showy and easy to spot. Do they mean a tree is going to die? Most likely not! Cedars lose needles every year. Ponderosa pines lose needles every year." Doc walks down the hill back toward the log deck. "Think!" he says. "What little creatures live in these holes in live trees? In dead trees? Did you know that fungus consumes bird feces and keeps these nesting holes clean?" The kids are scrambling, looking for fungi. "Understand how all the parts work. Every part is important, from the smallest to the largest. Can't you see the forest for the trees?"

"There are two layers to the Forest Service—the honest part, and then there's the administration." We are back in Doc's office at the University of Idaho. "People in the Forest Service are taught to lie. The official line is that problems are internal problems. Let's keep them in the family. Hell, that was true when I worked for the Forest Service back in 1956, in Columbia, Missouri, at the beginning of my career. It's still true today." After four years in Missouri, Doc moved to Idaho and the university. He's been there ever since, working on understanding disease and insect interaction on an ecological basis. "Back in the beginning of my career, the emphasis was all agricultural. When you had an insect infestation, you applied sprays. Everything was direct intervention. The problem is this: you can't name a single problem in the forest that you can fix like that." Doc emphasizes time scale—nature's time scale for a forest, 250 years. "Gentle manipulation—moving a stand toward root-disease resistant species. That takes time."

"All the parts have to be there for a forest ecosystem to work. The old and the new. The problem is today we're only looking at the transitional phase, the growing of trees quickly. My great-grandfather was a full blood Iroquois. He took me out in the woods and would ask me, 'How does ladybug fit in? You think that yellowjacket is bad, because he might sting you. But yellowjacket eats the aphids, which would take over your garden.'" Art pauses.

"This forest health 'crisis' started with a memo from former chief of the Forest Service, Dale Robertson, issuing a statement saying that forest health might be a good way to get the cut out. What I say is that both forest health and fraud begin with an 'F.'"

Former Democratic congressman from Idaho Larry LaRocco picked up on the forest health issue and advanced his own bill. Doc testified in front of Congress back in Washington, D.C. "I told them that there was no forest health crisis. We've done actual field studies, and looked at the Forest Service's own data. Currently, in the Inland Northwest, three-quarters of one percent of all trees are recently killed or dying. As trees die, they are replaced by other trees. On top of that, there are many trees that may have some symptoms of root disease, but are in no danger of dying."

Root diseases and insect outbreaks are cyclic, Doc says, and turn into outbreaks only rarely. Additionally, while there is much discussion about trees dying from root disease, the positive benefits from disease and insects are never discussed. Root disease creates small openings in the forest canopy that trap and hold winter snow, creating a water bank for dry years, and operate much differently from clearcuts, where rain-on-snow sends torrents of water running downslope over a short interval. Dead trees provide shelter and nest sites for woodpeckers, which are natural agents of bark beetle control. Dead trees on the forest floor shelter new trees, lichens, mosses, bugs, and fungi that build soils. Biomass is kept in the forest system. "Hell, wood-mining, this continuous removal of logs without replacing key minerals and nutrients, destroys the forest. Why are these people in denial of reality?"

Art talks about the real forest health problem. "High grading, removing the genetically superior stock and allowing weaker species and individuals to take over a stand, that's the real problem. Soil destruction and roadbuilding, even chemical dumping—why aren't we worried about these issues? The outcome of all those actions is longterm stress. When we actually go out and count trees to record root disease activity, we always find poorer recovery on these managed sites. Recovery from root-disease is common on less disturbed patches of ground."

Forest Service disease reports often are also distorted, Doc says. They record any tree with a thin top or yellowing needles—trees that may have symptoms, but may not die for decades. According to his research, root disease was actually at a historic peak in the early '70s. But that was also when the Forest Service had all the old-growth timber it could cut. No one said anything about tree disease. They didn't have to. They were getting the cut out. "The way the Forest Service generates its statistics goes something like this. In the town of Moscow, where we live, there are over 24,000 people. At any given time, one percent will be sick. Twenty percent will be old and dying. If you go to the cemetery and count all the graves, you would probably come up with a figure of fifty percent of the people being dead. Counting graves in the cemetery is similar to what the Forest Service does to estimate numbers of dead and dying trees. I've seen surveys where the Forest Service was counting dead trees that had been killed in the 1910 blaze. One of the reasons for those types of errors is that there are very few surveys done by people actually walking the forest. Most are done aerially."

Doc is concerned about social issues, too. He stresses that most problems in the woods are due to pressure from large, corporate loggers. "When I testified about this whole 'forest health' bunk, I also told Congress that I wanted to see something to help the small logger—small sales set aside for individuals. In my opinion, that's the other 'forest health' problem. No one back in D.C. was interested in making legislation for that."

"What's really bad about all this forest salvage legislation and this newly passed rider is the real anti-democratic side of it all, banning citizen appeals to stop and change timber sales, and suspending all laws and judicial review. It's fundamentally fascist, that's what it is." Doc stops for a moment, then grimaces. "You'd better start believing that the next thing they'll do is start telling you how to pray."

LuVerne

T HE FIRST THING that you notice about LuVerne Grussing is that he is big. Wide shoulders, bald top with blond hair on his sides, big long arms, and thick hands, he moves quietly, smiling. LuVerne is the outdoor recreation planner for the Bureau of Land Management (BLM) office in Cottonwood, Idaho, and is one of the new wave of resource professionals who are slowly making their mark on the federal agencies across the country. He runs a program to develop amenities rather than timber and mineral resources on the lands under his supervision.

Originally from Minnesota, where he worked with inner-city youth, LuVerne moved to Cottonwood in 1978. "What happened was I took the civil service test and got this job with the BLM," LuVerne says. "The first day on the job in Idaho, within three hours, I was on a raft on the Lower Salmon for four days, from White Bird on down. I thought I had died and gone to heaven."

The Lower Salmon River is currently being considered for designation into the Wild and Scenic Rivers System, established by the Wild and Scenic Rivers Act of 1968. The act was designed to protect the best of the best river systems in the country. However, in order for a river to be designated, it must run a gauntlet of levels of scrutiny. A study must first be done by the agency of the federal government that may be responsible for managing the future designated river. Such a study documents the "Outstandingly Remarkable Values" (ORVs) present in a given reach of the river. This determines the eligibility of a river for inclusion. Piggybacked on top of eligibility is the determination of classification of a river. Three categories are available: a stretch of river can be designated "wild" if there are no roads accessing the river; "scenic" if the river is crossed only by roads; and "recreational" if a road runs up and down the bank, or if there is extensive development along the river.

After eligibility comes a determination of suitability, more a political determination than an objective, biological, or aesthetic opinion. Local landowner support, opinions of adjacent communities and other federal and state agencies, and number of designated rivers in the vicinity all factor into the agency's recommendation. The suitability recommendation is then forwarded to the involved state's congressional delegation. If there is support among the voters in the state and the delegation is not especially retrograde, a bill supporting inclusion into the system is then drafted, and must navigate the complex legislative branch of our national government before it finally ends up on the President's desk and is signed into law.

The Wild and Scenic Rivers Act does carry within its text certain protections. No new dams or diversions can be constructed on a Wild and Scenic River. No new development can occur within a quarter mile corridor along the river on public land. Environmental watchdog groups can sue if they perceive that the river's ORVs are threatened. But there is no watershed-level protection for any rivers yet designated. Small streams running into larger protected rivers are not equally protected. As a rule "traditional" uses are typically grandfathered into the protection of a river stretch, even if these uses destroy the river. Old mining claims on public land can still be maintained as active claims. According to Tim Palmer, author of *The Wild and Scenic Rivers of America*, as of August 1992 only 223 rivers totaling 11,276.6 miles were in the National Wild and Scenic Rivers System and related national systems, constituting only .3 percent of total stream miles in the United States. Only 1 percent of streams over five miles in length is protected. Compare this with 200,000 miles of river channelized, additional untold hundreds of thousands of miles polluted by PCBs, sewage, and mud, and thousands of miles of rivers buried behind dams.

No other federal mechanisms exist for protection of river corridors, outside regulatory oversight given the EPA by the Clean Water Act. Some states, Idaho included, have state-level river protection systems, but these are usually minimal, and to date not recognized by the Federal Energy Regulatory Commission (FERC), the federal agency in charge of authorizing permits for damming rivers. If a state wants to protect a river, but the federal government thinks that it should be dammed, then the permit can still be issued. Additionally, in a conservative state such as Idaho, moneyed special interests and developers control the environmental agenda of the public lands and rivers inside the borders. Politicians home for reelection brag about poor behavior in Washington, D.C., regarding exploitation of our public lands, and scream to the voters about the "rights" of Idahoans to deforest, despoil, and destroy federal lands, lands belonging to all

Americans. The Lower Salmon Wild and Scenic Designation process, what should have been one of the most noncontroversial pieces of environmental legislation in the history of the state, is a case in point.

The Lower Salmon had been originally recommended for designation into the Wild and Scenic River system before LuVerne's arrival in Cottonwood in 1978. The study had been completed in 1974 and went to Congress, but the legislators did not act on the recommendation until 1980, with the Central Idaho Wilderness Act, designating the Frank Church/ River of No Return wilderness. The exclusion of the river segment was part of a conference committee compromise—the Panther Creek Roadless Area, up by the confluence of the Middle Fork of the Salmon, and the Main Salmon River, was included. The Lower Salmon, from Long Tom Bar to its meeting with the Snake at the bottom of Blue Canyon, was denied protection to pacify Idaho Senator Jim McClure. Part of this had to do with the attitudes of local landowners. When the Forest Service completed the study for the entire river, local opposition was fueled by Forest Service misinformation, particularly having to do with the condemnation clause in the Wild and Scenic Rivers Act and the protection of tributary streams given by the legislation. "The real situation with the Wild and Scenic Rivers Act is much simpler," LuVerne says. "Protection freezes the state of the river in time—it protects the status quo, and most people living along the Lower Salmon want that."

The condemnation clause in the Wild and Scenic Rivers Act states that a government agency can use the power of condemnation to secure easements and property within a designated river corridor to preserve the qualities of the river. The government can only use that power if less than 50 percent of the quarter mile river corridor protected by the act is owned by the government.

The condemnation clause has been the source of much criticism of the act. But in this country every day, land is condemned for public construction, most notably miles and miles of set-aside for roads. Indeed, when one considers the use, "condemn" is a good word to describe it. Barely an eyebrow is raised when a new highway goes in, or an existing one is broadened, and a berm gobbles up another twenty feet of someone's yard. But to "condemn" an acre of land to preserve it for posterity, to set aside a quiet spot along a cool river for shade, for wildlife habitat, or heaven forbid for an endangered species or for beauty is an outrage. The sad fact is that more miles of streams are contaminated by mine acid in this country than are preserved by the Wild and Scenic Rivers Act. The question of balance, painted by corporate America, is indeed one of no balance, but not in the method that they portray it—there is no balance for preservation.

For a few years the Wild and Scenic process for the Lower Salmon was dormant. No dramatic development occurred in the river corridor. The conference committee reports said that the Lower Salmon would be considered for protection later on its own merits, and gave the BLM the continued mandate to manage the Lower Salmon as a de facto Wild and Scenic River until Congress voted on the river again. One of the key elements of protection concerning the river was statutory withdrawal of the land along the river from mining claims. Save for a couple of sites around Florence, no significant gold had been found in the stretch, but unless the banks had been withdrawn, the 1872 Mining Act would make it possible for people to stake claims for various mining operations.

Nothing happened concerning protection. In 1984, the BLM realized that the time-limited withdrawal for mining was about to expire. Because LuVerne believed that mining as it had occurred was not compatible with Wild and Scenic inclusion, he then took it upon himself to seek a BLM administrative withdrawal from mining of the river banks. This, in itself, was no small task. These were the wild west, James Watt years in the Department of the Interior, and a de facto moratorium had been declared on any withdrawals. LuVerne was quiet and patient. He cultivated a good relationship with the State Department of Lands, which by Idaho law, officially claims the streambed, and got it to withdraw the streambed for any kind of mineral activity from Hammer Creek on down, including leasing for sand and gravel. This move stirred no controversy on the state level. LuVerne only encountered resistance from the Interior Department, whose bureaucrats were trying to lift as many withdrawals as possible. Finally, in a consensus-building move, several river outfitters in Utah and Colorado cultivated Assistant Secretary for Minerals David O'Neal, and built support for LuVerne's proposal. It was granted in 1985 for a twenty-year period.

This left only the roaded section from French Creek to Hammer Creek unprotected. Here, the state had no inclination to withdraw the streambed; there were twenty-three existing mining claims on the BLM ground, and several other claims waiting to be developed. This interest signified that there were a set of different economic priorities for this stretch. LuVerne was patient. He set about building a consensus for mineral rights withdrawal. After meetings with the local citizenry, the scenic and recreational values prevailed. The Riggins and Grangeville chambers of commerce endorsed mineral rights withdrawal, and the French Creek to Hammer Creek reach of the river was removed from possibility of new mining entry on the riverbanks. However, the streambed, owned by the State of Idaho, was not withdrawn from mining.

Once these withdrawals were in place, LuVerne made a major push to move Congress toward designation. He started floating staffers and congressional representatives on the river. "We did the soft sell in the offices. Once we were on the river, the lower canyons did the hard sell." Cy Jameson, director of the BLM from 1989 to 1992, supported river recreation and encouraged the process. By cultivating his friendship with Representative Larry Craig and staff person Missy Guisto, LuVerne folded Craig into the ranks for pro-preservation, unusual for a man with one of the worst environmental voting records in the United States Congress. Craig introduced a bill to add the river in the House. The bill was not able to move all the way through Congress that year because of calendar constraints.

LuVerne's hopes were high when Craig was elected to the Senate in 1992. He was banking on the fact that Larry LaRocco, a former staffer of Senator Frank Church, and now representative from the first district, would move legislation through the House, and Craig through the Senate. However, upon being elected to the Senate, Craig insisted that a no-condemnation clause be inserted in the legislation. Condemnation had never been an issue on the Lower Salmon. Through land swaps, purchasing of scenic and development easements, LuVerne had accomplished a true *fait accompli*—a noncontroversial piece of environmental legislation in Idaho.

I tell LuVerne that I think Larry Craig was trying to set precedent with the Wild and Scenic Act. He wanted to remove the condemnation clause from the act, and figured that this might be a tool to disable the act. LuVerne looks out the window, across the parking lot, hands behind his head. "Condemnation for land was precluded anyway for the Lower Salmon. When the government owns more than 50 percent of the banks, you can't use that power." He shrugs his shoulders.

Both LaRocco and Craig introduced the bill supporting designation. However, the bill never got out of the House Interior and the Senate Energy and Minerals committees because of the condemnation language. It was all pointless. Land acquisition and easement procurement had proceeded to the point where condemnation was not even to be considered. No issue had become the major issue.

LuVerne continued doing legwork, arranging meetings with landowners and Larry Craig. In the end, the only local resistance came from the contingent that figured any federal interference was bad. LuVerne hired a person to do nothing but land acquisition and exchange using money from the Land and Water Conservation Fund. Because there was local resistance to adding public land in a county already predominantly public land and removing more tax base, land trades were arranged whenever possible.

At this point in 1993, the bill became a legislative football. Larry Craig refused to back down on the condemnation language. Other players got involved—Wendy Wilson from Idaho Rivers United, Beth Norcross of American Rivers, and Skootch Pankonin, a Washington, D.C., lobbyist, tried to rewrite the language and grease the legislative skids. Larry Craig refused to budge. LaRocco introduced the bill again the next year. It passed in a House vote, but time ran out at the end of the session. The bill has yet to come around another time.

"It's such a non-issue." LuVerne is complaining. "That's the frustrating part. Designation is not going to change the way the river is managed. The river has been managed as a de facto Wild and Scenic River since 1974. It's simply come down now to a matter of principle. Everyone agrees that the values are there, the existing uses are going to continue, are well accepted, and generally non-controversial, and we'll continue to manage as we have over the last twenty years. And we'll continue to preempt controversy through our land acquisition and exchange program. It's just frustrating. Why no designation? Why not?"

Andy, Greg, and Mike

"Y OU KNOW," I SAY, "being considered 'reasonable' in Idaho is not necessarily a compliment, especially when it comes to environmental
issues." Andy Boyd, Greg Gollberg, and Michael Murray, graduate students at the University of Idaho in the School of Forestry, all advocates of
stopping fish stocking in high wilderness lakes, are sitting around me in a
circle. Cessation of such activities in wilderness is widely viewed as one of
the most unreasonable of all environmental priorities.

Greg, originally from Texas City, Texas, on the Gulf of Mexico, witnessed an entire marine ecosystem from Houston to Conroe be completely
trashed in the span of a short twenty years. "When I was a kid, you could
walk to a sand beach and catch whatever fish you wanted. Now, there's
nothing." Michael, from upstate New York, speaks next. "When I was
young, I had a cousin who lived in Idaho and was a forest ranger. Ever
since third grade I've wanted to come here." Andy chimes in last. "I don't
come from a town. I come from a freeway exit—number forty five off the
Long Island Expressway."

The group originally formed as a chapter of the largest conservation
organization in the state—the Idaho Conservation League (ICL). All were
interested in wilderness management. "There were three issues that we
were trying to move ICL to action," Greg says. "First was the adoption of
the Northern Rockies Ecosystem Protection Act. The second was grizzly
bear reintroduction. The third was wilderness management—in particular
fish stocking in wilderness. We picked wilderness management because we
perceived that it was the one place where people weren't involved. Everyone's
always interested in allocation—getting more acres into the wilderness system. We want more big 'W' wilderness, for sure. But there are already
more than 100 million acres of designated wilderness, and only one national organization dedicated to monitoring usage and impacts—Wilderness Watch. With this issue, we felt that we could make the biggest impact
for the ecological good."

Mike says, "Fish stocking represented one of the biggest blatant violations of wilderness law, policy, philosophy, and ecology. In the Wilderness Act, in the very first section, it talks about 'preservation and protection (of lands) in their natural condition.' Ninety-five percent of all high mountain lakes in the Western U.S. originally were fishless. In the Selway/Bitterroot, that number was more like 98 percent." But going against fish stocking in Idaho is like going against history. Stocking has been going on since Western man showed up 125 years ago. Miners and loggers originally stocked lakes for a food source, and the states started aerial stocking in the '40s, right after World War II. Some people argue for only stocking locally occurring cutthroat trout in the lakes, eliminating brook and German brown trout from such programs. Concerns have been voiced for fish below the lakes, since brook trout can hybridize with both downstream cutthroat and bull trout. "But," Michael says, "a fish is a fish, no matter what kind it is. Cutthroat weren't originally in those lakes."

"One third of the lakes in the Moose Creek District of the Nez Perce Forest in the Selway/Bitterroot have been stocked with brook trout. They're tenacious, and out-compete virtually everything else in the aquatic ecosystem. Before you know it, you have high population densities that can dramatically alter the prey base. Even from a fisheries perspective, these lakes are often overstocked. They once found a twenty-four year old fish from one alpine lake that was only nine inches long. What kind of fishing experience is that?" Michael continues. I relate to what he is saying. I, too have caught six-inch brookie after six-inch brookie from high lakes in the Gospel Hump Wilderness.

The group approached the issue by sending a letter to all the forest supervisors involved with the Selway/Bitterroot Wilderness. Since something such as fish stocking has the potential to change dramatically the ecological balance of these delicate systems, they asked if there had been any National Environmental Policy Act (NEPA)-required environmental analysis performed, and asked for the copy of the environmental analysis for the current year's fish stocking. The group knew that there had almost certainly been no review done. The purpose of the letter was to start a dialogue. "Our first goal was not to take them to court, which we could easily have done. And probably have won, made them stop, I might add," Andy says. The Forest Service responded positively, agreeing that their concerns were legitimate, and hosted a meeting involving Liz Close, the wilderness coordinator from the Forest Service Region One office, Dan Ritter, the Selway/Bitterroot wilderness coordinator, Rich Clough, representing

Montana Fish, Wildlife and Parks, and Ed Shriever for Idaho Fish and Game. All attending were personally sympathetic, and the general outline of the issue was discussed. A second meeting was then proposed.

The students agreed to host the second meeting. Invited were all the principal players: Larry Peterman, the top administrator from Montana Fish, Wildlife and Parks; Steve Huffaker, Fisheries Bureau Chief of the Idaho Fish and Game commission; a representative from the Forest Service; Grant Simonds, president of the Idaho Outfitters and Guides Association; and a representative from the Backcountry Horsemen, Tom Walton. Greg comments. "It's important to remember that in the past, even Sierra Club members have done it. Members of ICL have stocked lakes, in particular the Boundary Backpackers. Don McPherson of the Backcountry Horsemen stocked lakes for over thirty years and was a Johnny Appleseed type."

Plans were progressing smoothly for the second mini-summit when the Boise paper, the *Idaho Statesman*, ran a piece on the issue. The coverage was balanced and fair. The paper talked with Greg, ICL, and the Forest Service and gave the story a full page in the outdoor section. The headline read "We're Not Against Fishing." Karl Brooks, then acting director of ICL, heard about the story and started backpedalling furiously. Fearful of alienating allies and stirring up controversy, he sent a letter to the editor of the *Idaho Statesman* pulling the organization's support, saying that he had grown up fishing alpine lakes out of McCall. He then proceeded to label the group "just a bunch of college students." The group felt betrayed—they had done everything within their power to confront the issue and remain noncontroversial. Michael looks at me, frustrated. "Technically, there aren't even any 'alpine' lakes outside of McCall. They're subalpine. It can be difficult to communicate these issues."

After this, some major players started backing out of the second meeting. Larry Peterman and Steve Huffaker, the two primary fish stockers, didn't show. But Grant Simonds, the Forest Service, and Tom Walton were there. Grant had initial negative reactions to the proposal and claimed that the agencies were backing out of deals made on grandfathered uses of the areas. Tom Walton joked, "How do you catch and cook salamanders?" But he later said that personally he didn't have a problem with stopping fish stocking. Greg told them that the group would be submitting a proposal to the Forest Service to phase out fish stocking, and was trying to be considerate to all sides involved. The peer-reviewed proposal would go to the Forest Service in April. The group broke with ICL and incorporated a new group, the Ecocentric Wildlands Management Institute.

"We have to take a different approach to solving these types of problems," Greg says. "With us, litigation is a last resort. You can be sure that a lawsuit does not build bridges. We also feel strongly that at least part of the conservation community should move away from just getting more wildlands, and start paying attention to management of what we have in the present system. We're all supportive of such efforts as the Wildlands Project and the Northern Rockies Ecosystem Protection Act. But we also need to consider management. The environmental community and the country need to realize that the Wilderness Act is not enough. Ecological integrity has to be the cornerstone of our concerns."

A year has passed since Andy, Mike, and Greg made their pitch to the Forest Service. Their proposal sits, mothballed, in the wilderness management division of the regional office. "I sure thought it would be a novel thing if you got the Forest Service to change without a lawsuit," I remark to Greg. He laughs, and shakes his head.

Part III

Crisis

As fish biologist Chris Frissell says, "If there was a free lunch, we ate it a long time ago."

The following essays are my stories of current issues involving the present ecological crisis in north-central Idaho. They are almost purely elemental, involving earth, wind, fire, and water and their various manipulations by humanity, driven by local economic need as well as policy invented in Washington, D.C.

We live in a time where the bill is coming due for all of our excesses regarding the land we live on, and these essays reflect this idea. There are prices to be paid, both ecologically and personally. These are stories of the bill collector.

Salmon River Mining

MARTI KNEE-JERKED. Hell, she's some woman, image-wise—big, loud, conservation's Mae West—but she knee-jerked. And I know that they, the opposition, don't love us, hate us even, always looking for a weakness. Marti goofed and sent out an inflammatory flyer concerning mining on the Salmon. Now there's hell to pay. Big time.

A miner's claim was transferred on the bed of the main Salmon River, somewhere between Long Tom Bar and Riggins, the part that LuVerne Grussing had not been able to withdraw from mining while he worked on the Wild and Scenic River process. It looked like someone was going to develop it, suck up the river bottom with a big tube, spit it out, take the gold, and ruin the river. Marti, on the staff of Idaho Rivers United (IRU), filed for the mining withdrawal again with the state Department of Lands. The state owns the riverbeds in Idaho. She hadn't prepped us, then went on vacation. Meanwhile, the miners protested and asked for public hearings. It was her ballgame. But she bailed and went to Baja, and now we're stuck with these hearings. There's one in Grangeville on Tuesday night, and I know no one is going to go but me, at least from the environmental side. I haven't got the facts. It's going to be hard to get in someone's face and talk to all those damn crotchety miners. I know those guys—the wise users will also be there. Hell, Marti's right—who would want to mine the Salmon anyway? All of the good stuff is gone, the big nuggets, the motherlode.

Tuesday night in Grangeville. I get lost because the meeting isn't being held where they usually are. I stop at the gas station. "Where's the senior's center, Ma'am?" I ask. She gives me directions—wrong, of course. I'm wandering down in the industrial district, then finally out on the county road. I finally see the senior's center, all lit up with a full parking lot. I called Whale, my friend who talked at the other public meeting held last night in McCall. He told me he had a Rodney King day—just got all beat up. Even the outfitters didn't protest, at least not much. People had climbed all over him about a figure Marti had wrong on the amount of money coming from the small sand-and-gravel operation on the river. She said only $1,500 total was coming in from the lease, a figure that I will find out later that the Department of Lands had given her. Turns out it's more like $6,000 each year. Money talks in this neck of the woods. I could care less about the money. I am thinking about the river.

I walk into the senior's center. The Department of Lands representative is up front, biasing the crowd even before the start of the hearing. "I don't know why we're here tonight. I can't understand these people. You know that I know all of you—I'm on your side. I don't know who this IRU is either." All of the miners and wise users are complaining, calling IRU an organization from California, the worst insult that one could give in these parts. I see my old friend, Gary Lane, an outfitter, elk teeth around his cowboy hat, and his friend, another outfitter, wearing a black, weatherworn Stetson drooping down around his ears. LuVerne is there too, and I say hi to Gary and LuVerne, and shake the other outfitter's hand. I bend, whisper to LuVerne and the other outfitter. "Am I going to get my ass kicked after this is all over?" The cowboy leans over, gives me the voice of solidarity. "They'll have to kick my ass, too." I am an unlikely gunfighter tonight, wearing my wrinkled clothes and Carhartt's coat. Grease is under my fingers; I changed my oil before I left Troy tonight.

I sign my card to testify last. I am called first. I get up, my Peterson's guide for freshwater fishes in my hand, my notebook tucked up under my armpit. I walk up to the mike. I start talking, then look up. In the front row is an old friend, probably not on my side tonight. I make eye contact. "Why, hi, Al, how's Georgia?" I ask. The crowd is quiet, confronted with a personal connection. I wave the book above my head, talk about darters. Hundreds of them in this book, I say. Small perches, all about one to five inches, beautiful, godawful beautiful, greens, blues, reds, oranges, like a tropical fish store on the plasticized plates stuck in the middle of my field guide. Kentucky and Tennessee river systems, a lot of them, up in Ohio, too. Destroyed, lost to mining and agriculture. I tell them I know that most of them are probably glad that 50 percent of these types of darters are gone. I tell them that I don't see the Salmon as a dredge mine, or a big placer site, or a gravel pit. I see it as a beautiful river, one of the last left in the country, maybe one of the last in the world. I tell about falling in love with my wife on the Salmon, and wanting it to stay for my children. I want to connect to them, to the things that they know, to the whole idea of continuity of generations.

Thirty people testify after me. Almost all want to mine the Salmon. A young woman testifies, gutsy. She doesn't practice speaking in front of people every day. She says she loves the river and can't see how mining is going to help. She lives close, in Cottonwood. Tim Cochnauer, the regional head of Idaho Fish and Game, tries to tell the people that destroying the fish will cost the people money, that salmon and especially steelhead are worth big money in Idaho for all the tourist dollars that they bring in. They call for his resignation. The part-owner of the gravel pit speaks. She says her gravel pit does no harm, that every Sunday when she drives to church she sees screaming rafters, drinking, carrying on. If people are worried about visual quality, clean that up. She is right. I ask LuVerne how much impact comes from the two sand-and-gravel operations. He says "minimal." Miners get up, give wild testimony on how mining is beneficial for fish; one miner from Red River takes the mike, waves a study over his head, and says it's scientifically documented. The real story is that miners have turned over the entire streambed of the Red River at least three times and there are few fish there. The chair of the Idaho County Commission testifies, tells everyone that he's sorry that they have to be here, and wishes that they could be home watching TV.

I stay until the end, honor-bound. I must defend IRU, and I can't do that by leaving early. I get into lively discussions quickly. Some of the more progressive miners want to talk. I get in their face. I am big, too, and use it to my advantage. I am quick to agree with what they say that is right, and disagree when they are wrong. Exaggerating my facial gestures, I try to understand and have compassion too. I promise to check on grandfathering the little sand-and-gravel operators. I leave at 10 p.m. It is a long drive back to Troy. I am still alive.

Two weeks later, I talk to Marti. I recommend grandfathering the little sand-and-gravel operators and letting them keep their operating permits. She agrees and apologizes, and says she will refile the withdrawal petition. I tell her that some of those folks wouldn't love us no matter what we said. She says that someone from Division of Environmental Quality who was there says that I got one set of big balls, talking to those miners. I laugh, flattered. They obviously could not tell. I was desperate.

Children's Crusade

This huge territory—larger than Holland, rich in minerals, endowed with abundant rainfall and breathtakingly beautiful vistas, and rich with the seeds of the temperate zone's most varied forest—was turned adrift at the mercies of the marketplace. With no national planning to assure the continuance of forest growth and productivity, the preservation of water quality and the survival of a viable and regenerative population, the region was dragged through boom and bust toward ruination. Its natural resources were squandered and its people were victimized and exploited in a manner that might have reddened the cheek of a Genghis Khan. It was done in the name of capitalism and free enterprise though, in truth, only the profits were capitalized; the losses were socialized, with the staggering social overhead attendant upon such economic and political irresponsibility thrust onto the general taxpayers, including those of future generations.

—Harry M. Caudill, *The Watches of the Night*

CRAIG, MY ENVIRONMENTAL INTERN, is standing in a cold August downpour. His hands are outstretched, poking out of his cheap green raincoat. I stand facing him and the dilapidated trailer on the Land, the old Comstock mine property used as base camp by the Earth First! Cove/Mallard campaign. Around us is logged-over second-growth lodgepole forest, with water puddling underneath the branches on the sparse, rocky soil. It is the beginning of Wild Rockies Week 1995, a seven-day congregation of activists that usually ends with some kind of mass-arrest protest scenario, followed by a wild party after everyone manages to get out of jail. Though I am very familiar with the campaign, there are a lot of faces unknown to me up here this year. Many folks have only recently arrived in Idaho, residents of other communities, involved in other issues, shuffling around in the outdoor set's version of poverty: cheap raincoats, shoddy clothing, discount hiking boots. Lycra and GoreTex are not popular with the Earth First! crowd.

Gary Macfarlane, one of the campaign organizers, asked me to come up here to teach a class on timber sale monitoring for Wild Rockies Week. Gary has been living in my barn all summer. He used to be a mainstream type, had a car, a job with the Utah Wilderness Association, and a wife. But he quit two years ago and moved to Moscow. Something needs to happen now—not next year—to stop the destruction, he says. I owed Gary one—he had taught Craig about environmental activism all summer long, and I felt if there was a way that I could return the favor, I would. But I am uneasy at camp. There has been continual protest concerning this area. Yet, in four years of raising hell, we are nowhere close to protecting it. And with our legal means almost run out in the courts, there appears nothing that can happen besides making the Forest Service pay for cutting this area.

The rain has been coming down in sheets for days. Walking around the old trailer, I think it impossible to find a campsite not in a puddle. The lodgepole forest sure doesn't offer much protection. I suggest to Craig that he pitch the tent on a slope, as I turn to talk to another organizer. She tells me that they've had problems with newcomers getting hypothermia this summer. It's been cold, and many of the Earth First!ers are not experienced campers. I walk to the kitchen, greeting the familiar faces I know from my few past visits to the Land, as well as their brief sojourns in Moscow. Around the cooking fire, people are smoking cigarettes and swapping stories about different ecological battles. There must be at least forty people here, but no one is talking about the history of this campaign, though, as if the past had been suspended and the issues surrounding Cove/Mallard had mysteriously materialized with the arrival of the latest pickup truck or VW microbus. I sit down on a bench next to a small, pretty blonde woman, who can't be more than twenty-one years old. "My friends all wanted to come up here for this," she confides. "Cove/Mallard is so—you know, like, terrible."

I hear Cindy, longtime Earth First!er and camp mom-from-hell, bellowing at her boyfriend. I walk over to her, give her a hug, and pull a carton of Marlboro Reds out from beneath my raincoat. "How much I owe you?" she says. I tell her nothing monetarily, that I have brought a rented electrical generator to camp to run a P.A. system and my slide projector. I'm going to leave the generator up in camp for the week, and I don't want it vandalized. "Earth First!ers and equipment, Cindy," I quip. "I don't have enough money to replace this." Fourteen dollars for a carton of cigarettes seems like cheap insurance to me. "Don't worry," Cindy says. "Those goddamn hippies won't even get close to this thing."

This most recent chapter in the battle over the Cove/Mallard area, a wedge of land bordering the Frank Church/River of No Return, the Selway/Bitterroot, and Gospel Hump wildernesses, started in 1989, when Steve Paulson and Ron Mitchell of the Idaho Sportman's Coalition filed the original comments and appeal on the Cove/Mallard project prepared by the Red River Ranger District on the Nez Perce National Forest outside Dixie, Idaho. Eighty million board-feet of timber were to be cut, with sixteen thousand logging trucks hauling away the forest. One hundred and forty-five miles of new road would have to be built for the sale. Furthermore, this recycled version of the infamous Jersey/Jack project had been shot down with a lawsuit back in the early '80s. The litigation ended up going all the way to the Ninth District Federal Circuit Court of Appeals, with a victory for the environmental side. Many involved with the debate, including Idaho's former governor Cecil Andrus, say that the Cove/Mallard area was traded to the timber industry informally in return for not attempting to block the Central Idaho Wilderness Act of 1980. And the Senate committee report on the act does state that both Cove/Mallard and Meadow Creek should be examined for timber harvest. But those lands were not formally released by legislation to be cut, and Senate committee reports are nonbinding.

Steve had pointed out problems with the Cove/Mallard timber sale, mostly concerning the survival of the gray wolf in that area. Because the wolf was listed as a threatened species under the Endangered Species Act (ESA), the Red River Ranger District staff was required to consider the effects of the sale on the gray wolf and its recovery. An environmental impact statement was written concerning the sale, along with a biological evaluation concerning the gray wolf. That report determined that there would be impacts on possible den sites, the number of elk in the area (a primary source of wolf nutrition), and the wolves' ability to evade hunters due to the extensive roading and logging. However, the biologist on the project returned a finding that the sale would have "no effect" on the wolf. The ESA specifies no effect on reproductive capability for any threatened or endangered species. "Wouldn't destroying possible den sites affect the wolf?" Steve had argued.

But legal problems arose with Steve's plea to the Forest Service. Steve had not written the formal appeal. He had only been granted status as an intervenor, meaning his comments only piggybacked on top of Ron Mitchell's appeal. The appeals regulations required the Forest Service to read Steve's comments, not to address them, inasmuch as they were not placed in the body of the appeal. The Forest Service perused, then ignored his opinions. In addition, the Ecology Center of Missoula, which usually appeals this type of project, had missed the appeal deadline. The Cove/Mallard EIS had fallen behind the bookshelf in the office, and had been retrieved too late. The sale went forward, with timber sold to Shearer Lumber Company in Elk City.

Failing to convince the Forest Service, Steve wrote the original plea for help in the *Earth First! Journal* in the spring of 1992. His cry fell on deaf ears in the mainstream environmental community. But the Ancient Forest Bus Brigade, an Earth First! support group, responded after Phil Knight of the Native Forest Network out of Bozeman, Montana, convinced members around a campfire at an Earth First! rendezvous in Southern Colorado that Cove/Mallard was the next big fight. Recruiting the Bus Brigade was a coup in the fight to save the area—the Bus Brigade, a self-contained base camp, had the ability to support activists involved in civil disobedience and direct action campaigns by serving as a food center, lodging, and logistical source. The summer of 1992 started slowly, with a handful of activists conducting in-your-face civil disobedience in and around the area. It culminated with three activists being arrested for mooning the Forest Service, under the charge of providing a hazard to traffic. The media had a field day with the mooning charge but paid little attention to the monster timber sale itself.

By 1993, Ramon of the Bus Brigade was able to purchase a twenty-acre inholding, called "the Land" by activists, on the Comstock Mine next to the Cove/Mallard area. The previous year, Forest Service Law Enforcement had harassed activists as they camped in the national forest adjacent to the timber sale. With the private land acquired, everyone went to work planning the summer 1993 campaign.

However, the Earth First! contingent was not alone in preparing for the summer of 1993. The Forest Service was also hard at work, contracting with Highland Enterprises for construction of the Noble Road, one of the main trunk routes into the roadless area. When elk calving season ended in early summer, the bulldozers moved in. Hundreds of activists from around the country arrived to participate in the campaign. More than sixty were arrested in demonstrations ranging from sitting in fifteen-foot tall tripods constructed of lodgepole trunks to locking down individual activists' heads to bulldozers and Forest Service vehicles by using U-shaped bicycle locks around their necks. Legal action by the Sportman's Coalition included filing suit under the ESA, the NFMA, the NEPA over the timber sale. To Earth First!, there appeared to be reason to fight—stop the sale for this summer, and maybe it would be stopped for good.

District court judge Harold Ryan did not hear the legal case over Cove/Mallard until 1994. Ryan granted a preliminary injunction over the timber sale, with the instruction that the Nez Perce National Forest would discuss the impacts of the project to threatened chinook salmon with the National Marine Fisheries Service, in charge of recovering populations of the fish. The summer was quiet, and the talk at base camp was one of possible restoration projects on the Comstock Mine property. However, in late 1994, Judge Ryan grew ill, and the case passed to Judge Allan McDonald, who dismissed it and lifted the injunction. Roadbuilding and logging both commenced in 1995, and protesters started civil disobedience actions to stop the development.

I walk back to the fire, sitting down next to Mike Bowersox, one of the Seeds of Peace organizers here at camp. Seeds of Peace travels to different protest sites around the country, providing food and nonviolence training to activists engaged in different campaigns. Mike, short, dirty, with his blond hair mashed into ratty dreadlocks, is a veteran of Ward Valley, the nuclear test site in Nevada, and many other actions. His pants have huge holes in them, and his glasses sit sideways on his face. He is one of the most intelligent people I know. He has been up on the Land for two years. "It's raining, Chuck," he says, slouched in a beat-up director's chair. "Dirt is sliding off the Noble Road. Big Mallard Creek is silting up, fish are dying. Loggers are logging. What else do you need to know?"

I mix and mingle, talking to people. Some plan to get arrested on Wild Rockies Day, this Friday. I assume it has something to do with blockading the Jack Road, though I don't know, and don't really want to.

I ask them why. One tells me that his parents were antiwar activists, that this kind of thing runs in the family. "What about this place? Does this place matter to you?" I ask. It's the issue, he tells me. Another person is a peace activist. She's getting arrested for reasons of nonviolence. Mike tells me he's going to get arrested this year. I think that Mike is getting arrested for the sanctity of this place. Another person is an AIDS activist; this is the place he has decided to stake himself out.

"What about the land?" I say to myself, walking away from the crowd.

"I started hiking in the '60s, up in the Adirondacks," Ramon says. But it wasn't until he divorced for a second time that he took to the road, hiking and wandering the West. As he traveled, he started to notice change everywhere on a massive scale that he hadn't seen before. It was the classic Western story: more development, more timber harvest, more everything. "It angered me," Ramon says. "But I had no idea about what to do to stop any of it."

Ramon had, however, heard about Earth First!. He had gone to an Earth First! rendezvous with his son in New Mexico in 1989. There he met Judi Bari and Darryl Cherney, two of the chief organizers of Redwood Summer. He admired their passion and commitment, as well as their determination to do something about the destruction of ecosystems. "Action is what is necessary, not letter-writing, not talk-talk-talk. Just knowing that made life difficult for me," he says. He went back to his insurance business, still having conversations with people about environmental issues, but still remaining fundamentally uninvolved.

While talking to people in his social circle, Ramon would try to get them to ask him those magic words, "what can I do." The answer that he would give was always the same: what you can do is read the *Earth First! Journal*. He would pay for their first subscription. "Read that for a year, then figure out what to do yourself," Ramon says. "But it wasn't satisfying. It wasn't really action, and I didn't see any results. I didn't see any of my friends having any life changes, and in fact, neither was I. I was still selling insurance, driving an expensive car, and making cocktail party talk."

Things started changing after Ramon attended Earth Day in Santa Barbara. Being an early-riser, he arrived before most of the crowd. "I remember a young man named Jesse, with fiery green eyes, circulating petitions for the California Forests Forever Initiative," Ramon says. The initiative was an attempt to issue a taxpayer bond to buy Headwaters Forest, a huge grove of redwoods yet to be cut, three thousand acres of private land owned by Maxxam Company and its subsidiary, Pacific Lumber, with a surrounding ecosystem of fifty thousand acres. Ramon offered to get people to sign petitions. After he had filled up the first set, he found Jesse again, who gave him more. (The Forests Forever Initiative failed in California, by a mere couple of thousand votes, but it was a year when no bond issue passed.)

At the end of the day, when he returned the petitions for the last time, Jesse said that Ramon ought to come to Redwood Summer. He told him about massive demonstrations in the redwoods to stop Pacific Lumber from cutting down the Headwaters grove. Ramon asked him how many people would be there. Jesse said a hundred thousand. "That sounded great!" Ramon says. And so he made plans to go.

But a problem arose. Ramon had already signed on with his son back East to expand his corporation to the West Coast, and had promised him two years of his labor. So he called his son to ask if he could take two months off to go to Redwood Summer. His son reminded Ramon of his commitment, and naysayed the idea.

"I felt bad—chagrined, really, but I had also promised my son that I would do this, and no one likes to welch on their son," Ramon says. "So I stuck with my promise. Then, one evening, I was having dinner with him when I heard that Judi Bari and Darryl Cherney had gotten bombed in Oakland, in June of 1990. At that point, I said 'That's it—they're bombing us.' I told my son that I was going to Redwood Summer. We got into a big argument, because his automatic assumption was the same as the Oakland police and the FBI—that Judi and Darryl were carrying a bomb, that Earth First!ers are terrorists. Of course, my automatic assumption was that the FBI did it, since the Earth First!ers are a threat to the status quo in our society. He hasn't spoken to me since."

After he had decided to go to Redwood Summer, Ramon took a Greyhound bus up to the base camp near Laytonville. He fell asleep on the bus, overshot it, and ended up in a redneck town in timber country in northern California. It wasn't a problem—Ramon was an insurance salesman, and had no problem talking to a bunch of loggers, making spotted owl jokes in the bar. The next day he took the bus back down the road and found his way into camp, looking for the crowd of a hundred thousand people. But instead of the multitudes, there were only a couple dozen people milling around. His heart fell. If there was safety in numbers, these were not numbers.

Ramon participated in a nonviolence training session the next day, practicing role-playing. First, he was a logger, later a cop. His confidence slowly returned. He took a break and wandered down by a stream in the campground. Suddenly, a young man came running, visibly shaking, scared, because people had been in the woods, blocking the roads to keep trees from being logged. The protesters had been awake for 48 hours, and they needed more people immediately, and were looking for volunteers. He looked at Ramon, and said, "Tell me I don't have to go." Ramon looked back at him and said, "You don't have to go. You're just the same as me, we've only been in camp for two days. Take it easy and see what happens."

"You're absolutely right," the young man replied. "But I'm going." And he turned around and was off. Ramon stood there looking at the water for a few minutes and thought, "I don't have to go either."

"But before I knew it, I was in a pick-up truck, headed for Mendocino County, a famous place in Earth First! history," Ramon says. "Navarro Ridge, a big stand of redwoods—well, not any more, they're all gone."

After being arrested and spending two days in jail, the authorities finally let the protesters go because of a jail solidarity technique—not giving their names to the arresting officers, which made arraignment difficult. "After that, I figured all arrests would be like that, which wasn't necessarily true," Ramon says. Ramon's second action at Redwood Summer involved occupying a log deck. A security truck came up, so the group spread out on the road, unrolled a banner, and just stood there to stop him. At one point, the driver threatened that the protesters were going to go out of there in pieces. He blew his whistle and loggers started coming out of the woods with chainsaws. The group just sat down in the road. In no time at all, the protesters were having a conversation with the loggers, waiting for the cops to come, swapping cigarettes. The tension was greatly reduced, but when the cops showed up the situation deteriorated. "I didn't know what to expect, and I don't think anyone else did either, but I remember cops walking up the road, twenty of them in twos, with batons, and face shields," Ramon says. "They had raised an army to arrest us."

Ramon met soon-to-be Bus Brigade member Billy Packer at that action. Billy, a commercial tuna fisherman from Massachusetts, was his action partner, and the two together were the oldest guys present, by a factor of thirty years.

"I also remember meeting with Jake Kreilick, of the Native Forest Network from Missoula, as well as Phil Knight, Tim Bechtold, and Dan Funsch. Everyone else was in handcuffs, except the Montana crowd. They were in handcuffs and restraints. They impressed me. I can remember thanking Jake for coming all the way from Montana to save my redwoods. Jake made some comment 'that's OK Ramon—some day, you'll come to my town and help us save our place.'"

Redwood Summer ended, and Ramon went home. But less than a year later, in March 1991, Billy showed up at Ramon's front door and announced that Ramon had to quit his job, renounce all of his worldly possessions, buy a school bus and take it on the road, doing actions. Billy wanted to give environmental sermons at churches, and Ramon was going to get him in the door. Ramon asked him if he could make that decision himself. Billy said "take your time, I'll just camp in your front yard." In the end, Ramon gave him a couple of thousand dollars, and Billy went back East and bought a 1975 International school bus.

After Billy returned with the school bus, the newly formed Bus Brigade attended a regional rendezvous in Northern California, where they picked up Russell Poe. "*Outside* magazine said that our main claim to fame was showing up at actions and drinking beer—the Ancient Forest Beer Brigade," Ramon says. "Our concept, though, was to give activists, many of whom had to work at city jobs, a way of support, by virtue of the bus providing food and shelter if they needed it."

After acquiring Cindy, an ex-logger's wife, the Bus Brigade supported the Peace Walk from Las Vegas to the Nevada Test Site, delivered over a ton of food to the embattled Navaho at Big Mountain, and attended Redwood Summer II in California.

After that summer, Billy had the idea to go south for the winter, to Nevada and Arizona, and link up with the snowbirds, old people in their Winnebagos, many of whom they had met in the past two years. "All of them love to whine about how things are changing all over the world. Their special places from their childhood were all ruined with developments. I thought that these people would be sensitive to what we were doing but just didn't know what actions to take. I was going to raise an army of RVers and bring them back to the hands of Judi Bari, and say 'Here, do what you can with these people,' in what I assumed would be Redwood Summer III, in the summer of '92," Ramon says. "But nothing came of it. I couldn't activate the older folks."

In the fall of 1991, the Bus Brigade attended the Earth First! rendezvous in Durango, Colorado. They had heard about Cove/Mallard from the *Earth First! Journal*. Some members of Earth First! had considered starting a campaign, but there were serious logistical problems associated with a major action in central Idaho. At that point, Ramon volunteered the bus.

"I remember my first day at Cove/Mallard," Ramon says. "Steve Paulson walked up to me. 'Let's take a walk,' he said. I told him that I was busy. Steve said 'take a walk first.' Half the time when Steve and I were walking, we weren't talking—we were just feeling."

The year 1992 was crazy. The Forest Service harassed the twenty-some protesters from the beginning. After Erik and the mooners got arrested, the trial in Boise made national papers—a federal trial for mooning. "And that's when I got involved with the media—it was a hot story," Ramon says.

Toward the end of the summer of 1992, the protesters were sitting around camp trying to keep warm one afternoon. Because of recent forest fires, they had decided not to do actions. A car pulled up, and out stepped a man from Kamiah who had been a hunter all his life. He told the group that he still hunted, but only with a video camera. As he was leaving he asked if there was anything he could do.

"Well," Ramon told him, "as a matter of fact there is. We're not getting anything done up here this summer because we're operating on Forest Service land. They are in our face every day, harassing us with video cameras. They walk around threateningly, take pictures of the women taking showers and going to the bathroom. They always come around dinner, it seems, always in the evening. What we want to know is this: is there any private land for sale in the area?" The man told him of a place, but he was not sure if it was for sale. "He gave me the name of a person that we could contact. That person put me in touch with the seller. It was only a short period of time before we had twenty acres in the middle of the Cove/Mallard cut area."

That piece of land turned into the camp for protests in the summer of '93. A woman in Florida and her husband had originally bought it as a hunting retreat, along with four other couples. The first time she visited, she got off the airplane in Lewiston and immediately started telling her husband how quaint the wilderness was. Then they started driving up the road, through Kamiah, Kooskia, and Dixie. She looked at the trailer, which had been hauled up to the land, and then started making some food for dinner with her husband. Her husband asked her if she wanted to go back that night, or the following morning. "Right now!" she said. They turned around and fled.

"But she also didn't want it to be clearcut," Ramon says. "When she found out that one of the partners had been approached by Jim Miller, the Dixie local who owns the Lodgepole Pine Inn, to log it, she was appalled. Jim Miller wanted to cut the land and pay off the mortgage. She went to the other four parties who jointly owned the land and bought out their shares over the period of a year."

"In order for Cove/Mallard to be saved," Ramon says, "we needed national media attention. So I unplugged myself from camp and moved to Moscow. Things went from there. Lots of people arrested—over sixty, with long probation periods or jail time. Native Americans, people from respectable professions, and old women were the three types of people I would have liked to have seen more of at Cove/Mallard. In all three categories we were unsuccessful. We tried, but only got one Native American. Law enforcement doesn't know how to deal with Indians. They are subject to twice as many laws as whites, but whites still don't like arresting them. It makes bad press. The other thing was old women. We found a group called Great Old Broads for Wilderness. We wrote them and sent them money. They sent us a T-shirt. Their action seems to be that they go to D.C. and present T-shirts to congressmen. That's fine, but I wanted some of them on the front line daring the cops to arrest them. We saw pictures of them— they were in their seventies and eighties, looking feisty and spirited. But we couldn't even get the president of the Great Old Broads to respond to our letter. What is the point of having this great resource if no one's going to do anything?"

"I've been asked what direction I would like to see the environmental movement go, as well as whether action and nonviolent civil disobedience is the path that we need to take," Ramon says. "The first order of business is to stop. And if I had to say what the *raison d'être* of Cove/Mallard is, I guess that is what this is all about."

The weather was sunny, that August 17, 1993, Earth First!'s official Wild Rockies Day. Outside the infamous "mooning" event, August 17, 1993, was one of the few days that the Cove/Mallard campaign attracted national attention.

Steve Paulson was driving his car up the FS 222D road to the Earth First! encampment when he passed three young men, millworkers and loggers, standing in the road. Steve stopped to talk peace, not knowing that those three had already chased two other activists.

Immediately, he was surrounded by ten timber workers in a circle. Out of the crowd a fist hit him above his left eye. Then came a second punch from a fist wearing a hardened metal object. The metal knob punctured his skull, and Steve dropped unconscious immediately. While he was on the ground, he was kicked, with one rib broken, as well as blows to his back. In the background, he woozily heard murmurs, "don't kill him." Somehow, he managed to revive himself, jump up, and plead, blood rubbed all over his face. Donald Alan Cooper, the logger who punched him, said, "The time for talking is over." One of the other loggers jumped in to protect Steve and promised his safety. Another logger started swinging, but missed. Steve retreated, jumped in his automobile, and sped up the road to camp, where, by coincidence, the ABC Nightly News film crew had been doing a story on the campaign. As weird luck would have it, the ABC crew, at camp at the time, filmed Steve staggering into camp. His blood-covered face appeared nationwide on the news clip about Cove/Mallard.

The Idaho County sheriff never formally arrested Cooper, even though Steve filed a complaint and the prosecuting attorney filed an assault charge. The court proceeding was delayed twice by Cooper's refusal to show. The second time, the judge finally issued a bench warrant after fifteen minutes of waiting for Cooper to arrive. Steve, disgusted, left with his partner and some friends for lunch across the street. When they were exiting the parking lot after their meal, the prosecuting attorney flagged them down, told them that Cooper had arrived, and asked Steve to return to court. In the trial, the prosecutor only filed for misdemeanor assault, even though Cooper had been arrested and served time for a similar charge in Alaska. Cooper admitted guilt, said he had not been provoked, and confessed to a problem with alcohol. The judge commiserated with the defendant and suggested in an avuncular manner that the defendant might try attending Alcoholics Anonymous meetings. Cooper was given only twenty days in jail.

"My next-door neighbor used to take me fishing," Erik Ryberg says. "On the way back, I could see the Siskiyou Mountains, outside my home in Ashland, Oregon, which at that time still had trees on them. He would point out over the mountains, and say 'That's some big country out there.' Then when I became old enough to have a bicycle, I would push it all the way up from Ashland, to where I could ride around and see. And then it became obvious to me that it wasn't big country at all. My neighbor would talk about how a fella could get lost up there, and I would think that it wasn't true, you couldn't possibly get lost. It was small."

Erik's Siskiyou Mountains are now mostly scalped, casualties of the lost timber/spotted owl war in the Cascades. Outside the parks and a few small roadless areas, the old-growth forest is gone. Many of the small towns that prospered off the destruction of the last forests have also collapsed, victims of timber overharvest and resource depletion, as well as corporate propaganda about the state of the timber supply. "I remember Medco, a local timber company out of Butte Falls, vowing that they had been logging their private holdings carefully," Erik says, "that they had timber to last forever when all this spotted owl stuff hit. A year later, they said that they had logged all their land, and basically closed the town. They weren't tooled for anything except big, old-growth trees."

After graduating from the University of Rochester in 1983, Erik hitch-hiked around the Pacific Northwest, climbing the Cascade peaks. On one trip, a woman named Elaine Rees picked him up. "She was an old hippie, with long grey hair, driving a VW bus. She talked about how she lived in a house built out of driftwood for years near Coos Bay, with no running water. She was putting together a wilderness area proposal, the Hawksie/Walksie Wilderness Area. She let me stay in her house. Her only furniture was a bed and a writing table. I had been giving money for a while to groups like Greenpeace and the Wilderness Society, and had always felt like there was nothing I could do except give money. Elaine was the first real environmentalist I had ever met—not someone who lobbies in Washington, D.C., but someone who did it on her own. Hawksie/Walksie is now a wilderness area, called Hawk Mountain. She didn't have a degree in biology, or work for the agencies. She didn't have any money. She just applied her brain, figured out what she wanted, and got it."

After attending graduate school at the University of Virginia, where he became associated with Earth First!, Erik moved to Phoenix, Arizona, and got involved with the Mt. Graham campaign. The protests revolved around construction of a number of telescopes by a consortium of universities, government agencies, and the Vatican, headed by the University of Arizona. The U.S. Forest Service, the agency in charge of managing the area, had closed off the mountain during preparation of the telescope site, ostensibly for the protection of the Mt. Graham red squirrel, an endangered species unique to Mt. Graham.

The entire red squirrel population on Mt. Graham consists of two subpopulations that live on two parts of the mountain, one high elevation and one low elevation. Populations thrive or decline depending on the crop of pine cones occurring at different elevations. If there's a bad cone crop up top, there is generally speaking a good cone crop down below, and vice-versa. The squirrels don't truly migrate up and down the mountain, but as the various populations rise and fall, the greater population re-inhabits the area occupied by the lesser population. With the telescope construction, the Forest Service permitted the removal of all the habitat up top. The excuse offered by the agency was that there was plenty of habitat four hundred feet in elevation below. But that decision rested on a fundamental fallacy. They weren't just cutting the habitat in half; they were taking out an entire component.

The activists at Mt. Graham used protests against cutting down the forest on the top of the mountain to stall site preparation activities while waiting for an injunction from the Ninth Circuit court against the Forest Service to stop the telescope construction. The situation was touch-and-go. The protesters never knew when they would wake up and find out that the chainsaws were running.

At one protest, people had locked themselves to gates with bike locks and to trees with lock-boxes (steel tubes in which people stuck their arms and then handcuffed their wrists). Erik was up on the mountain that day, hiding in the forest surrounding the action site with a camera. Such behavior is typical protest protocol; having people in the woods with cameras can prevent violence by the police making arrests. A large protest was planned, with more than two hundred individuals in attendance.

"But once they started cutting trees, all hell broke loose. The plan just collapsed," Erik says. "People who were supposed to stay hidden and protect the people who were locked to trees didn't do it. They ran out screaming—it was total havoc. We were pretty convinced that when they cut those trees, we were watching the last step in the extinction of the endangered Mt. Graham red squirrel. There was one kid named Larry who ran screaming at a logger and tackled him. The logger was trying to cut down a tree. He turned and chased Larry. Larry leaped into the tree, like I had never seen anybody do, and started climbing it, while other loggers were trying to cut the tree down. There wasn't any of this dumb hippie shit—people were yelling and screaming. We abandoned those ones who were locked to the trees, left them to their own fates."

Law enforcement arrived and started yanking people out of trees by their feet. Erik stood there, dumbfounded. He told the sheriff that all the people who were cutting down the trees were violating the Endangered Species Act and should be arrested. Instead, he was charged with violating the Endangered Species Act, along with a county charge of criminal trespass. They found him guilty, and fined him $700. Since Erik wouldn't pay, he was given thirty days in the Graham County jail. "The first cell we were put in was this squalid, dark hole filled with eighteen people," Erik says.

"They served us chicken once that wasn't cooked all the way. We all got sick. There were eighteen people on two toilets, one that didn't flush, shitting and puking. It was terrible. It was dark, no windows, one little light, people sleeping on the floor. Some people were doing six months—it wasn't just a holding cell." After catching and mailing a big cockroach to the sheriff, with a threat to send roaches to the local health department, Erik was transferred to the Safford federal correctional facility, a high-security prison.

After he was released from jail, Erik started hanging out in the Mazatzal Wilderness Area outside Phoenix. There was a small spring that he loved, called Mineral Springs, which formed a small stream that flowed above ground for a half a mile before going underground for another half a mile. The Forest Service had plans to sink a concrete culvert in the spring to pipe water to cows. When Erik found out about that he became furious and requested all the documentation on the project. There was a sensitive species of concern, the Chiricahua leopard frog, that would have been hurt by the development. The Forest Service maintained that the frog would only be displaced momentarily while those developments proceeded. "I talked to the wildlife biologist," Erik says. "He had never even been up to the spring, and didn't even know that there was flowing water." Erik wrote his first appeal and won, but that was followed by project revision and another decision. In the end, he lost. "Mineral Springs is probably a mudhole with cows around it now," he says. "It used to be a spring with ferns and vegetation. The Forest Service biologist didn't care—he just signed off on the projects."

Erik finally loaded everything in a LandCruiser and drove to Missoula to work on the *Earth First! Journal*. At that time, Cove/Mallard was starting up. The *Wild Rockies Review*, a local environmental publication, printed maps of the cutting units for the sales, along with small graphics of burning bulldozers. Underneath the maps was a little paragraph that said "this is a giant timber sale, in a very important wildlife corridor. This is exactly where the roads are going to go, the trees are going to fall. You know what to do."

Camping out in the Nez Perce Forest during the Cove/Mallard protests in 1992, there were twice as many Forest Service law enforcement officers as protesters. "They'd come right up to us and stick their video cameras right in our tents," Erik says. "They were harassing us constantly, trying to get someone to assault one of them. They watched us twenty-four hours a day. But one thing I noticed—they wouldn't follow us into the woods. They were afraid of the woods, and still are."

Erik was arrested twice that summer, the first time for crossing an unconstructed, closed road. The Forest Service had closed a road that didn't exist—no survey stakes marked the intended byway. He was out in the woods with some friends, looking for candystick, *Allotropa virgata*, a sensitive plant, whose presence could help delay the timber sale. Law enforcement was waiting where the trail crossed the road. "It was crazy," Erik relates. "They came out with guns drawn on us, from both sides, then made us get on the ground and handcuffed us. One guy stood there with his gun directed at my head while the other one put the cuffs on. They were all wearing bullet-proof vests. It went through my mind that they were just going to execute me."

Later, in September, in a particularly ill-fated action, James Barnes locked himself to a gate. The Forest Service ended up dismantling the entire gate, leaving James locked to a post as they drove equipment by him. For a grand send-off, Erik and three others mooned James. One escaped into the woods; the other three were later cited by the Forest Service for creating a safety hazard, but the judge ultimately dismissed the case.

After the summer of 1992, Erik went back to Missoula, writing appeals with the Ecology Center. He returned to Cove/Mallard the following summer, 1993, with only a hundred dollars in his wallet.

"What a summer 1993 was," Erik says. "It was a rolling calamity. Every day, I would wake up and ponder what fresh hell would happen that day. What thing that I can't even imagine will go wrong?" Erik was the camp coordinator, the person who kept the basic framework of a campaign alive, trying to make sure that people didn't get botulism from the food.

On August 2, Erik was driving down the road with one of his brake lights out. Forest Service law enforcement stopped him and gave him a mandatory appearance in Boise. Later that day they stopped him and surrounded his truck, shoved him around, and accused him of being in the closure while some protesters were setting up a satellite camp, a remote camp away from the Land. They told him that they were going to get him and that he was going to go to prison.

Tensions finally erupted on August 3. Erik had been up the previous night working on a friend's truck when a Forest Service rig drove up on the property. The encampment had a gate down below, and the campaign organizers had made a verbal agreement earlier that year with special agent Mike Merkeley, in charge of Forest Service law enforcement, that law enforcement wouldn't come on the Land without a search warrant.

When Erik saw the Forest Service Suburban rolling up the drive, he walked down toward the gate. Other Earth First!ers were already approaching the vehicle. He questioned the two Forest Service law enforcement agents concerning their violation of the agreement, and asked for their warrant. "They had their nametags covered up with their pocket flaps," Erik says. "It was kind of frightening—we didn't know who they were. My first reaction was 'just get the hell out,' but they were stuck, because they had driven up this road that wasn't really a road. My friend Catfish got behind and directed them.

When the Suburban got to the bottom of the hill, Erik sent Catfish back for a camera. He told them that they had to tell him who they were and what they were doing, or they had to stay until we got a picture of their license plate. The officers at first said OK, but then changed their minds and began to leave. Erik believed the gate was still in place, and that they would have to bash up their Suburban to get over it. But when he rounded the corner, he noticed that they had taken it apart and set it off to the side of the road. Erik got in front of their Suburban and said, "We're going to keep you here until we get the information." The officers kept driving and pushing him. So Erik got under the front tire. The vehicle stopped. The officers got out and pulled him away, but he got back under the wheel as soon as they got back in the truck.

"It's funny how things got carried away," Erik says. "I was lying down there under the wheel, and thinking that they were going to drag me out again. Now, there's a lot of room underneath one of those big green Suburbans, and I was looking at the oil pan, right above my head. And I thought, I'll be danged, I've got a crescent wrench in my pocket, that'll keep them here. So I got up and said, 'I'm going to drain all of your oil out of your oil pan, so you should turn off your truck.' It was an idle threat, because it would have meant spilling dirty motor oil all over Rhett Creek. But it backfired, because they instantly jumped out of the truck and dragged me all the way down the embankment, took my glasses off, and threw them away. I started screaming my lungs off, and people started running down the hill."

Now the Forest Service officers had a situation on their hands. Before they just had one person under their Suburban. Now they had a crowd of people surrounding their rig. The officers handcuffed Erik and put him inside. Now the vehicle was seriously stuck. One officer got out with his shotgun and said "Get the hell away from my truck" as he cocked his shotgun and pointed it at people around the vehicle. "That was the totally wrong thing to do," Erik says. "At that point, everybody jumped in front of his gun. It was kind of funny to me, because he believed that if you pointed a gun at somebody, they would get out of the way. He ran around with his shotgun, and pretty soon, three more people were locked to the front of his truck. These guys' day was just going bad. They were scared. They called for reinforcements, and locked themselves inside the truck." A number of activists started rocking the vehicle. Some of the activists wanted to flip the Suburban upside down and take Erik out. Catfish, a level head, prevailed, and calmed the crowd. Erik remained inside.

After several hours of waiting inside the vehicle, Erik told the officers that he had to pee. He asked to be let out, or he was going to urinate in their Suburban. They wouldn't release him. So Erik told them, "You're just telling me to piss in your Suburban." And they said "well your hands are handcuffed." Erik said "I'm not going to be able to aim too good." But they didn't count on the fact that Erik is really flexible, and can double-joint his shoulders. He got his hands around to his front, unzipped his zipper, and sprayed their radio. The officers started shaking their heads.

The reason for the Forest Service officials being on the land was later revealed as a "courtesy call" to bring activist David Pacheco news of his grandfather's death. Erik was found guilty of obstructing a federal officer and sentenced to two months in the Latah County jail.

Kelley and I visited Erik in jail, my first friend behind bars. We went inside into the holding area, metal clanking behind me, into tight halls of sensory-deprivation yellow. When I was called, I gave my driver's license to the jailer and walked through the door of steel bars to the visitation area, a huge wall with three windows one-foot square, double-Plexiglassed with phones hanging on the walls. The jailer brought out Erik, ecstatic to see friends, dressed in his bright orange prison fatigues. He grabbed both phones—Kelley took one, I took the other. Then, for the fifteen minutes allotted, I poured forth my best effort at comedy and story-telling. Next to us, a young trollop rubbed her breasts on the Plexiglas window, smearing her lips at her check-kiting boyfriend. I went home to nightmares. Erik returned to the constant, banal blather of eighteen hours of television on weekdays, twenty-four hours on the weekends, and candy bars for good behavior.

Erik lives now in McCall, Idaho, waging another personal, legal war on the Payette National Forest. In the aftermath of the fires of 1994, the Forest Service is launching a full-frontal attempt to enter a number of pristine areas under the excuse of salvaging dead timber. Erik is appealing the sales. "You know, Chuck, I am the best last man in the trench," he says. "Everyone else will have abandoned the fight, but I'll still be here. I keep fighting these projects, over and over, but reincarnated, they come back."

In my college days, I used to read pulp fantasy novels, by authors like Michael Moorcock, with dark heroes, like Elric of Melnibone. Elric was an albino prince, neutral, with a magical sword, Stormbringer, that would eat the souls of the enemies he killed. These reincarnated timber sales seem to have a life of their own, I think. And then I see Erik, getting arrested on the front lines, working late into the night, appealing timber sales, over and over again, fighting reprocessed versions of the same monster. As he curses his fate, shaking his fist at the gods, I can see Erik praying. Praying for Stormbringer.

It is the fall of 1995, and the protesters who were arrested in the Jack Road are now congregating on the federal building steps for their trial. There are twelve of them total, some old campaigners, some new, that stood in the road on August 18. Two were perched atop twenty-foot-tall lodgepole tripods. The rest were similarly fixed to the tripods and gate with bike locks.

I had heard stories of the arrest scenario—how the Forest Service and local sheriff had deputized loggers to help arrest the protesters, how one of the law enforcement officers had kicked the leg of one of the tripods, which could have caused it to collapse, possibly killing the protesters. I am here for moral support. Erik Ryberg is here also, with Kelley, covering the trial for the *Earth First! Journal*. The protesters are charged with being inside a closed area inside a National Forest.

As I walk into the trial, in the middle of the proceedings, I see a crammed jury box, but no jury. The protesters are being tried simultaneously, and each protester has a lawyer, twelve total, throwing motions, deliberating, yelling objections to lines of questioning. The only difference between the pandemonium that occurred at the demonstration and this, I think, is that this is legal. One lawyer states that the timber sale is illegal, and the defendant was obstructing this illegal process. Another lawyer states that his client was policing timber sales; the Forest Service had previously denied anyone associated with the campaign from legally witnessing the cutting down of the forest. Another lawyer, obviously less skilled, argues the "idiot" defense, that the protesters didn't know they were in Idaho because it wasn't printed on the map, a legal requirement. As I leave for work, the judge is admitting evidence into the record never before allowed in these types of cases.

I return to the courtroom the following day, seating myself toward the front in a walnut-veneered bench. Kelley and Erik are sitting behind me. Erik's face is downcast. "They should fire all their lawyers and go *pro se*," Erik says. "They're screwed."

That night, Erik and I talk about the protesters. I question their sincerity. Some of the activists have spent hardly any time at all on the Land. How can someone who has only recently arrived at a place feel compelled to submit themselves to imprisonment for such a place? Where is the identification with the Northern Rockies? How can we expect other people to see the wild Rockies as an entity if our own protesters see it as an issue?

Erik shrugs and frowns. "Everyone up there, Chuck," he says, "has lost something. Some of those kids are from Oregon, others from the Midwest. Think what happened to those places. What about you, Chuck? Why are you in Idaho, working on the Clearwater? A lot of them don't know what to do. They just know that they're losing something else, something important to them. And they've chosen to come to Cove/Mallard to express that loss."

When I was young, I would go to the grocery store and stare at the photographs on the side of beer six-pack containers, covered with pictures of blue skies, moose surrounded by tall grass in front of big timber, with tall mountains in the background. Maybe I, too, am in the West for the love of an idea.

The trial drags on for another two days. The protesters are sentenced alternately to one, two, or three weeks in jail, depending on past arrest records. As the protesters are released, some make the decision to return to school at the University of Idaho. Others work in the small office dedicated to the campaign. Many leave for their homes.

Peace returns—until next year. More will be back.

A Handful of Ashes

In 1942 there came a truly tragic forest fire—by far the worst that mankind had ever witnessed. Crazed, screaming animals flew, galloped, ran and crawled from hideous tongues of flame, stopping only long enough to warn their friends. Some were burned. Many wept. They lost their families and their beautiful, happy homes. This was the conflagration in Walt Disney's animated motion picture, "Bambi"—a work identified by Roderick Nash, professor of history and environmental studies at the University of California at Santa Barbara, as "The most important document in American cultural history bearing on the subject [of fire management policy]."

—Ted Williams, "The Incineration of Yellowstone," *Audubon*, Jan. 1989

THE SUMMER OF '94 was a big fire year out West. But even so, the Clearwater Country did not burn like central Idaho did. Only scattered places like Hidden Creek, Minnesahka Creek off of Smith Ridge, or up on the Powell District in the Selway/Bitterroot took to flame. Two of the Clearwater's largest fires started in clearcuts, in logging debris, one in the checkerboard nuclear zone on the Plum Creek intermingled lands, where a log loader exploded. But regardless of the size of the fire, when smoke drifted into the towns on the edge of the wild, the fires were big news. The papers were filled with various accounts of how bad the fire season was. What they did not say was that only .5 percent of the Northern Rockies took to flame. This, the worst fire year, called by the timber industry a "natural disaster" and the result of "improper management," provided justification for a massive campaign to salvage dead and dying timber across the forests, including the roadless country.

The fires were not new to me. I can remember fire from my youth on the Kentucky hills, on the Ohio river breaklands covered with oak forests. I can still remember the black of the sky, the outlines of trees along ridges with fire behind them, the acrid smoke and red on the river. I was only thirteen then, too young to join the fireline like the older boys in my high school. There was money to be made, fighting the fires, and white smiles against blackened faces printed on the front page of the newspaper belied any hint of tragedy left by burning hillsides.

My sister, a wetland ecologist familiar with Eastern ecosystem dynamics, tells me that fires naturally burn in the oak savanna, giving the prairie a second chance for survival beneath the forest canopy. I never thought of fire in the forest as bad—more like someone talking about the weather. Good or bad, trees burn. Back in Ohio, beneath open canopies of red oak and buckeye, fire is the price for open, uncluttered space.

But since moving out West, I have never seen a fire in lodgepole, or watched the brush burn in the ponderosa pine understory. When fire came last summer to the Salmon River breaks, to French Creek and the South Fork of the Salmon River, they closed the roads ten miles out from the fire perimeter. McCall was a war zone, with people wearing yellow coats and canvas pants ferried to the front far away. Helicopters buzzed overhead, dodging slurry bombers taking off from the airport with loads of red borate to spray on isolated stands of timber. I could not even get close.

And even when the farmers burn their fields in a wet year with no fire danger, they still close the roads, leaving only the smoke to fill the air. I am told where to go, where to drive, and when to stay away. In the West, we are in denial of fire.

Forests burn in the West, covering big pieces of the landscape. We can no more stop fire here than we can persuade the clouds to rain. And because of this, the forests and natural communities have adapted. Ponderosa pine forests in open glens burn every ten to twenty years. On the border of the grasslands of the Palouse, the Nez Perce used to burn the fields every year, depending on preference of place for spring or fall grazing. The lodgepole forest burns every one hundred years, has to for the tight, resinous cones of that conifer to burst open and reseed the area. The Douglas fir/ cedar/grand fir community, inhabiting wetter landtypes, does not burn as often. But even these groves can withstand fire. Their age alone, often 250-500 years, demonstrates survival through all but the hottest seasons. Western larch, often one of the first trees to reforest a fire site, claim the ridgetops in this country. You can see the streaks of yellow on a fall drive as trees drop their needles after the first hard freeze.

Even the mathematics justify fire. The Clearwater National Forest grows 440 million board feet of timber a year, most unrecoverable to humanity. In a heavy harvest year, logging may take 150 million board feet of this total. This amount of logging scars the land and wastes the streambeds.

But a more sustainable cut of 40 million board feet logged still leaves 400 million every year that nature produces. In a dry climate during a dry year, the fungus and bacteria that break down the forests into soil cannot haul away the excess biomass. The forest must have fire.

Animals have evolved around fire, building their nests in the spring, and raising their young in dens and cavities during the wet, early summer. When the inevitable drought comes in late July, and the forest dries out to the moisture content of kiln-dried lumber, the birds, the squirrels, and the insects are gone, running in front of the hot wave that swirls up the mountains. Elk, deer, and bear retreat to the rivers, out of the high meadows. Moose stand unconcerned in their wetland bogs. Fires rarely burn the whole forest, occasionally burning a hillside, mostly twenty- to forty-acre patches, a scattered mosaic across shrublands and early-successional forest.

The difference between the impact of man simulating fire and the impact of fire alone in the forest is dramatic. Fire puts no pressure on the soil. There is no analog to the weight of a Caterpillar D-9 tractor in nature, nor comparison between the compaction of roads versus the brush of a hot wind passing briefly over a landscape every twenty or fifty years. On fragile soils, roads and roadcuts persist for ages.

Fire also leaves behind big, standing snags to protect the birds, creating places for woodpeckers and cavity-nesters to homestead. Fires provide logs that block the paths of streams, creating new pools for fish after nature cleans the ash and erosion out of the streambeds.

Logging leaves only stumps. Fire cannot be simulated by logging, hauling away the trees by skidder, or flying huge logs by helicopter, taking away biomass and minerals. Logging crews leave behind only the small branches, the kindling for fire to come again, because there is no economic sense in hauling anything away by air but the bole of the tree. Roads built with the justification of fire salvage are used by the industry the following year to haul away green trees out of the forest.

Where fire burns too hot, shrubs such as ceanothus cover the fire site and rebuild the soil, adding nitrogen over a ninety-year age, enriching the land to critical mass to support the next wave of the mixed conifer forest. Ninety years is not too long to wait.

The U.S. government has historically tried to suppress fire in the West, and these efforts were very effective for a short period of time, right after World War II, because of increased manpower, communication, and equipment previously not available. For the first time, the country could fight fires effectively in remote areas such as backcountry wilderness. It was also a time that was critical in terms of fire cycles. Forests that had commenced growing after the last dry cycle, that had grown to a size and density where fire would typically sweep through and thin out the newly grown stands, were spared the torch. Grazing also dramatically affected the ratio of herbaceous grasses and shrubs to the number of small evergreens in the forest. Because cattle prefer to eat grasses instead of small trees, young trees, not nearly as flammable as the grasses, overtook the forest floor. Small fires typically spread quickly through grasslands underneath pine boughs. But when land is overgrazed, this avenue for understory burns is eliminated, creating longer fire cycles and more catastrophic burns.

Congress passed the Gorton/Taylor salvage rider during the summer of 1995, ostensibly to preserve "forest health" and prevent fire. The timber industry says it can prevent fire by chopping down trees. If you chop down the entire forest, fire is no longer an issue. The salvage rider gives the Forest Service amnesty, setting it free of obeying laws such as the National Environmental Policy Act, or the National Forest Management Act, or the Endangered Species Act when it prepares its timber sales.

Just as territorial governor William Gilpin of Colorado thought that he could legislate the fact that "rain follows the plow," we have another generation of politicians who have decided that they can litigate the laws of physics. They can do this, these Western senators and congresspeople, because they believe in the myths of the people of the intermountain West. The cult around fire and fire suppression is "The Big Gung-Ho Thing." And in this myth, the worst of the character of the West is embodied, paid for and propped up by the U.S. government, in bad forest management, fire suppression schemes, in the actual firefighting itself, and finally with post-fire salvage logging.

Ben's house is cool, dark, and neat. It is spring, and clouds hang low over the mountains in Boise, where we are visiting. I skied with Ben last year up in the Wallowas, and we made our acquaintance around a steel-plate stove in a small mountain cabin, an anachronism buried under eight feet of Oregon powder. Ben talked about firefighting. He is an Idaho native, raised within the boundaries of the mythos. He started fighting fires in 1984, after four years in the navy. He was planning on going to college, but when he got out of the service, he hired on with a BLM fire crew in Salmon, Idaho.

"You know that old saying, 'Black forest, green paycheck,'" he laughs. "There was good money to be made, even in 1984, a slow year. We fought a couple of fires, just around Salmon. I remembered one time they choppered us into Lens Peak—it was nothing but a giant rockpile. We had to cut a snag down and dig it out. They paid us anyway. Anytime you're out there and you're on it, you're getting paid. I remember the next day, the helicopter came in and brought us hot breakfast. It was pretty uptown."

The next year was different, a hot, big fire year. Ben was assigned to Helitack, an elite helicopter crew flying to remote areas to fight fires started by lightning strikes. During that time crews could still fly into wilderness areas. Ben's job was to make sure the firefighters and their equipment got on- and off-board safely. Having grown up in Salmon, he knew the country and would usually be the navigator, sitting next to the pilot and pointing out landmarks.

"Initial attack fires, we would get those, because they were small," Ben says. "But the bigger fires, like the Lake Mountain Fire, south of the Salmon in the Williams Creek country, as well as the fire complexes along the river—we had help. On Lake Mountain, where we were fighting the fire, bulldozers would be right behind the guys, cutting the line. One day, about midday, the fire just blew up. I remember the borate bombers coming in, but the fire was so hot, so massive, that the borate probably crystallized before it even hit the ground. We had to move our entire fire camp and do an emergency evacuation. By the time it was all over it seemed like it ended up burning where it wanted to go anyway. Sometimes, we'd be on these fires all summer long, and they wouldn't be officially declared out until the snow hit. With Lake Mountain, all you could do was sit back and watch it go."

The mentality behind firefighting is driven by mock macho war heroics, Ben says. Firefighters view the fire as the enemy, working round-the-clock in twelve hour shifts. But what makes it different from war is that the fire isn't shooting back. A firefighter gets the thrill of the Big Gung-Ho Thing, without the bullets. And that attracts people looking for a thrill. "One of my crew bosses was an old Vietnam vet, and he was so gung-ho that he was dangerous," Ben says. "He would draw us into situations that were really scary."

But in a typical fire season, as far as acres are concerned, a lot more gets burned than gets saved. "I can remember half the pictures on TV from the Yellowstone fire," Ben says. "People were sitting around, leaning on shovels, watching it burn. When a fire gets that big, we'll spend a lot of money on it, but it's going to go where it wants to go."

Moneymaking in the fire business goes on, even during slow, wet years. "In a slow year, we would milk small fires," Ben says. "When a fire might be relatively out, they'll milk it right down to the last ember. You jump on the bandwagon, like everyone else, because you know there's going to be really good money at the end of the year. Sometimes in a slow fire year, they might spend more time than in a hot year. Kind of the attitude that 'we've got a fire, let's ride this one out.' That's not always the case, but it's there."

Ben stops. It has become darker outside. He talks about how it all made him sick in the end, how the waste, the abuse got to him, how he doesn't want to fight fires anymore. But I think about my feelings, the unattainable opportunity to fly low over the forest in a helicopter, seeing the puff of white smoke in the distance, and coming to terms with the landscape on a scale that explains the continuity in the ground. In the distance, I see holy mission, and monetary reward at the end of the line. My training and my understanding hates the result. But my perspective understands the seduction.

Leon Neuenschwander, a forestry professor at the University of Idaho, says that we have already lost 70 percent of the original ponderosa pine ecosystem in the West, the one we identify with our open, park-like forest that used to fill the low-elevation country in Idaho. Most of it has been lost to wheat farmers, grazing for cattle, and the early destructive timber harvest techniques practiced by Potlatch and others. It's the big trees, the huge old punkin p-pines that held the whole thing together, he says. Once those trees are gone, the ecosystem and its biodiversity vanishes. And to top it all off, we are in a drier climate cycle and the ponderosa pine borders marginal dry areas, those likely to turn to scrub anyway. Currently, there is a trend to warmer weather, similar to the last cycle from the late 1800s to the 1930s that ended in the dust bowl. That cycle also ended up with really large forest fires, which shaped the current fire policy of the United States. Leon's theory holds up concerning the Clearwater Country. The great fires of 1910, 1919, 1937 created the Great Burn country drained by Kelly, Cayuse, and Weitas creeks that swept all the way up to the Coeur d'Alene watershed.

"We don't know whether we're in a long period of permanent climate change, or just in a forty-year cycle," Leon says. "But one thing for sure, the greatest environmental stress is in the driest part of our forests." That's where people are moving, where they want to live—the wildland/urban interface. In nature's view, the wildland/urban interface is winter range for migrating animals. But whether it's from houses, agriculture, winter range for migrating animals, or whether it's ranches or timber harvests, the areas that get hit first are the lowlands. And of all the different types of lowland ecosystems, the ones that get it the worst are these forests.

Leon's work concerning fire ecology mostly concerns the Boise National Forest, down south past McCall, and he is quick to note that the fire frequency is different in old ponderosa pine than in the lodgepole and mixed conifer forests of the uplands of the Clearwater Country. But the Boise experience is true for much of the land where we actually have our homes—we have chopped down the trees and excluded fire. These forests have undergone a dramatic change. The ponderosa pine ecosystems have been converted to brush, even-aged tree plantations, and farmlands. These, along with the effect of this dry period, have created a homogeneous landscape that begs for large fires.

Fire in these dry forests has changed from its evolutionary role and historical place, from a frequent visitor of every twenty years to rarely or never. In the past, fire created the landscape mosaic and site diversity essential to ecosystem resilience that allowed the ground to recover. These fires were typically small. But the exclusion of fire over a hundred years causes fires to grow to the point where they are now catastrophic and lethal. The big trees, the icons of the ponderosa pine forest, even with their thick, pyrophobic, bark are not surviving. With the loss of these big trees, the structure in the ecosystem is being eliminated.

"We're creating a new ecosystem that's non-forest. Sure, there will be brush and seedlings and young trees, but we're now in a cycle where the big trees are gone, and the fires burn the brush fields." Leon sighs. "We are losing ponderosa pine ecosystem at the rate of 4 percent each year."

It's not just fire, Leon says. Logging is wide-scale, hauling away the big trees by tractor, skyline, and helicopter. Regardless of the television ads by such timber companies as Boise-Cascade, the timber giants are not changing their logging practices. They are still harvesting old-growth ponderosa pine, exacerbating an already bad situation. They take the big trees, leaving the smaller ones behind, creating dense stands of young ponderosa mixed with the true firs, which are more flammable and not likely to survive a large fire. Often the shorter firs, hiding in the understory, carry the flames up into the crowns of the few larger trees left standing. These crown fires burn large areas, simplifying the ecosystem over thousands of acres. The problem is not just Idaho's. Everywhere there is a ponderosa pine forest— eastern Washington, California, southern Idaho—there are the big fires. When the ecosystems will break is anyone's guess.

In the wake of the 1994 fire season, salvage logging, the logging of a site after the trees have been scorched by fire, has been promoted by some as a solution for wildfire in the West. But salvage logging is an economic issue, not an ecological issue, Leon says. "The justification for salvage logging is the rural community sets of issues involving sustaining local economies. Most of the justifications that have been given for the ecological basis for salvage logging are exaggerations of the benefits. Most prominent of those is reducing the fire hazard. Salvage logging marginally, if at all, reduces the fire hazard, and in some cases it may even increase it."

In order to avert this crisis and the loss of the ponderosa pine ecosystem, Leon wants to return fire to its original role in the ecosystem. Gently at first, he wants to start small prescribed burns—fires set by land managers— during wet years, initiating them in the springtime before wildlife has set up their nests and when the danger of a fire burning out of control is low. And we need to start doing this now, he maintains. On the Boise National Forest, only a twelve-year window remains where any management activities can make a difference for preservation of the ecosystem. After that, the combination of fires and logging will have destroyed so much of what is left that the forest won't be a forest any longer—it will be fragmented, disconnected islands that can no longer support the wildlife that depends on this ecosystem type. The old-growth ponderosa pine will be gone.

A wet, gray snow, hangs tight off the ridge overlooking Little Payette Lake where Erik and I hike to see one of the fire sites for the Fall Creek timber sale. A big chinook wind had blown in last night over the mountains, passing like a shadow over Oregon, southern Washington, Hells Canyon, then here, into the giant yellow pine country, the wet high-elevation spruce country, the edge of transition between rock and ice outside of McCall, Idaho.

I had seen the chinook coming on my friend Mike Beiser's weather map, in the orange, yellow, and blue paired vortices of clouds that pushed off the edge of Hawaii. Mike, a seasoned sailor and mountain rescue expert, traced the lines of the swirls with his fingers, then admonished me about the avalanche danger. Mike worked Teton Mountain rescue before his job as the director of the Outdoor Program at the University of Idaho. I saw the rain on the screen and Mike's face. I came anyway. It's been raining in Idaho this winter, a confused season, El Nino for the fifth straight year. I wanted to winter camp and needed the break. I would visit Erik anyway. I took my border collie, Mary.

Erik and I put our snow shoes on at the truck. I have never snowshoed before, and my green aluminum Sherpas seem disjointed and clumsy. Long-legged Erik strides in old, fish-shaped Michigans. I plod deeply in the slush. He floats.

The trail is steep up to the ridge, to the sale unit for the Fall Creek Analysis Area on the McCall District of the Payette National Forest, part of the Blackwell fire, a huge complex of wildfires that swept the hills around McCall last summer. In the Payette National Forest, if a tree burns, it must be cut down. I want to see the fire sites and evaluate myself. I want to view a world of black and white. I must hike in the winter.

Erik leads the way with slow, methodical strides on a secondary road up a thousand feet to a view over Little Payette Lake. At first, I am happy to stay on the road. Though we are far below tree line, there is a delicate comfort in the notion of civilization here. The road grows steeper. I take off my coat and hat, then pack them in my small fanny pack. Erik meanders ahead. Mary flounders in the snow. We are talking about women again, confused. Then fire. Then the salvage plans. We laugh cynically about the Forest Service's publicity flyer on the fires. They proudly proclaim $63 million dollars spent fighting the fires, $41 million in property saved, $7 million pumped into the local economy in McCall and 780 temporary people hired. All for a fire that ended up being put out mostly by cooling weather and fall snows.

The Blackwell fire, containing the Fall Creek area where we are snowshoeing, along with the Chicken and Corral Creek fires, outside of McCall to the east and north, burned hot in the summer of 1994, covering some of the wildest country in central Idaho, the Secesh drainage, and a huge hunk of whitened granite uplands. Fire ran through the high elevations—sparse lodgepole and subalpine forest. In the case of the Blackwell fire, the Forest Service established the burn perimeter as surrounding 48,300 acres. But just because the Forest Service drew a huge line around all the patches of land touched by fire in no way meant it all burned.

The land inside the perimeter was graded as low, medium, or high burn intensity. Even in the areas marked "high intensity," the service admits that there were patches of trees left standing. A lot of the country burned in a mosaic, the thirty- to forty-acre patch size that typically characterizes fires in the Northern Rockies. In the initial post-fire assessment, the Forest Service noted that most of the high-intensity burn ran through the subalpine fir, which would seed back to lodgepole pine, the first seral tree species to reclaim the landscape after a fire. Most of the land is several thousand feet above sea level, some of the tallest, wildest country in Idaho.

The draws and creeks are where the big trees survived, the ponderosa pine and spruce. Those are the ones that the Forest Service wants to log. The Payette National Forest already has a huge salvage agenda for this coming summer, involving building new roads and dozens of helicopter landings to harvest the dead and "dying" timber, whatever that means. It's all got to be done quickly, they say, or the wood will rot and be of no use to man. For man, for humans—that's their worry, regardless of the fact that man got along fine without this wild country since the beginning of time.

They want to log French Creek and the South Fork of the Salmon, two of my favorite places in the Salmon River drainage. They got locked out before, in the '60s, because all the roadbuilding on fragile ground ended up destroying the fishery in the South Fork, one of the premier salmon and trout fisheries in the world. Even by their own admission, they had done a bad job. They were constrained by language in their own Payette Forest Plan. They don't want all this scorched peckerpole lodgepole. They want yellow pine—the big stuff. Even if they don't get it this go-round, they know that the road network will allow future sales of live trees. They don't care about ecosystems going extinct. Looking at the budget in the initial assessment, I can see why. The timber budget is several orders of magnitude above all the money spent for fish and wildlife. It's in the millions of dollars. More millions, after the fact, after spending $63 million just putting out the fire. "Post-fire recovery," they call it.

Erik turns to me and points up the hill, motioning that this is where we leave the road. I am reluctant. I tell Erik to take a bearing with his compass. I am cautious. The road is a security blanket, and leaving it in the winter troubles me. But I quickly notice that as we climb only a hundred feet back into the trees, the sickening whine of the snowmobiles from the valley floor below dies away. Erik bounds ahead. "We can't get lost here. All paths lead down." I follow. Up another five hundred feet in elevation, we stop. I tell Erik how to dig an avalanche pit. He nods and eats a piece of cheese, then bounds off, sidehilling. Even with snowshoes, we sink two feet into the fresh slush. But away from the road, the forest opens up and becomes more complex. There is a lay to the land that is natural, uninterrupted to the eye, that is not present in the corridor.

"Over here. I can see the burned trees," Erik calls out, directing. On this patch—it can't be more than two acres—there are some burned trees, and snags too. The boles of the oldest ponderosa pines, though charred black, still have bark structure. The youngest trees, with short, slender black trunks and yellowed needles, have died in this fire. But the big trees are strong Only the bottom needles are brown. The tops remain a subdued green, survivors for another year in a fire cycle ecosystem. I take a picture for my mother. We eat, drink Old Granddad, and make the usual favorite-relative jokes before starting down.

Erik goes bounding down fast, jumping past the remains of the fire, into ice, the snow, toward a stand of old growth, headed for the creek. The snow moves in, solid and white. The clouds drop over the lake below our heads. He drops out of sight, into the draw, behind the old ponderosas, hiding behind a Doug fir, then a spruce. A spruce? I see his tracks, and pause. As I stand, the forest starts to change.

I slough through the deep snow, slipping through a grove of yellow pine, young, then old. The wind blows as the sun rises. The fires burn with a red smoky haze. Hundreds of years pass. The yellow pines, with their flame-resistant bark, hold the moisture on the southern slopes, blocking the wind off the ground. A slow, wet winter comes again. Young spruce, shaded from the high elevation sun, start their procession to the sky under shelter from the yellow pine. As I reach out, closer to the creek, the spruce grow, tall, wide, five feet in diameter in front of my arms. Summer comes again, and fire passes above me, high on the ridgeline, away from the draw. The spruce have claimed the wet bog around the creek back from the yellow pine.

Erik, waving his camo hat off his head, is pointing at a blue mark on one of the big spruces. I stop and strain my eyes. It is there, under the branches, hidden in this place with no trail nor road. Erik leans forward like magic, using no poles to stop his fall. "I think this is state land. These trees must be part of a planned timber sale up here. Probably be cut down in the spring."

It is a high water June, and Kelley and I are on the road, driving up Rattle-snake Grade to McCall. We are headed south, to Gooding, to raft the Jarbidge and Bruneau with our friend Gail. I love the desert canyon country, and relish the opportunity. Kelley is reluctant. The water is high.

We stop for lunch outside McCall, and pull off on the side of the road next to a small, grassy field so that the dogs can run. I tell her Charlie Ray's story about a big state lands fire-salvage sale up the Warren Wagon road outside McCall, probably up in the Corral/Blackwell complex. Charlie said most of the trees were green, but the guy that he was talking to, a logging truck driver, didn't really care. Charlie had admonished me, "Chuck, the thing that guy cares about is having a load to haul every day. He don't care about what it is, just as long as he gets paid."

As we stand in the stiff breeze, the dogs run, stretching their legs, oblivious to the traffic. Log trucks start rolling by. They are carrying big pickles, old-growth ponderosa and spruce, with "state" spray-painted on the ends. Every now and then, a log with fire-scorched bark peeks out of a load, sandwiched in between huge, fresh timbers.

"It's starting," I say, turning away from Kelley, to the mountains lining the edge of the valley and a quickening sky.

Save the World by Christmas

I'M OUT OF CONTROL THIS MONTH. My schedule is full, my life dictated by a stupid looking little book with flowers on the cover and dates in the middle, bought by my wife. If I slip, I'm screwed. I've got no slack in the system.

Larry McLaud—I call him the Trout Man—and I drive through the Floodwood State Forest, off the west shore of Dworshak Reservoir. It's hacked bad, real bad, some of the worst land management in the state, what we call nuclear forestry. Clearcuts for miles, cut over decades. Driving along, I start seeing a pattern, a wave, like ripples running out from the small mill communities of Pierce, Elk River, and Clarkia. That's Clark-ee. Say it right, or show you don't belong, that you're an outsider. Walk into one of the two small mom-and-pop restaurants/bars just off the highway. Ask the stupid question: "Is this Clar-ke-ah?" If you're in the wrong bar and wearing something made by Patagonia, you might, just might, get your ass kicked.

The latest push in Congress, by our own homegrown Idaho Republican Senator Larry Craig, is to give the federal lands to the states. Ostensibly, state governments respond to local citizens' concerns, says Craig; the people who live close to the land should be the ones who manage the land. No more Clearwater National Forest. How about the Pierce Local Forest? With most of the timber gone, and the forest supervisor weakly fending off attacks from locals wanting to finish the job of deforestation, I shrug my shoulders and conclude that this is already the state of things. Local people already get the lion's share of the input when writing the forest plan, the governing document that specifies how the forest will be managed. There also seems to be no problem with constructing more off-road vehicle (ORV) trails to satisfy endless local demands of the Blue Ribbon Coalition, a national off-road vehicle promotion group.

Craig knows all of these things. And he also knows that in Idaho, citizens interested in actually maintaining an ecosystem, individuals concerned about wildlife, water quality, and harvest levels have no opportunities for input to modify, change, or stop decisions on state forest land. Everything is done by the managers, who respond only to the state Department of Lands and the state legislature. The Idaho legislature meets only two months a year, in the winter. The pay is small, and no ordinary citizen can leave their job for two months and expect to keep it. But a rancher, miner, or logging operator can get away for two months during winter slack time.

Our legislature, always vigorously arguing for separation from federal constraints to increase freedom and democracy in Idaho, has outlawed citizen input in such matters as state lands planning. You can't even sue over a timber sale on state ground in Idaho. State lands are supposed to be managed for the maximum financial gain, they say, the money going to support the public schools and other state institutions. But the charter says nothing about the length of the term of this fiduciary decision. An old-growth cedar can live more than 600 years. What will future generations say about the ruined stump desert that they will inherit? Is timber the only resource of monetary value in a forest?

Every stream the Trout Man and I drive by today is annihilated, choked with silt to the point of geomorphic threshold and beyond, the load of dirt so great the stream actually changes its channel. The industry and state have thrown their pennies on the collection plate to assuage their consciences. These pennies are called "Best Management Practices" (BMPs) and include various provisions such as buffer strips along streams, how many logs must be thrown in the stream to create new pools, the number of trees per acre that must be left in order to satisfy the Idaho Forest Practices Act, and other palliatives, written by industry for industry. These BMPs have proven so effective that Idaho now has 962 stream segments of concern under the Clean Water Act. Most of the streams in the roaded country are trashed. As we drive along Stony Creek today, the occasional log has been tossed into the channel. This supposedly creates more pools in the creek to "mitigate" for pools filled in with silt and stream courses damaged by multiple crossings by log skidders and bulldozers. Trout need slow, deep waters to winter in and rest. The timber industry knows this. But the bastards won't get out of these watersheds until the last trees are cut, until the forest is replaced by bare earth and shrub fields. The new, man-generated pools are also filled in with dirt. The streams have been transformed into raceways, constant riffles, evenly spaced by the dictates of gravity and an unchanging, manmade geology. "Boy, any fish swimming in here would get tired really quick, Trout Man," I say, looking at him hunched behind the wheel of his pickup. "Don't worry, though," I say. "The fish are all dead, anyway."

The Trout Man nods, driving carefully. "We have to come up with a story, a rap, Chuck. Something the media can relate to, something they can use for their readers," he says. We stop at a new cedar clearcut notched into a mountainside. The land is swampy, and a huge slash pile, filled with the familiar aromatic stink of wetland death, blocks the skidder road. On the side of one slash pile—it's got to be at least twenty-five feet tall—is spray-painted in neon orange the words "Bob's Barbecue." We walk around the side of the hill, looking for the stumps. We find them, a quarter of a mile down the trail. Cedar didn't get cut out of this country the first time, or even the second time the loggers came through. The first loggers were only interested in white pine, most used for home construction. It's only relatively recently that the vogue has shifted to cedar. Up on Moscow Mountain, next to my house, a friend's subdivision has mandated natural wood to cover your house and roof. Never mind that cedar catches on fire at the drop of a hat, easier than any other wood, burning hot and fast. It looks great, doesn't rot easily, and no one's asking where it comes from anyway. This patch of cedar was the last piece of real forest cover back on this mountainside—a horrible loss of a small oasis, I think.

The state doesn't cut all of its lands like this, though. Up on Priest Lake, the state owns the whole east side of the mountain, and I have seen it, gold and green, perfect Rocky Mountain colors. But then again, rich people own cabins up there, and can actually see the job that the state foresters are doing. But down here it's out of sight, out of mind in this Third World part of a Third World state.

The Trout Man is standing in the mud, sinking slowly in his boondocker boots, hunched back, stressed shoulders, hands on hips, cussing up a mean streak. I am only sad, blue. It must have been beautiful here, I think, this one last small spot. We look at the map—there's Potlatch ground out here, too. We're close to the border between state and private land—that we know. But we can't tell any line of demarcation solely by looking at the management. The destruction of the forest is panoramic.

We cruise for another twenty miles up by Boehl's Cabin, some weird little historic spot in the middle of the clearcuts, and crest the rise, on Potlatch ground for sure, then down in the valley of the Little North Fork of the Clearwater. Logging trucks are hauling the logs off a half-square mile clearcut of old-growth cedar. The Trout Man and I pull off the road to let them pass, snapping artistic post-apocalyptic photos of the trucks above the opening. In the background, the angry chainsaw bees buzz, punctuated by the occasional crash of a tree falling. Like a pathologist on a lunch break in the morgue, the Trout Man hands me a tomato and cheese sandwich and asks me again for ideas for a media campaign. I bite off a chunk, look down at the Little North Fork, and shrug my shoulders at the roadless country in the distance. I tell him my idea about explaining the pattern over the landscape, try to inculcate a feeling for the magnitude of the problem, instead of doing the dead-child-in-the-gutter form of media relations—taking someone to your worst possible spot. The Trout Man says that it might work. I disparage the notion that anything is going to help this beautiful, desperate, and hopelessly out-of-the-way place.

Back in town, we work. We contact the media and set a date for a tour. Coming along are two reporters—one local and one regional, a friend who recently left Moscow. The week is filled with meetings, seminars, letter writing, my full-time job, but no break. On the weekend, I work on the book.

Two weeks later, on a Friday, we go out with the press. The trip runs smoothly. Our homework and prior planning pay off. The weather rains, but the gray lifts off the top of the mountains. One reporter has brought along a photographer who can take pictures of the view, the clearcuts moving out from Clarkia meeting the clearcuts advancing up from Pierce. Midway through the trip, I ask him what he thinks of all this. He is a young man, only in his mid-twenties. He says he is neutral. We drive up the mountain, then down into the Little North Fork again, stopping at the edge of the huge cedar clearcut. Next to a giant slashpile at lunch, I can hear him mumbling to himself, "horrible. This is just horrible." We stage closing comments on the bridge over the river, me in front of the camera, mouthing lines memorized, the spontaneity of discussion in the car replaced by canned discussion for the evening news. Looking at the clearcuts, I tell the reporters that the issue is not "log versus not log." The issue is "do we want to apply this type of management, this version of nuclear forestry, everywhere?" The reporters, used to casting certain issues in defined frameworks, stare at me. I am praying that the message gets through.

Tuesday brings a front-page spread. The Trout Man and I exchange high-fives in the bar, me in the photo looking worried, despondent in front of a clearcut. I show the article to my wife. She looks worried. "Good shot of you. Anyone can recognize you now. Don't you think that there are consequences for that type of behavior? What if someone wanted to shoot you?" she says. I pay no attention, out the door for more interviews for the book. I tell her about a quick dash up to the Middle Fork of the Clearwater at the beginning of next week for some timber sale monitoring—just one more week of this, honey, I say. She turns away, cold.

All Monday, I work at my regular job, then jump in my car at the end of the day and stop by the house for a moment on my way to the Middle Fork. Cruising a clearcut off Big Smith Ridge the following day, I start faltering. I turn to Bill Bob and Gary and tell them I am going home. I need to get to work—my paying job, as opposed to this, I kid them. Students are waiting by my office door when I arrive, with questions. I work late. The next morning, up at 3:30, I fly to Seattle—more job business. I collapse in my plane seat on the return flight, deboard at Lewiston, and drive home. I arrive at 10 p.m.

Black circles ring my eyes. Kelley comes out of the bedroom. She looks at me, slumped on the couch. We, or really she, is busy with her kitchen remodel. "Any time for me?" she says, anger resting on the edge of her words. Mary rings my feet neurotically, circling and butting my hand with her head, begging for a pat. "Any time for the dogs? For the house? Only time for other people that call you with stupid requests, like going to the Clearwater and looking at clearcuts? Those trees are already chopped down. What in the hell is the point of that? Am I the only person you can say 'No' to?" I shrug my shoulders, staring blankly at the wall in our empty room. "I had to move all the furniture out of both the kitchen and living room. Where were you when I needed you? What about your dog? Am I supposed to take care of everything? What's your problem, anyway? What do you think all of this is going to accomplish?" I drop my head in my hands, mumbling, migraine headache moving up around my temples. I don't know.

She turns around, heading for the bedroom, stiffly shaking her head. "Is this your plan, your delusion that someone made you Jesus Christ for a month? A year? The rest of your life? Do you really think that you're going to save the world by Christmas?"

Apocalypse Now

Then there might be an answer to the question I am asked most frequently about the diversity of life: if enough species are extinguished, will the ecosystems collapse, and will the extinction of most other species follow soon afterward? The only answer anyone can give is: possibly. By the time we find out, however, it might be too late. One planet, one experiment.

—E.O. Wilson, *The Diversity of Life*

IT'S BEEN RAINING for the past two weeks now in late November—a strange, warm rain after a cold October. We had thought that winter was coming early this year, with a premature freeze killing the tomatoes in Kelley's garden in late August. But it warmed up at the beginning of November and started to rain instead, a Pineapple Express, a wet wind from Hawaii, coming up and meeting another moisture-laden snowstorm from British Columbia. It's been soaking the soil hard, and as I sit here in my office, it looks like the rain is picking up.

Two weeks ago, one of the banks of Quartz Creek up on the North Fork of the Clearwater, outside of Aquarius campground, slid big time, in what is commonly called a blowout. A blowout is an unknown force of nature to most people, happening when a road gives way, or a mountain of supersaturated soil suddenly slumps into a creek bed. When all of the trees have been chopped off a slope and there's no vegetation to soak up the rain, water builds up, both on the hillside and in the stream, past a critical point. Then the dirt liquefies and turns into a wall of mud and boulders. Roaring downhill and through the stream, it scours out the channel of an entire creek. All that's left are ragged rocks along the stream banks and a huge alluvial fan of gravel and debris at the confluence of the stream and the river. Blowouts can take out the huge trees that grow along the banks, too, although most the drainages that blow had those trees cut a long time ago. I've never been present when a blowout has actually occurred up in the Clearwater Country, but I am sure it is a riverine form of an avalanche, cleaning out everything in its path. An unimaginable number of fish get killed in that kind of thing.

The whole watershed of Quartz Creek has just been hammered, kind of a classic Forest Service pick, pick, pick with timber sales in a fragile watershed until catastrophe happens. Well, catastrophe came—the real thing, with the whole mountainside giving way, creating an earth dam on the creek more than sixty feet tall and six hundred feet wide—400,000 cubic yards of dirt and rocks. The Forest Service folks down on the Clearwater told no one. They just closed the road and dropped the cloak of silence on the whole affair. How they expected to hide the whole thing from the public is beyond me. Word is that the creek, now a reservoir over an acre in surface area and growing, is starting to cut down through the earthen dam.

We'd been telling the Forest Service that the creeks like Quartz Creek were going to blow for years. They knew they would, too, but denied it. I think a lot of people just considered it a price of doing the business of deforestation. But they couldn't tell the public that. They had to maintain the myth of a perfect world up there on the Clearwater. And they pretty much had, because no one goes up there to see the stumps anyway, except misanthropes and Jeremiahs like me. If you stay on the roads, the beauty strip of trees along the edge hides the betrayal. All that was true until November 30.

I am talking to the Trout Man on the phone. We're trying to work out the details of getting some press to see the slide, maybe take a few pictures and hammer on the overharvest problem that caused Quartz Creek to blow out in the first place. It seems like the same old "how are we going to fuck with the Forest Service" conversation that the Trout Man and I have had a thousand times. "Good cop, bad cop, Larry," I say. "I'm in a pissy mood today anyway. I'll be the bad cop," I tell him. "I'll call Art Bourassa and tell him how outraged I am, then you call him and maybe he'll take you up there." Larry thinks it's a good plan. He's been trying for the past week to get a reporter up in the air with Project Lighthawk, the group that flies environmentalists over ecological disasters, but the weather has not been cooperating. Quartz Creek is steep country, rugged and straight up-and-down, and if you plan on flying in there with some little fixed-wing Cessna, you have to have stable air. He tells me the plane is just a little 180, underpowered with three people on board. I know we don't have the money for a helicopter, and even if that was an option, we'd have to have a big one. I hang up and call the North Fork Ranger Station in Orofino.

"Is Art there?" I ask politely, hoping to get past the receptionist. She starts babbling, excited, telling me that Art is out in the field. "Quartz Creek?" I ask, figuring that the mass of dirt and mud is finally starting to move. Shit, I think, maybe there goes my picture of the dam. I start thinking what would happen to the North Fork when all that dirt moves downstream. "Skull Creek," she says. Skull Creek is the drainage below Quartz Creek. She continues, rambling. "Canyon Work Center might flood," she says. "The North Fork might be in record flood. A bunch of debris has moved down into the river, and it's rising fast." She speaks abruptly, saying that all over the forest roads are slipping, slumping, obeying gravity and the condition of fragile soils. The entire roaded front is sliding toward the sea. I start firing questions at her, places, mile markers, amounts, flows. "Who are you, anyway?" she asks, self-correcting. The cloak of silence drops again. I give her my name and phone number, and tell her to have Art call me.

Hanging up the phone, I call the reporter at the regional paper, telling him that the heavily roaded and logged drainages on the Clearwater are all letting go. Roadcuts all over the forest are slumping onto roads, and roads are sliding into creeks. The day of reckoning, what we've been saying is going to happen when there are too many roads and too few trees, combined with rain-on-snow, and nothing to hold it back, is happening now. We need a helicopter, I tell him. I hang up and call Al Espinosa. "Give me your top ten list of drainages that are going to blow, Al." He rattles off the list, watersheds that he fought for during his whole career and lost. I cut him off, telling him that the reporter will call him. I call Larry. We start calling all the district rangers, working staff, receptionists, anyone who can tell us anything. The road and stream blowout list starts matching Al's list—Orogrande Creek, Skull Creek, Smith Creek, Pete King Creek, Canyon Creek, Papoose Creek up on the Powell, and Squaw Creek. Lots has happened that no one even knows about. A roadless drainage blew onto US 12, knocking out the road. The Lochsa is going for record flood. The Selway is raging, over ten feet on the gauge up by Paradise, four feet higher than even this spring's flood stage.

The Trout Man and I work the phones all day long, calling reporters, sources inside the agency, and fellow environmentalists. "A day of prophecy, Larry," I say. "That's our message." I meet him at the bar at 5, strangely vindicated, exuberant, both of us exchanging high-fives. Larry scores a National Public Radio story hit, a ten-second sound bite on the unraveling of two entire river systems. I get a major byline quote in the *Spokesman-Review*. "Years of bad land management by both state and national agencies came home to roost today," I crow. "The Clearwater is in the middle of a major aquatic extinction spasm." I run around the bar the next night, telling everybody we need a helicopter, making bad jokes while laughing and drinking, slapping my hand and singing "wop, wop, wop."

For a moment, I am sixteen again, high on bad dope, drunk on cheap beer, driving my big gray Ford Bronco down on the river side of the levee, next to a brown, flooding Ohio River. Running and screaming with my friends along the road, we are throwing our beer bottles into the river, dodging washed trash on the matted, muddy grass against the backdrop of the Kentucky hills and the huge roadcut from the new four lane along the south bank. I am dizzy, high, exultant, and nihilistic. Then, for a moment, the blood level of alcohol in my system drops, and I think of the upper Lochsa salmon redds destroyed, maybe the last of the Clearwater chinook smolts being washed out to sea—quite possibly the end of the salmon in the Clearwater Country.

Is this what Armageddon feels like? Losing half your country in the river? Please, oh please, tell me this: what will keep the pieces of my soul together when the wild country is gone?

Epilogue
Why

genocide: the deliberate and systematic destruction of a racial, political, or cultural group.
— *Webster's Ninth New Collegiate Dictionary*

> Who then, or what, is the splendid blond beast? It is the destruction inherent in any system of order, the institutionalized brutality whose existence is denied by cheerleaders of the status quo at the very moment they feed its appetite for blood.
>
> The present world order supplies stability and rationality of a sort for human society, while its day-to-day operations chew up the weak, the scapegoats, and almost anyone else in its way. This is not necessarily an evil conspiracy of insiders; it is a structural dilemma that generates itself more or less consistently from place to place and from generation to generation.
>
> Much of modern society has been built upon genocide...[and] systemic atrocities are for the most part not even regarded as crimes, but instead are written off by most of the world's media and intellectual leadership as acts of God or nature whose origin remains a mystery.
>
> It is individual human beings who make the day-to-day decisions that create genocide, reward mass murder, and ease the escape of the guilty. But social systems usually protect these individuals from responsibility for "authorized" acts, in part by providing rationalizations that present systemic brutality as a necessary evil.
>
> —Christopher Simpson, *The Splendid Blond Beast*

AL ESPINOSA AND I are headed for the yearly Wild Rockies Rendezvous held at the Teller Wildlife Refuge on the backside of the Bitterroot mountains, put on by the Alliance for the Wild Rockies. A grassroots organizing group, every year the Alliance re-drafts and pushes the Northern Rockies Ecosystem Protection Act, known as NREPA, which would designate the remaining federally owned unprotected roadless country in Idaho, Montana, and Wyoming as federal wilderness. NREPA then gets shut down by the local congressional delegations who are all beholden to the various timber, mining, and grazing concerns that put them in office. It is no matter to me on this day, though. It is a warm, sunny September day, and I am anxious for the camaraderie of those of like minds and different stories. As we pull into the parking lot, I can see the Bitterroot divide—bright, steel, and glowing in the sunshine—and imagine my Clearwater River tumbling down off the back.

Saturday rolls around, still beautiful. I spend fifteen minutes talking to Carl Pope, the executive director of the Sierra Club, asking him why the club is not doing more to protect over a million, forested, connected acres in the Clearwater Country. He makes some vague promises, then pats me on the head. I ask him if he even knows where the Clearwater Country is. He shakes his head "no." I point up to the divide only twelve miles away. "Over there, Carl," I say. "Inquiring minds want to know."

I wander over to a mini-fair set up in front of the events barn. This year, the organizers have invited a raptor rehabilitation group to set up shop on the lawn. I stroll over to the exhibit. A great horned owl with a wing blown off by a large caliber shell is perched on a wooden tee in the middle of some boxes; people are patting it on the head. I look down in a small box. A tiny saw-whet owl looks back. "Don't get too close," the organizer warns me. "She'll peck." I briefly consider the honor of being pecked by something as rare as a saw-whet owl.

The majority of the birds here today are the victims of chemical contamination from agricultural pesticides, the woman watching the birds explains. I reach out at my turn to pat the owl. One of its wings has been shot off. It swivels its head as I touch it, then flops onto the ground, laying on its back, squirming. "He has balance problems," the keeper explains. My stomach sinks. I move over to the red-tailed hawk. In place of one of his eyes is a scarred deformity. Birth defects, I am told.

I walk away from the exhibit, out to a cornfield, only stubble now. Along with Dave and Kathy Richmond, two activists from Challis, Idaho, I watch a golden eagle hop around the field, jumping over the short remains of the stalks. "Why doesn't he fly?" I ask Kathy. Apparently, the problem is more of the same—he probably dined on a poison bait predator control carcass, and the toxic contamination has destroyed his sense of balance. The eagle bounces in wide circles—no danger of him getting away.

The Richmonds and I talk for awhile. I have immense respect for them. Being an environmentalist in a place as redneck and hostile as Challis and championing their current cause—eliminating bear baiting in Idaho—

requires real courage. I ask them why they do it, and they respond with the usual answers: love of place and creatures; tired of seeing all of it mined, logged, and destroyed. They turn the tables on me, asking the same question, Kathy smiling in her fresh Western shirt. "The usual," I say. "Loss of place, personal redemption, trying to save my worthless soul." I pause, pointing to the eagle. "How can I not?"

Much is made in today's newspapers of the present ecological crisis, which finds itself embodied in microcosm in the current situation in the Clearwater and Salmon river watersheds. Environmentalists are fond of using the term "holocaust" in describing the present state of affairs. Despite media attention and constant pleas from activists to save the last remaining wild country, the public remains largely senescent, figuring the use of such terms is only rhetoric propagated by a "special interest" group—the environmental community—and should be given the same intellectual weight as the glossy pamphlets handed out by timber industry front groups at county fairs. The truth must indeed lie, in this ostensibly centrist society, in the middle.

The unfortunate fact behind this interpretation of the situation, however, is the profound denial about the existence of a phenomenological reality—the underlying assumption that there is no real truth. According to this worldview, environmentalists have their opinion, just as the timber industry, and both are exaggerating. Hills aren't really being clearcut—they've stopped doing that, haven't they? At least that's what the ad copy says. The debate is then corrupted with nonsense labels that posit a certain human economic system viewpoint that have nothing to do with the issue, such as left-wing, right-wing, conservative, or liberal. Though there are certainly angles, deforestation of the Clearwater Country is not primarily about class struggle.

The sad fact is that in spite of evidence that major global crisis is rapidly approaching, signaled by such events as global warming—and the incumbent increase in average ocean temperature along with the ozone hole over both North and South America—the American public remains largely inured to the state of affairs existing in its own backyard. It is easy to talk about rainforest deforestation in Brazil, or nuclear horrors in Russia. It is harder to face the reality that the Cascade Range in Washington and Oregon, with its spotted owl and coho salmon crises, is largely deforested. The old-growth groves of Douglas fir and western hemlock are gone.

The spotted owl, such a potent symbol of the environmental movement in the Pacific Northwest, didn't become that solely because environmental organizations were looking for some way to shut down the timber industry. The spotted owl is on the endangered species list because we, as a nation, stood blindly by as corporate giants such as Weyerhaeuser actively destroyed one of the great temperate rainforests in the world.

But is it holocaust and genocide? In order to answer this question, it is necessary to examine dynamics from past examples. This leads one necessarily to examine the most dramatic example of the form in the twentieth century—the German holocaust perpetrated against the Jews.

In Daniel Goldhagen's book, *Hitler's Willing Executioners,* the author persuasively makes the case that Germans actively participated in the holocaust. He authoritatively dismisses the argument that Hitler and the Nazi elite forced the German people to participate in the holocaust, or that German culture was uniquely predisposed by virtue of the German stereotype of orderliness and submission to authority to commit unquestioningly the crime of Jewish extermination. Most people in Germany believed that Jews were undesirable and that something needed to be done to get rid of them. Hitler, with his gift for anti-Semitic rhetoric, mobilized this sentiment and directed the debate toward marginalizing the Jews economically and socially, depriving them of their businesses through the Aryanization programs of the mid-1930s—in essence turning them into social lepers. Additionally, Hitler made the case for elimination of the Jews based on genetics; the ersatz, widely accepted "fact" that Jews were an inferior race and the source of evil in German society logically demanded their extirpation. Not only the ultra-violent and loyal Nazis killed helpless men, women, and children; ordinary people such as casually recruited police battalions and acting troupes had no emotional or intellectual problem joining in the extermination.

Goldhagen also makes the very important point that attempting to understand Germany in the 1930s and 1940s through transference of our values onto the German people will inevitably provide no understanding of the situation. Americans who have come of age in the post-World War II era tend to think of the German people during that time as psychotic monsters, a nation of the mentally disturbed, or a people so dominated by a charismatic megalomaniac that they **had** to kill the Jews. However, at that time in Germany, it was acceptable to kill Jews. Certainly it was encouraged; it was even a logical extension of contemporarily held beliefs. One didn't have to be a psychotic killer to participate, and the vast majority of those who manned the elaborate system of concentration and work camps were not. What the Germans clearly demonstrated was that given the appropriate cultural underpinnings, people—any people—are capable of doing anything. There is no universal code of morals held by all people at any given time. What is considered wrong or evil now was not necessarily considered wrong in times past, and in fact may have been deemed absolutely necessary. But just because a culture endorses a particular belief does not mean that it is "right" in any long-term, truly universal sense of species or planetary survival. The only thing that is certain is that cultures with defective values will inevitably collapse over time, becoming catastrophic victims of their own bad judgment. Certainly Nazi Germany exhibits that characteristic.

The experience of the Jewish Holocaust is, unfortunately, applicable to the current ecological holocaust ongoing in the remains of our old-growth forest, because it explains **how** human beings could destroy so much that is beautiful on such a wide scale. One of the most commonly used conventional wisdoms for denial of the situation in the Clearwater is that timber communities and the Forest Service are not filled with evil people and by extension they couldn't possibly be destroying the Clearwater forests. Things couldn't possibly be as bad as activists like myself say—those Forest Service people are nice folks, and Congresswoman Helen Chenoweth sounds reasonable when she trumpets that she would rather hug a logger than a tree. Arguing against the legacy of clearcuts, blown-out roads, and exterminated fish populations in the Clearwater by noting that lumber firms, the state Department of Lands, and the Forest Service are all filled with nice people with families is like arguing that every Gestapo member beat his wife. Through there is no question that societal dysfunction contributes to events of genocide—whether involving chinook salmon or Jews—reducing this down to individual dysfunction is profoundly irrelevant. Defining the deforestation of the Clearwater in terms of some kind of character test for the majority of the players will inevitably fail to provide any usable societal lessons.

We can judge the real ecological situation in the Clearwater by examining what is happening to the members of the original ecological community. This information lies outside the realm of opinion; science and surveys can establish a verifiable picture of current events. And this picture is not pretty. The majority of coldwater biota in the Clearwater is threatened with extinction. Chinook salmon, bull trout, steelhead trout, and westslope cutthroat trout are either on the endangered species list or are objects of various legal machinations to place them there. The presence of chinook salmon and steelhead trout on the list is even more troubling; both are not only indicators of ecological health, but also keystone species and primary sources of nutrients for what is biologically a rather sterile ecosystem. The fact that **all** native coldwater salmonids are on the list is an indicator that problems in the Clearwater are attributable to more than the barge/hydropower system on the lower Snake and the Columbia; habitat degradation caused by logging, road building, and the construction of Dworshak Dam clearly has taken its toll. In a region named long ago because of its remarkable water quality, the fact that the primary residents of such clear water are going extinct is a hallmark of this chapter of human-induced genocide.

Things are probably no better off for the land-based denizens of the unique old-growth forest remaining in the Clearwater. The majority of classified "sensitive" or indicator species, including northern goshawk, flammulated owls, Townshend's big eared bats, and others are all imminently threatened. But because these species are not game species, their numbers are not tracked nearly as closely. By virtue of not being tasty, these beautiful creatures are destined to go extinct without notice.

It is not only fauna threatened with extinction. Both western white pine and western redcedar are threatened with imminent extirpation, both by the fact that their wood is extremely merchantable, and western white pine also by an introduced disease. Thus, we also have the feature of incidental genocide rearing its ugly head.

Of course, wolves and bears were successfully exterminated long ago in the Clearwater region, the victims of aggressive "animal control" programs generated by the nature-destructive culture of the pioneers of the area. In so many ways, the circumstances surrounding their demise mirror the dynamic of the Jewish Holocaust better than any. Like the Jews, both wolves and bears were demonized to the point of hysterical fantasy, allowing heroic status to be heaped upon the hunters who killed hundreds of these intelligent, and in the wolves' case, highly social animals. The fact that this attitude remains in place today is an unpleasant anachronism of life in Idaho. Letters to the editor fantastically testify to the enormous killing abilities of both wolves and grizzlies, animals that the vast majority of Idahoans have never seen outside a zoo. As I write these words, hearings concerning the draft plan for reintroduction of grizzly bears in the Selway/Bitterroot Wilderness could not even be scheduled in Salmon, Idaho, because local law enforcement could not, or would not guarantee the safety of U.S. Fish and Wildlife Service employees. Even the head of the state Fish and Game Department, Steve

Mealey (formerly the Boise National Forest Supervisor and known in some circles by the nickname "the Butcher of the Boise"), has said that his department will actively resist reintroduction efforts.

Some may resist the application of the label "genocide" to the extermination of a given animal species. After all, they're only animals, the argument goes, and comparing the fate of wolves, grizzlies, or flammulated owls to the fate of the Jews under the Nazis might at best be disrespectful, and at worst, specious and evil in itself. Yet this view is also a function of current cultural values, not something written in stone across all races and ethnicities of people everywhere. For example, many Native American tribes considered all members of the animal and plant kingdoms their brothers, while having no qualms about exterminating neighboring tribes of humans.

If there is something that we as a society can learn from the experience of the holocaust, it is that it is **necessary** to posit a large enough set of differences to fuel any exterminationist campaign. In order to sell their genocidal campaign, the Nazis used genetics, defining the Jews as a separate, subhuman race that threatened to pollute the superior Aryan race. Animals and plants, of course, have less ability to disguise themselves—it is obvious that they are different. Yet instead of respecting that diversity, our culture is loaded with value-derogatory phrases: "he behaved like an animal"; or "they're only animals"; and all the other manifest destiny-laden and ostensibly biblically produced reasons we can muster. By doing so, our culture sets the table for genocide. It may sound hackneyed to say that we have to respect animals as lords of their own kingdom. But without adoption of this value, humans seem unable to stop themselves from destroying this other world.

Some people in our present society must be presented with more concrete evidence of genocide before accepting this argument. At the end of World War II, when Allied troops liberated the camp system in a defeated Germany, photographs galore were published to expose the attempts at destruction of the Jewish people. Pictures of heaps of bodies seem to have some effect on today's society. But if that is what is required to prove the case, environmentalists will never be able to plead for all the beautiful creatures left on this planet. When rare species starve to death, or freeze because of lack of suitable habitat, their bones and bodies are not neatly piled in heaps for photographers. Their fate is more silent. They melt back into the clay from which they came.

Our culture is deeply schizophrenic when it comes to dealing with these issues. This nation has passed biodiversity protection laws. The Endangered Species Act is one of the most far-reaching pieces of legislation regarding the rights of animal and plant species ever drafted. The letter of the bill guarantees species the right of survival, if only at a minimal level. And most polling information shows that there is a remarkable consensus among Americans that the environment is important; laws, regulations, and special designations are held by the majority to be good and worthy. Our remaining wild landscapes are part of our national identity. But the same culture also glorifies 5,000-square-foot houses, the unlimited use of paper, and little or no restriction on personal freedom. Americans don't like to be told where they can ride their dirt bikes. Wood for those houses has to come from somewhere. And often, when the agencies in charge of endangered species actually attempt to limit a given person's plans and enforce the standards required by the ESA, politicians and the media cry "regulatory reform," or the oft-heard battle-cry, "people first!"

This sends a split message to timber country, giving economic and moral encouragement to the communities at the heart of the current deforestation effort. Loggers can make $50,000 a year for their eminently dangerous work, and to travel to a timber town like St. Maries, Idaho, during the fall of 1997 is to see fields of new Dodge Ram pickups, the current vehicle of choice. The federal government continues to appropriate money for more roads into roadless areas of the national forest, supporting money-losing timber sales that make no economic sense, while barely considering the damage done to the land. Funded by dollars from Washington, D.C., huge buildings house the large staffs of the Clearwater and Nez Perce National Forests in Orofino and Grangeville, buildings filled with people whose major job is developing excuses for chopping down the remaining forest. One district ranger, a supposed progressive in the agency, while discussing with me the deforestation, resultant landslides, and destruction of one of the last major steelhead spawning areas in Idaho at a recent open house, reminded me of Americans' desire for "goods and services" as well as wild country. She is enmeshed in the culture.

People who want to go beyond words and actually apply a conservation ethic can't last in today's Forest Service—the case of Al Espinosa as well as others that I interviewed for this book has convinced me of that. I walked a sale with a bright young woman biologist recently. She treated me fairly, seemed genuine enough, told me about a geographic information system mapping project she had completed, as well as a variety of assessments she had done for various plant and animal species. During the drive back to the office she turned to me pleading, knowing that I was writing a book. "Please don't say that I said anything bad," she said. "I'll lose my job." And it goes without saying that any corporate logger who stands up to the status quo of deforestation would receive his or her walking papers, or worse, the next day. The only people involved in the timber business who seem to have an environmental ethic are the horse loggers, a group ostracized outside the mainstream of current timber practice.

We must remember, though, when dealing with the Forest Service, that we, the citizens of the United States, are the ones who give the district rangers their jobs. And it is our job to give them their walking papers. The Forest Service and the welfare timber communities they marginally support will stop when the last tree is chopped—or because federal timber is such a subsidized resource, they'll stop when we stop sending them a paycheck. Make no mistake about it—the Forest Service will never change on its own.

But the question then arises: why can't the Forest Service change? And more importantly, why can't it admit that it has made horrible decisions in managing the land? Why can't it admit that it is wrong?

Once again, by referring to the example of the German holocaust can we find some answers. Christopher Simpson's book, *The Splendid Blond Beast*, discusses the economic and cultural underpinnings for genocide in the Third Reich. At the beginning of the Nazi period, while many Germans had a cultural underlayment of anti-Semitism, many were also ambivalent about extreme eliminationist solutions to the Jewish "problem." In 1933, when the Nazis came to power, they immediately started an "Aryanization" program of ostensibly buying Jewish businesses at cents on the dollar, then selling them to German companies. Many heads of German businesses were initially suspicious of the Nazis. The reasons for this varied, not necessarily having anything to do with persecution of the Jews. Most were suspicious of Hitler's desire to have all business owned by the fatherland. However, the leaders thought they could control that particular Nazi propensity. Participation in Aryanization started slowly at first, but rapidly gained speed. After a while, not participating in the Aryanization program left companies at an economic disadvantage to the ones that were making off with the stolen Jewish booty. Economic incentive, amplified by the cultural groundwork of anti-Semitism, allowed Aryanization to pick up speed.

The result was to take a group of relatively amoral individuals, only marginally inclined toward the end goal of Jewish elimination—the heads of German corporations—and economically enfranchise them into a political, cultural movement. After time had passed, it became evident to the business leaders that if the Nazi party fell from power, the business leaders' heads would also roll because of the collusion between the two. Thus, it became important for those leaders to completely support the Nazis' cultural and social agendas. If that cultural agenda failed, there would be hell to pay with the rest of the world.

The Forest Service, the timber industry, and timber communities are largely in the same boat as the German business community during the Nazi period. Some individuals in these groups may express regret or remorse for the legacy of deforestation during the past thirty years. But the vast majority are now both culturally and economically enfranchised in the business. On the staff of the Clearwater National Forest, virtually every person with a permanent job facilitates logging. Hydrologists, wildlife biologists, and fisheries scientists all spend a majority of time analyzing the effects of timber sales and preparing sale documents. Engineers lay out and maintain roads for logging trucks. Timber sale planners and silviculturalists do the down-and-dirty work of laying out sale units. Even recreation specialists analyze the effects of timber sales on trails and river corridors. Getting out of the timber business would result in the vast majority of these people losing their jobs. And saying that there would be hell to pay if they admitted their sins to the American people would be an understatement.

Timber communities are also directly enfranchised into the destruction of wildlands. The most obvious example of this is the high-paying jobs provided in the woods, or the less lucrative, but more stable employment provided in the mills. But also of importance, though much more insidious, are the various federal payments-to-counties programs authorized under legislation such as the Knutson-Vandenberg Act. Originally enacted to encourage reforestation efforts, the Knutson-Vandenberg Act stipulates that 25 percent of all timber sale receipts go to counties to compensate them for loss of property tax base, since property taxes can't be assessed on federally owned land. In short, the more acres cut, the more money in the local coffers. If no trees are cut, then there is no money to run schools, fix roads, and maintain infrastructure in what are largely poor, underdeveloped areas. Add to this cultural priorities, such as loggers' competitions and fairs, and naming school mascots after timber industry iconography, and one has a complicated societal quilt interwoven with economic incentives to cut more trees.

It is certainly true that the timber industry's interest in federal timber is purely economic—corporations are largely ruled by their bottom line. The industry enjoys a huge federal subsidy from the existence of the Forest Service. The Forest Service plans roads, lays out sales, performs various economic viability analyses, then puts timber up for sale under extremely limited competitive circumstances. By rights, anyone with the financial means can bid on a timber sale. But because of the limited value of the timber sold, as well as the fact that it is illegal to export raw logs from national lands, the company with the mill closest to the sale area usually possesses an unbeatable financial advantage in the bidding process. This discourages broader competition, delivering a virtual buyer's oligopoly on sales. And when the supply pipeline is full, timber goes for what the buyers want to pay. Add to this the fact that the Clearwater and the Nez Perce forests both have a certain timber volume set aside for small business, and competition is even further reduced.

Economics matter; but cultural support with defective myths provides the ideology to run the machine. Workers believe in the endless abundance of the frontier; added to that are the hysterical fear of fire and insect infestation. Such myths of holy cause are necessary not only for the Forest Service and local timber communities; since the whole operation is losing money hand over fist (not that economically fair compensation would serve as a justification for the loss of the old-growth forest), they are necessary to sell the whole program to a relatively uninvolved national Congress. When you are a deficit-running operation, as the Clearwater most certainly is, the timber industry and Forest Service can't tell the truth. It simply would not justify the status quo.

The question of how to construct a sustainable timber industry has yet to be answered on a large scale anywhere in the U.S. It is possible to do some logging without wholesale destruction of ecosystems. But in the Clearwater, because of the extensive damage that has already occurred, a sustainable industry would have to be dramatically scaled back. And none of the major players—Potlatch, the Forest Service, Plum Creek, the state Department of Lands—or the many medium-sized operations present in such towns as Princeton, Kamiah, and Kooskia show any interest in changing business-as-usual.

Should citizens push for abolition of the Forest Service? There will always be an agency in charge of managing our national lands—this book adamantly opposes giving these treasures to the states or private concerns—

but incentives for clean water, species diversity and abundance, and stable ecosystems with management for the animals, the plants, the rocks, and rivers must be established above the need of the bureaucrats and their sup-plicants currently in charge. A fire must sweep through the agency and clear out the backward timber managers running the current program. And this source of renewal, kept out of the agency for so long, is long overdue.

Where are the mainstream environmental groups, such as the Sierra Club and National Wildlife Federation? If the Clearwater Country is as signifi-cant as I have made it out to be, why are these large organizations not fighting for its preservation? Though there are notable exceptions, by and large the national groups have turned their back on the wildlands in Idaho. As of this writing, over eight million acres in the state are still roadless and would qualify as federally protected wilderness. But Idaho as a state has little national name recognition. The referent known to most is the slogan of "famous potatoes," a legacy of an agricultural industry with arch-conservative J.R. Simplot at its center. National groups can't raise money off places that no one knows, even if they are worth saving. Even the major state-based groups in Idaho fall into this trap. Lots of wild country in the center of the state has poor name recognition, so campaigns often center on rivers that run next to roads, or wildlands next to populated areas. Fighting for areas without constituencies is difficult work, and the prob-lem with the conservation movement in Idaho is that there are few people, plenty of issues, and the worst political climate toward environmental is-sues of any state in the union.

What also exacerbates the situation with mainstream groups on the national level, and to a lesser extent on the state level as well, is that the national environmental groups and the Department of the Interior have turned into parallel career ladders for people in natural resource policy. Individuals with little connection to particular landscapes move back and forth between the Department of Interior or the Forest Service and the national groups, depending on political climate and which party is in of-fice. There are notable examples, such as George Frampton, ex-head of the Wilderness Society, who, as the Assistant Secretary of the Interior under Bill Clinton, engineered much of the ESA-weakening policy now advo-cated by Bruce Babbitt and the Clinton administration. Don Barry, an old staffer at the World Wildlife Fund, has taken Frampton's place during the second Clinton term. Steve Shimberg, staffer for Senator John Chafee and defender of the Kempthorne-Chafee discussion ESA draft, is now senior vice president at the National Wildlife Federation.

To an environmentally leaning public, such placement back and forth might be considered a good thing. After all, the "revolving door" between lobbyists and other federal agencies is well established, and it might make sense that having "our guy" in Interior making the policy is better than having that same individual sitting in a supposed advocacy group. But what actually happens is darker. Environmental groups, if they are doing their job, should be advocating against the status quo, pushing for stronger protection for more wildlands and wild things. These types of actions should inherently be making the agencies and their rulers uncomfortable.

Instead, individuals inside the mainstream environmental groups become reluctant to attack the agencies perpetuating the destruction precisely because they know that their career track might well run through those agencies some day. Access to politicians and career bureaucrats is also considered important—a privilege easily denied if an activist is considered unpleasant or a bad actor.

The public also tends to believe that these agencies are run by "radicals," and that agency employees, especially under a Democratic president, define the cutting edge of what is possible. Nothing could be further from the truth. It should be remembered that Al Gore was the one who gave the nod to the notorious Gorton-Taylor timber salvage rider, the Al Gore who, in the eyes of mainstream America, is as green as anyone need be. By coopting the progressive label while simultaneously subverting the progressive platform, such mainstream activists marginalize the true grassroots. And while the rhetoric of more radical organizations such as Earth First! tend toward the "collapse of the industrial state" theme, the reality is that the majority of issues such as "zero cut," the campaign to stop any logging on our **national** lands (not all logging, everywhere), had their genesis in the fringe, are inherently rational, and are economically, if not politically, palatable. The unfortunate fact is that the majority of large environmental groups have become part of the Splendid Blond Beast, and are going to have to undergo redefinition if they are to confront the challenges of the new millennium.

To be fair, some national groups are starting to reach out to the grassroots. Defenders of Wildlife runs its GREEN (Grassroots Environmental Effectiveness Network) program, which provides on-line updates to conservation battles around the U.S. The Western Ancient Forest Campaign lobbies under the title of a grassroots umbrella group. And Save America's Forests has always been a group that grassroots forest activists have been able to count on for pushing a true no-compromise, wilderness preservation position. The national groups do marginally counter-balance the increasingly corporate-bought legislative and executive branches of government. But holding these national environmental organizations responsible for all the problems with deforestation in the Clearwater is a "blame the victim," or more appropriately, "blame the bystander" mentality. The large timber and mining corporations and their purchased political agents are the real bad guys.

The fix for these problems is easy to state, if not to implement. The bottom line with the national groups stops with the membership. For too long, the majority of people have sent in their "clear their conscience" payments to a national conservation organization, and in return have had their mailboxes filled with glossy magazines and further solicitations for cash. Members are going to have to demand ways of getting involved—because in my experience, members of most environmental organizations are usually more radical than their boards of directors.

There are issues that this book has neglected that are also playing important roles in the future of the Clearwater Country: the influence of the Christian Patriot and radical religious right on the management of our national lands, through their proxies in Idaho's congressional delegation; the effect of the 1864 Northern Pacific Railroad Land Grant Act through the behavior of its corporate child, Plum Creek Timber Company, which owns huge square-mile checkerboards of land on the northern and eastern boundaries of the Clearwater Country; or equally important, the interaction of the Native American tribes such as the Nez Perce in the future of this place. Anadromous fish have played, and will continue to play a huge role in environmental issues in the Clearwater, and the Nez Perce tribe, with its treaty-granted trust obligation of the federal government for preservation of hunting and fishing, holds one of the strongest cards in any hand for preventing future environmental degradation. All these topics are worthy of books in their own right.

Since the body of this book was written, much has happened on the front lines of environmental crisis in the Clearwater Country. The Forest

Service, currently the keeper of the last clean spawning streams in the area, is planning huge timber sales in the last of those roadless areas. On the Nez Perce Forest, the Wing-Otter timber sale will destroy the best remaining spawning habitat on the South Fork of the Clearwater. On the Clearwater Forest, huge logging projects on White Sand Creek, the keystone drainage of the upper Lochsa, and Fish Creek, which drains into the middle Lochsa and provides 15 percent of all the juvenile steelhead production in Idaho, are on the block. Two huge projects on the North Fork district, the Fish Bate timber sale and the Fern Star timber sale, will fragment the majority of the remaining coastal disjunct habitat on the North Fork of the Clearwater, as well as providing huge clearcuts within view of the river. Rare plants will perish; species already on the edge of extirpation will be pushed that much closer. On the national scene, Idaho's Senator Larry Craig is pushing his version of reform of the National Forest Management Act that would basically gut the law. Idaho's other senator, Dirk Kempthorne, is trying to deep-six the Endangered Species Act. Helen Chenoweth has taken up the cause of expanding motorized vehicle use in roadless areas, and there is great pressure to allow snowmobiles into the Great Burn during the winter. Nothing seems to matter to the executioners.

But there is reason for hope. Much of the land, though threatened, still stands. And this August of 1997 I went swimming in a clear Lochsa. With mask and snorkel, I floated down through a strategically selected riffle, seeing all my familiar friends—five or so cutthroat, two bull trout, a huge sucker hugging the bottom, and mountain whitefish tucked behind rocks at the end of the glide. As I was about to pull out of the current, breast-stroking while sucking air through my snorkel, I turned my head. To my left, barely out of reach was a lone female chinook salmon, green face and mottled red body, gleaming next to the surface in the light of a late afternoon sun.

There is no question that the patient is on the table, and her condition is critical. But I believe truly that she can live—if we would just quit stabbing her in the heart.

A hearty Grand fir heavy with cones along the Lewis and Clark Trail. *Gerry Snyder photo.*

Notes and Comment

Few books are as much fun to read aloud as "The Cat in the Hat," but it was not written to be read aloud, and it was not much fun to write. The book took Theodore Geisel—Dr. Seuss—more than a year to finish; he described the experience as "being lost with a witch in the tunnel of love," an analogy it is probably better to leave unpacked.

—Louis Menard, "How to Frighten Small Children," *The New Yorker*, October 6, 1997

THIS BOOK IS PRIMARILY an oral history of place. The references included in this section, while containing information pertaining to the Clearwater and Salmon river subdrainages, primarily have been written to describe other places and other catastrophes.

I have researched the majority of this book by talking to people I know and trust, what a working journalist would refer to as "good" sources. While I believe what the people in this book have said, I have included appropriately researched books, journal articles, and government documents that will substantiate the stories in the manuscript.

While good research is important and has been a foundation of my other career as a university professor, I have found that the truth about little-known places can only be obtained by getting out in the field and walking around. For me personally—after having flown, walked, and paddled through a good portion of northern Idaho and seen all the clearcuts I have seen—to still acknowledge that there is a debate about what is actually happening out there is more a symbol of the power of corporate and governmental propaganda than any real debate engaging citizens of the region.

Statistics and numbers lie; an example can be found in the Clearwater Forest's count regarding the status of old-growth forest left on the ground. The forest plan mandates that 10 percent remain. The forest staff recently did a survey involving examination of aerial and satellite photographs. The numbers came up to approximately 10 percent. When they sent ground-truthing stand examiners into the field to verify what the photo interpreters had predicted, they found diminishing percentages—less than they had originally estimated. The Forest Service has stopped doing ground-truthing of the remaining old-growth, instead insisting that it has enough information from its previous work to be assured that more than 10 percent remain.

Even numbers of acreage used for logging don't tell much of a story. Approximately half of the forest is roaded, and the majority of that is heavily logged. But when one stands on the end of the Lower Salmon road off of Smith Ridge next to the Mallard-Larkins Pioneer Area and looks at the country bounding down toward Dworshak reservoir, one realizes first that the real forest—the one with the big trees—was in that roaded half, and that this part of the forest is mostly gone. I have stood up on that point and thought about numbers and reality for a long time. I guess the point is this: read the books in the following section. They'll tell you part of the story. But get out and walk. Don't believe me—build your own rage.

Landscape

A Sense of Place

Maps I have found helpful for understanding the Clearwater Country are first and foremost the Clearwater National Forest and Nez Perce National Forest maps, published by the Clearwater and Nez Perce National Forests. The *Idaho Gazetteer* (Freeport, Me.: DeLorme Mapping, 1992) is also useful. The Clearwater National Forest map has land ownership information, so one can actually see who owns the clearcuts one is driving through. I have not found the standard United States Geological Survey (USGS) photo quads to be as useful, unless hiking off-trail, which is hard to do in the Clearwater Country, to say the least. Don't believe the trails drawn on the USGS maps, either. Inquire locally as to trail conditions before you hike, or be prepared for the worst. The 1:100,000 scale USGS maps can be useful for getting around on the road network if you don't have the *Gazetteer* or the forest maps.

Dr. Bart Stryhas of Kooskia helped me with the geology in this piece. Bart is a graduate of Washington State University, researched the Five Lakes Butte region of the Clearwater Country for his dissertation, and has worked for various gold mining concerns in the region. Also of interest for geology buffs might be the geologic maps published by the Idaho Geological Survey, specifically the *Geologic Map of the Upper North Fork of the Clearwater River Area, Northern Idaho* by Lewis, Burmester, McFaddan, Eversmeyer,

Wallace, and Bennett. For those interested in a more scholarly approach to Idaho geology, one can read "Basement Thrust Sheets in the Clearwater Orogenic Zone, Central Idaho and Western Montana," by Betty Skipp (*Geology*, v.15, Mar. 1987, pp. 220-224).

I have re-met two of the four boatmen with whom I took that first fateful trip down the Salmon. Jack Kappas is now a ranger for the Bureau of Land Management, supervising recreational use on the Salmon outside of Riggins. Gary Lane runs a small outfitting business out of Riggins called Wapiti River Dories.

Gary's illness, which my father diagnosed, was one of an intensely personal nature. When I walked into his shop a number of years ago to thank him again for that first trip, I asked him if he remembered me (knowing full well that he wouldn't, given only limited information). When he replied with the standard guide's response—he had rowed thousands of customers over the years—I smiled and told him that I could make him remember me. He looked at me out of the corner of his eye, as I started out with "Remember that trip when you came down with that infection..?"

He jumped up, looked at me, and yelled "I remember you!"

Lolo Creek

My first trip down Lolo Creek was with a crew of yahoos in the spring of 1991. We were so excited, all of us kept racing forward to paddle off the next horizon line. Lucky for us, it turned out to be a year without many logs wedged in the drops. Even with the introductory timber cuts, Lolo Creek is still one of the prettiest places in Idaho.

Mallard-Larkins

The Mallard-Larkins is one of the best places to witness the failure of the Forest Service's multiple-use philosophy. Up on the mountain on the north side of the North Fork of the Clearwater River, it is impossible to deny the scale of forest destruction on the south side.

I was originally sent the story of the wild goat by a biologist on the North Fork District. After talking to Keith Haley, I was convinced that it had to go in the piece, especially after being harassed by the local fauna on our trip. I never did send the letter written in the piece to Art Bourassa, but did confront him with the issue. Art, in a way that he has never seemed to be when talking about chopping down trees or building roads, was both defensive and apologetic. He has since told me that the goat biologists have been informed to lift their salt blocks up with them when they fly.

Cayuse Country

I originally met Steve Paulson at a Clearwater Forest Watch meeting, and we have since become good friends.

The red wolf information in the piece comes from a phone conversation with Curtis Carley, as well as his 1975 report, *Activities and Findings of the Red Wolf Field Recovery Program from Late 1973 to July 1, 1975, U.S. Fish and Wildlife Service Report.* Additionally, I used information from the *Red Wolf Recovery Plan* (U.S. Fish and Wildlife Service, 1989). The gray wolf information comes from *The Reintroduction of Gray Wolves to Yellowstone National Park and Central Idaho: Draft Environmental Impact Statement* (Helena: U.S. Fish and Wildlife Service, July 1993). Interestingly enough, there is little difference in the content of the letters regarding support for wolf reintroduction between the draft and final EIS.

Meadow Creek

Most of my Meadow Creek history comes from Dennis Baird, who sat at the table for the negotiations for both the Gospel Hump and the Frank Church/River of No Return wildernesses.

The information regarding Mt. Graham comes from talking to organizers associated with the protest, along with a videotaped interview of the Jesuit priest in charge of the project, who indeed said that the Catholic Church would be interested in baptizing extra-terrestrials if any existed.

For those curious, I had the USGS maps with me when I got lost in Meadow Creek. In a heavy forest with no visible landmarks, it is impossible to triangulate one's position.

People

Rowdy

Though I had the best of intentions of doing so, I haven't talked to Rowdy since our ride. I sincerely hope he is doing well, and enjoys this piece. The mill in Grangeville was bought by the Bennetts, and is now milling lumber and serving as a storage facility. Grangeville, in many ways, missed an opportunity to make the transition it will one day face. The information regarding Bob Krogh and his reasons for closing Ida-Pine also ran in the *Lewiston Morning Tribune* approximately a week after our ride.

Charlie (II)

The *Status Report: Columbia River Fish Runs and Fisheries, 1938-1993* (Washington Department of Fish and Wildlife and Oregon Department of Fish and Wildlife, August 1994), in dull numbers chronicles the death of anadromous fish in the Columbia River system. Proof that people were aware of the impending destruction of the fish can be found in the popular press during this period, such as the piece "Steelheaders Mourn 'Death of the Snake'" in the *Colfax Gazette*, on February 19, 1970, or the deception inherent in the decision-making process, discussed in an editorial in the *Lewiston Morning Tribune*, October 3, 1974.

Reed

When I interviewed Reed for the first time back in 1995, the idea of tearing out the four lower Snake dams was relegated to the fringe of the salmon restoration movement (see the July 18, 1995 headline in the *Idaho Statesman*—"Far-out Dam Idea Gets 'Seriously Considered'"). After writing the piece that appears in this book, I took Reed's revolutionary economic analysis to Idaho Rivers United (IRU), the state-wide rivers organization and one of the main salmon rescue organizations in the state. After lengthy and tumultuous debate, IRU's board endorsed dam removal.

Removal of the dams on the lower Snake has now become a serious possibility, no longer a fringe concept. The *New York Times* on April 21, 1997 ran a multi-column article on the concept, and on July 20, 1997, the *Idaho Statesman*, the largest paper in the state, began a three-day spread on dam removal and endorsed the idea. Reed, in the *New York Times* article, still said it best: "The Northwest is paralyzed by big money, and we have a bureaucracy that cannot act. It would be nice if the rest of the country would save us from ourselves."

For an in-depth history of the deception behind building the lower Snake River dams, read Keith Petersen's *River of Life, Channel of Death: Fish and Dams on the Lower Snake* (Lewiston: Confluence Press, 1995).

Al and Dan

The persecution of Al Espinosa and Dan Davis made the papers in the Inland Northwest for weeks. For representative coverage, see "'Combat Biologist' Calls it Quits," *Lewiston Morning Tribune*, January 6, 1993, as well as "Mumma-Cide II—The Purge Continues...?", (*AFSEEE Activist*, v. 2, no. 4,

Nov. 1992). Journalist Todd Wilkinson has also released a new book on the political perils of being a resource biologist, called *Science Under Siege: The Politicians' War on Nature and the Truth* (Johnson Press, 1998).

Kovalicky

Tom Kovalicky, no doubt a charismatic fellow, has always known how to appeal to the press. See "Nez Perce Supervisor Tom Kovalicky Cultivates a Forest with a Fishery," on the front page of the *Lewiston Morning Tribune*, March 6, 1988. In the piece, aside from some minor grumbling from the timber bosses, everyone across the spectrum sings Tom's praises. Interestingly enough, Governor Cecil Andrus also made a strong pitch for keeping Forest Service officers in one place for their career. "And don't keep transferring people. Man, for a while it was musical chairs in Idaho," Andrus is quoted in the Spokane *Spokesman-Review*, February 17, 1994.

Dennis

Dennis Baird is currently working on a history of the Frank Church/River of No Return Wilderness. The hearing referred to in the piece occurred on August 24, 1977 in Grangeville, in front of the U.S. Senate Subcommittee on Parks and Recreation, of the Committee on Energy and Natural Resources.

Good Old Bill Bob

Perhaps the best economic pathology of how the Forest Service manages to chop down 500-year-old cedars like those in Steep Creek is given by Randal O'Toole in *Reforming the Forest Service* (Covelo, Ca.: Island Press, 1988). Though I don't necessarily agree with all of O'Toole's free-market-based solutions, considering that most timber sales on national lands in Idaho are money-losers, a little free-market capitalism couldn't hurt.

Dan Davis and Johnna Roy of the Clearwater National Forest both confirmed Bill's goshawk story.

Uncle LeRoy

The history of the "Phantom Forest" scandal was amply documented in the press, specifically in the articles in the Associated Press, February 28, 1992, covering LeRoy's testimony in Congress. On June 16, 1992, another AP story talks about the House Interior Committee accepting LeRoy's phantom forest findings.

It is unfair to say that nothing happened from the "Phantom Forest" scandal. In the *Missoulian*, December 1, 1995, the Forest Service in the

Washington, D.C., office admitted that the Kootenai National Forest used phantom trees to inflate the allowable cut, and reduced the allowable sale quantity by 77 million board feet. The Kootenai Forest still denies the charge. In so many ways, it does not matter. I was studying a high resolution map of the Kootenai pieced together from U-2 photographs in August 1997. Save for a few small roadless areas, the Kootenai was chopped into forty-acre squares—the classic fragmented forest.

For a good introduction to progressive forestry, Gordon Robinson's *The Forest and the Trees* (Covelo, Ca.: Island Press, 1988) describes the legislative and silvicultural history that brought us to the current mess, as well as the basics of forest mensuration and silvicultural science. LeRoy's progressive forestry, learned by his observations in the woods, pretty much matches Gordon Robinson's prescriptions.

A thorough, detailed, scholarly history of the Forest Service can be found in Paul Hirt's *A Conspiracy of Optimism:: Management of the National Forests Since World War II* (Lincoln: University of Nebraska Press, 1994). Hirt is a professor of history at Washington State University and a colleague.

LeRoy's four revolutions to save the Earth are remarkably similar to the three revolutions Ed Grumbine discusses in his book *Ghost Bears— Exploring the Biodiversity Crisis* (Covelo, Ca.: Island Press, 1992). I asked LeRoy if he had ever heard of Ed Grumbine. He responded "no," but found it interesting that someone of like mind came to similar conclusions. I attribute this to "natural thinking" human beings confronted by similar problems left to themselves will naturally come to similar solutions.

Doc

In these parts, Doc Partridge is a legend in his own time, a maverick (now retired) in the College of Forestry, Wildlife, and Range Sciences at the University of Idaho. He has published guides for identification of tree disease such as the *Tree Defect Guide* (U.S. Dept. of Agriculture, Forest Service, Intermountain Region, 1994), which he wrote with his wife Catherine Bertagnolli. For further reading on the interrelationship of fire, insects, and disease in Western forests, see Chris Maser's *Forest Primeval: The Natural History of an Ancient Forest* (San Francisco: Sierra Club Books, 1989).

LuVerne

As a budding river advocate, I lived a good portion of the legislative process concerning the lower Salmon. Tim Palmer's book, *The Wild and Scenic Rivers of America* (Covelo, Ca.: Island Press, 1993), is an excellent primer to legal hurdles people face when attempting to add a stream to the Wild and Scenic River system, a process described in microcosm in this piece.

Andy, Greg, and Mike

Michael Murray, one of those interviewed for this piece, has written a popular piece on fish stocking of montane lakes, "Reconsidering Fish Stocking in Wilderness" (*Wild Earth*, v. 4, no. 3, 1994, pp. 50-52). He has also written a scholarly piece, "Natural Processes: Wilderness Management Unrealized" (*Natural Areas Journal*, v. 16, no. 1, 1996, pp. 55-61).

Crisis

Children's Crusade

Most of the piece on the Cove/Mallard crisis comes from my personal experience with the activists involved. The Spokane *Spokesman-Review* (Idaho edition), the *Lewiston Morning Tribune*, and the *Moscow/Pullman Daily News* have covered the campaign in-depth for the summers from 1993-1997; locking down to bulldozers and sitting in tripods make great press. Many of the original activists who started the campaign are no longer involved.

I have known both Erik and Ramon since 1992. In order to understand Erik's situation, consider the headline in the local paper, the *Upper Country News-Reporter*, from Cambridge, Idaho, June 1, 1995: "Terrorists Coming to the Payette National Forest." Reporter Luane Page writes "Earth First leaders are now living in the costly resort area of McCall and are holding rallies and secret meetings in preparation." Poor Erik—as of this writing, he is still alive.

Perhaps the best summary regarding the current problems with the Forest Service is the afterword of Chuck Bowden's book *Frog Mountain Blues* (Tucson: University of Arizona Press, 1994). In this, Bowden describes the Forest Service's concept of multiple use as

> a vision that must have been constructed by a pimp, a madam, or some other kind of professional consultant. I'll spell out what this concept really means. The Forest Service hosts orgies, and because it must satisfy diverse appetites in our culture, it plans for all tastes: we have a room for those who like whips, a place for the leather freaks, a venue for those who have fetishes of the foot and whatnot, an arena for those who crave them at an unseemly young age, and so forth. Under the mask of language, we call these depraved habits mining, cattle raising,

lumbering, hunting, fishing, and on and on. But just for an instant imagine you are a rock or a tree or a flower or an animal or soil. What does multiple use look like then? Well, it looks like a scheme for allowing Homo sapiens to have you in different ways. And when you have been had, it is not likely that you are going to be particularly grateful.

Chuck describes what is happening to the Santa Catalinas outside of Tucson as "but a little fragment of our failure." In this case, what is happening to the Clearwater is a big fragment, and a particularly sad one, considering the diversity of life contained in all the ecosystems present.

A Handful of Ashes

Having lived through the salvage rider and surveyed the sales set up by the Forest Service that fell under the rider, I feel that I am an expert in my own right regarding these matters. However, for those needing reinforcement, one can read Paul Roberts's June 1997 *Harper's Magazine* article, "The Federal Chain-saw Massacre," or outdoor writer Ted Williams's March 1996 piece in *Fly Rod and Reel*, "Congress's Scorched-Earth Policy." Salvage logging has now given way to the Forest Service's Interior Columbia Basin Ecosystem Management Plan (ICBEMP), which was originally commissioned to develop a recovery strategy for the failing anadromous fish runs in the area, which are being exploded alive by dam turbines as well as having their spawning areas silted in by logging and roadbuilding. ICBEMP's main recommendation? Massive job creation, road reconstruction, and doubling the allowable cut in places. Some folks never learn—especially if their jobs and culture are tied to whatever is causing the problem.

Save the World by Christmas

The only thing worse than having the Forest Service manage the landscape is to give it to the State of Idaho or Potlatch Corporation. The point of this piece was to state unequivocally that nothing is free.

As of this writing, my wife and I are still married.

Apocalypse Now

The flood damage in the Clearwater National Forest was all over the papers at the beginning of December 1995, and on through February 1996. See "Rains Devastate N. Idaho Forests and Watersheds—Officials Blame Clearcuts, Roads in Wrong Places for Most of Damage," in the Spokane *Spokesman-Review* (Idaho edition), December 8, 1995, or "More Logging Planned in Area of Mudslides—Environmentalists Call for More Study of

Planned Roads, Cuts, in Unstable Areas," in the *Spokesman-Review* (Idaho edition), February 19, 1996, for typical coverage.

Larry McLaud and I claim credit for breaking the story, though it was the informal activist network that put together the information. We are now just starting to deal with the consequences. The Forest Service, in the interest of obfuscation, placed on the flood study team Dale Wilson, retired USFS soil scientist who originally sited many of the roads that failed—similar to having a doctor investigate his own malpractice. Desperately trying to spin the "old roads bad, new roads good" or "we don't do that anymore" line, the flood study team, which also included a Potlatch Corporation hydrologist, took a group of us on a tour of road blowouts in the summer of 1996. When Dale Wilson started singing the same old song, I confronted him with a list of new roads that had also blown out. He stated outright that one of the examples that I had cited was a new road, true, but he, along with the district ranger, had made the decision to build it to old road standards, even though it was on fragile breakland soils—in my opinion, a direct admittance of malfeasance. The reason given was monetary—paraphrased like this: "Enviros are always giving us a hard time about below-cost timber sales, so we tried to make this one less expensive to prepare." This type of logic, what I call the "you're making me beat my wife" chain of thought, is pervasive in most arguments by the timber industry and sympathetic types.

Preliminary draft studies show that old or new road construction technique makes little difference—there are some places that one can't build roads. And it also follows that there are places that one shouldn't log. The forest-wide flood study, delayed twice, remains unpublished as of this writing.

Epilogue

Why

Two books dramatically changed my perception of the Holocaust and caused me to make what is on the surface a worn-out comparison. *The Splendid Blond Beast*, by Christopher Simpson (New York: Grove Press, 1993), offers an explanation of the economics of Holocaust; *Hitler's Willing Executioners*, by Daniel Jonah Goldhagen (New York: Alfred A. Knopf, 1996), tells the cultural tale. The main point is this: any of us can be participants in genocide if we suspend our sense of reality. And we as a society must act in concert if we are to prevent such things from happening.

Perhaps the best book explaining the dynamics of bureaucracy and the impasse that exists between mainstream enviro groups in D.C., and the grassroots is one about a man's military career and the Vietnam war: *About Face* by Colonel David H. Hackworth and Julie Sherman (New York: Simon and Schuster, 1989). Hackworth writes:

> And yet, even I could get a whole different picture of how things were going if I talked to the right people, and time and again find every reason to believe it. The starched briefers... snapped their pointers onto precise graphs and charts and invariably cited impressive statistics of... ever-widening success; the relevant information was always presented so logically and persuasively that I'd walk out of those briefings thinking I must be crazy. I'd seriously begin to question my own absolutely certain, on-the-ground observations and those of my team, in deference to those seemingly airtight official reports. Fortunately I'd only have to be back in the Zone for a few hours to recognize I'd been seduced, that what I'd heard was the same meaningless statistics, the same old artfully sanitized shit. But it showed the incredible power those briefings and reports had. If after all my years...I could still be taken in, at least momentarily, should it have been a surprise how easily and eagerly fooled the tourists still were?

Colonel Hackworth is talking, of course, about Vietnam. But after sitting through my share of national and state environmental conferences and board meetings, I could have sworn his words were meant for me, and anyone else in the grassroots environmental movement who has had to deal with the nationals.

Hackworth's other book of interest, *Hazardous Duty*, with Tom Mathews (New York: William Morrow and Company, 1996), profiles the enormous waste in the Department of Defense.

One of the few books that discusses the environmental implications of the 1864 Northern Pacific Railroad Land Grant Act is *Railroads and Clearcuts: Legacy of Congress's 1864 Northern Pacific Railroad Land Grant*, by Derrick Jensen, George Draffan, and John Osborn (Spokane: Inland Empire Public Lands Council, c1995). The book is filled with facts and figures detailing the deforestation of the railroad checkerboards on the northern flank of the Clearwater Country. The combined assets of Boise Cascade, Weyerhaeuser, Potlatch, and Plum Creek, are $20 billion. With the money from the B-2 bomber, a plane that will be based underground until the Apocalypse, we could buy out all the timber companies and restore the landscape. Money isn't the issue in environmental preservation and protection—it's will and priority. See *Hazardous Duty* for an analysis of the B-2 situation. Talk about burying money in a hole in the ground.

Kenneth Stern's book *A Force Upon the Plain: The American Militia Movement and the Politics of Hate* (New York: Simon and Schuster, 1996) is a scary introduction to the philosophies of America's Christian Patriots. Stern's main analogy, comparing the movement to a funnel, with Pat Robertson's Christian Coalition on the wide end and Timothy McVeigh on the narrow end, drives home the point that more people are enfranchised into this belief system than commonly believed. James Aho's *The Politics of Righteousness: Idaho Christian Patriotism* (Seattle: University of Washington Press, 1990) profiles in a very scientific way the various movements alive and well in Idaho currently. Aho makes the point again and again: these people are **not** crazy, but they are capable of believing some pretty wild things. The question that comes to my mind after reading the literature is this: will we learn the lessons of Nazi Germany before they happen to us directly?

David Helvarg's *The War Against the Greens* (San Francisco: Sierra Club Books, 1994) gives an extensive profile of the current players in the Wise Use Movement.

Three other books rate mention for their information on the Clearwater Country. *The Ridgerunner* by Richard Ripley (Backeddy Books, 1986), paints a colorful story and a beautiful picture of the Clearwater backcountry before it was turned into the frontcountry and logged. Two other books serve as adequate historical reference: *The Clearwater Story* by Ralph Space (Orofino, Id.: United States Forest Service and the Clearwater Historical Society, 1964); and *The Lochsa Story: Land Ethics in the Bitterroot Mountains* by Bud Moore (Missoula, Mt.: Mountain Press, 1996). Both Space and Moore were line officers on the Clearwater National Forest, Space the forest supervisor from 1954-1963, the beginning of the real logging go-go years on the forest, and Moore the Powell District Ranger from 1949-1954. Moore fills the end of his book with effusive praise for the agency and the rape of the upper Lochsa by Plum Creek and the Forest Service, hinged on a heavy subjunctive "if," as in "if the trees grow back." If you couldn't have guessed, I disagree with his assessment.

Appendix

Conservation Groups Involved with Environmental Issues in the Clearwater Sub-basin

ALL THE ORGANIZATIONS LISTED below are actively involved in attempting to save the remaining wild country of the Northern Rockies, as well as the Clearwater sub-basin. All are filled with truly fine people worthy of your support. I have included only grassroots organizations in my list. This is not intended as a slight to those national organizations such as The Wilderness Society, the Sierra Club, or Defenders of Wildlife, which all have helped in varying ways toward national wilderness preservation. It is, however, time to give the front-line warriors their due.

Clearwater Biodiversity Project
c/o The Idaho Conservation League
P.O. Box 9783
Moscow, ID 83843
peze@idaho.tds.net

Clearwater Biodiversity Project (CBP), headed by the author, is a small, grassroots group working on issues in the Clearwater Country. It specializes in short time-scale projects with a defined goal, as opposed to never-ending, single-issue campaigns. CBP has been instrumental in commissioning scientific studies, as well as public education efforts regarding environmental degradation in the Clearwater sub-basin.

Idaho Conservation League
P.O. Box 9783
Moscow, ID 83843
208-882-1010
www.desktop.org/icl
lmclaud@moscow.com

The Idaho Conservation League (ICL) is one of the main state-wide conservation organizations in Idaho. ICL lobbies the state legislature and works on water quality and wilderness allocation issues. Larry McLaud, the North Idaho ICL representative, and I work closely together on issues involving the Clearwater.

The Ecology Center of Missoula
801 Sherwood St., Suite B
Missoula, MT 59802
406-728-5733
www.wildrockies.org/ecocenter
ecocenter@wildrockies.org

The Ecology Center, directed by Bill Haskins, is one of the cutting-edge groups working on conservation issues in the Northern Rockies. Covering public lands management issues in Montana, Idaho, and Alberta, the Ecology Center provides Geographic Information Systems (GIS) support, technical expertise, and charitable donation pass-throughs for smaller grassroots organizations and activists.

American Wildlands
40 E. Main St., Suite 2
Bozeman, MT 59715
406-586-8175
mail@wildlands.org
www.mcn.net/~amwild/

American Wildlands (AWL) is another cutting-edge organization out of Bozeman with a current focus on preservation of native westslope cutthroat trout. AWL petitioned the U.S. Fish and Wildlife Service for listing of the fish under the Endangered Species Act, and has been mounting a public education campaign around the fish and its habitat. AWL is also involved with forest issues on the Clearwater and Payette national forests, and provides GIS support for grassroots groups.

Inland Empire Public Lands Council
517 S. Division
Spokane, WA 99202
509-838-4912
www.ieplc.org
ieplc@desktop.org

The Inland Empire Public Lands Council (IEPLC) is a nonprofit forest conservation organization based in Spokane, Washington, with more than 1,000 members. The Council has an active forest watch program, and works on toxic lead contamination resulting from mining in the Spokane/Coeur d'Alene watershed. Additionally, IEPLC runs public information campaigns on the legacy of the 1864 congressional grant of land to the Northern Pacific Railroad, the cause of mile-square checkerboard clearcuts across the roof of the Clearwater Country. Its publication, *Transitions*, serves as a reference of newspaper coverage of environmental issues in the region.

Idaho Rivers United
P.O. Box 633
Boise, ID 83701
208-343-7481
www.desktop.org/iru
iru@iru.desktop.org

Idaho Rivers United (IRU) is a state-wide rivers organization that focuses on hydropower and irrigation dams, wild fish issues, and river protection and planning. IRU also lobbies the state legislature regarding Idaho water policy and planning. The organization has been active in fights in the Clearwater sub-basin involving degradation of potential federally protected Wild and Scenic Rivers.

Alliance for the Wild Rockies
P.O. Box 8731
Missoula, MT 59807
406-721-5420
406-721-9917 (fax)
www.wildrockies.org/awr
awr@wildrockies.org

The Alliance for the Wild Rockies (AWR) is a transboundary grassroots network of member groups throughout Idaho, Montana, Wyoming, British

Columbia, and Alberta. AWR is the author of the Northern Rockies Ecosystem Protection Act (NREPA), the first conservation biology-based wilderness protection proposal, and holds the annual Wild Rockies Rendezvous on the last weekend in September every year at the Teller Wildlife Refuge outside of Corvallis, Montana. Its magazine, *The Networker*, carries ecological news across the Northern Rockies bioregion.

Friends of the Clearwater
P.O. Box 9241
Moscow, ID 83843
foc@clearwater.net

Cove/Mallard Coalition
P.O. Box 8968
Moscow, ID 83843
cove@moscow.com
208-882-9755
FAX: 208-883-0727

Friends of the Clearwater (FOC) is a small grassroots organization monitoring timber sales on the Clearwater and Nez Perce national forests. It writes comments and appeals on projects. FOC and the Cove/Mallard Coalition jointly publish the *Salmon/Selway Defender*, a twice-yearly publication discussing major environmental threats across the Clearwater Country. The Cove/Mallard Coalition coordinates logistics for the ongoing campaign to save the Cove/Mallard roadless areas on the Nez Perce Forest.

Idaho Sporting Congress
P.O. Box 1136
Boise, ID 83701
208-336-7222
iscsdd@rmci.net

Idaho Sporting Congress (ISC) is a 1,100 member sporting group dedicated to protecting national public lands. ISC has been involved with cutting-edge litigation to protect the Cove/Mallard roadless area, and filed the nation's first water quality lawsuit requiring that damaged streams across Idaho, including those in the Clearwater, be repaired. ISC also pioneered non-point pollution litigation of waterways—vitally important for stopping the timber industry from destroying the last of the Clearwater wild country.

Land and Water Fund of the Rockies—Idaho Office
P.O. Box 1612
Boise, ID 83701
208-342-7024
www.lawfund.org
lawfund_idaho@msn.com

The Land and Water Fund (LWF) provides legal help for grassroots groups for minimal remuneration. The Idaho office supports legislation involving water quality issues, water rights, and non-point pollution cases.

About the Author

Charles Pezeshki is an associate professor of mechanical engineering at Washington State University. An avid backpacker, whitewater kayaker, and environmental activist, he directs the Clearwater Biodiversity Project with his wife Kelley from their home in Troy, Idaho. This is his first book.

Index